# Qualitative Research in Theological Education

# Qualitative Research in Theological Education

*Pedagogy in Practice*

*Edited by*
Mary Clark Moschella
and
Susan Willhauck

scm press

Published in 2018 by SCM Press
Editorial office
3rd Floor, Invicta House,
108–114 Golden Lane,
London EC1Y 0TG, UK
www.scmpress.co.uk

SCM Press is an imprint of Hymns Ancient & Modern Ltd
(a registered charity)

Hymns Ancient & Modern® is a registered trademark of
Hymns Ancient & Modern Ltd
13A Hellesdon Park Road, Norwich, Norfolk NR6 5DR, UK

Scripture quotations are from the New Revised Standard Version
of the Bible, Anglicized Edition, copyright © 1989, 1995 by the
Division of Christian Education of the National Council of the
Churches of Christ in the USA. Used by permission.
All rights reserved.

British Library Cataloguing in Publication data

A catalogue record for this book is available
from the British Library

978 0 334 05677 5

Typeset by Manila Typesetting Company
Printed and bound by CPI Group (UK) Ltd

We dedicate this book to our students,
our colleagues and our families

# Contents

CONTENTS

# Acknowledgements

This volume is truly a collaborative work. It came about because of significant and greatly appreciated contributions from individuals and institutions. We are thankful to the Wabash Center for Teaching and Learning in Theology and Religion for its long track record of encouraging and funding activities that enhance teaching and learning in theological and religious studies. Particularly, we are grateful for its support in the form of a year-long project grant for the research that served as the impetus for this book and provided us with the opportunity to work together again. When I (Susan) conceived of the idea for the grant proposal, I immediately thought that my former colleague Mary would be the ideal facilitator, with her scholarship and teaching in the field of ethnography in practical theology. She fulfilled that role beautifully and skilfully, taking time away from her own myriad of responsibilities to do so. I'm appreciative of her untiring dedication to this project. We also acknowledge our authors around the globe for their participation in this endeavour, their rigorous scholarship, and their bold ideas and reflections contained in these pages. We trust these essays will be useful in continuing dialogue on pedagogy in practice and qualitative research.

Thank you as well to the faculty and administration of Atlantic School of Theology, Halifax, Nova Scotia, for hosting the symposium that brought some of the contributors together to engage in passionate conversations on the role of qualitative research in theological education. Kate Jones, who served as Research Assistant for the Wabash grant project, provided valuable and reassuring assistance with travel arrangements, hospitality, transportation, transcribing, and organization. Kate graduated from Atlantic School of Theology in 2017 after completing her own qualitative research study of bi-vocational ministry and is currently serving as a United Church of Canada minister in British Columbia. We extend our gratitude to SCM Press for seeing the potential of this work and agreeing to publish it and to David Shervington, our editor at SCM Press, for his always prompt professional advice. We also thank Rona Johnston for her meticulous editorial assistance and keen eye for detail.

I (Mary) would like to add my thanks to Susan, who initiated this project and worked with me to bring this volume to fruition. Our collaboration has been a source of great joy. My thanks go also to many colleagues and friends, including Eileen Campbell-Reed, Joyce Mercer, and Beverly Mitchell, as well as my online writing support group for sharing their ideas and encouragement. I also offer a note of appreciation to my students at Yale Divinity School, who with intelligence, creativity, and care venture out to study lived practices of faith.

We would also like to recognize the faculty and students in theological education and religious studies who harness the courage to teach research methods or to carry out qualitative research themselves, in order to move toward more relational ways of being and fuller understanding of our complex world.

*Susan Willhauck*
*Mary Clark Moschella*

# Notes on Contributors

Joseph (Jody) H. Clarke is Associate Professor of Pastoral Theology at Atlantic School of Theology, Halifax, NS, Canada

David M. Csinos is Assistant Professor of Practical Theology at Atlantic School of Theology, Halifax, NS, Canada

Elaine Graham is the Grosvenor Research Professor of Practical Theology at the University of Chester, UK

Brett C. Hoover is Associate Professor of Pastoral and Practical Theology at Loyola Marymount University, Los Angeles, CA, USA

Tone Stangeland Kaufman is Associate Professor of Practical Theology at the MF Norwegian School of Theology, Oslo, Norway

Bernardine Ketelaars is Professor of Missiology and Director of Lay and Pastoral Formation at St Peter's Seminary, London, ON, Canada

Boyung Lee is Senior Vice President of Academic Affairs, Dean of the Faculty and Professor of Practical Theology, Iliff School of Theology, Denver, CO, USA

Dawn Llewellyn is Senior Lecturer in Christian Studies at the University of Chester, UK

David M. Mellott is Vice President of Academic Affairs and Dean of the Seminary and Professor of Theological Formation at Lancaster Seminary, Lancaster, PA, USA

Mary Clark Moschella is the Roger J. Squire Professor of Pastoral Care and Counseling at Yale Divinity School, New Haven, CT, USA

Nichole Renée Phillips is Assistant Professor of Sociology, Religion and Culture at Candler School of Theology, Emory University, Atlanta, GA, USA

Apipa Prachyapruit is Assistant Professor of Higher Education at the Chulalongkorn University, Thailand

Anthony G. Reddie is Extraordinary Professor, University of South Africa, Unisa, South Africa

Siroj Sorajjakool is Program Director of Adventist Development and Relief Agency, Thailand, and Adjunct Professor, School of Religion, Loma Linda University, CA, USA

Todd D. Whitmore is Associate Professor, Department of Theology, and Concurrent Associate Professor, Department of Anthropology, University of Notre Dame, IN, USA

Natalie Wigg-Stevenson is Associate Professor of Contextual Education and Theology at Emmanuel College, Toronto, ON, Canada

Susan Willhauck is Associate Professor of Pastoral Theology at Atlantic School of Theology, Halifax, NS, Canada

# Introduction

## MARY CLARK MOSCHELLA

About two years ago, a group of theological scholars gathered at Halifax, Nova Scotia, for a symposium. Over samples of local seafood and dishes of poutine, we shared our experiences of teaching qualitative research in our diverse theological disciplines and educational institutions. We discussed both our own research projects and our various approaches to teaching qualitative methods and methodologies. We agreed that qualitative research is best learned by doing, that is, by students engaging in qualitative research, even designing and conducting studies themselves if possible. Teaching in and through the practice of various qualitative research methods is both perilous and inspiring: we shared stories of our tries, successes, and glorious fails.

Conceived and organized by my colleague and co-editor Susan Willhauck, this symposium, held at Atlantic School of Theology, was intended to take the measure of a growing phenomenon: the teaching of theologically grounded qualitative research methods and methodologies in seminaries, theological schools, and universities in the United States and Canada.[1] Willhauck sought not only to learn the extent of this teaching, but also to explore its effects upon the students, faculty, and educational institutions that have undertaken this work in a robust manner. What drives this trajectory in scholarship and teaching? Why ought theological education include in its curricula what Charles Marsh describes as 'disciplined attention to the detail and complexity of worldly life'?[2] And how do theological scholars' experiences of both doing and teaching qualitative research methods in their courses change them and their pedagogy over time?

As readers might imagine, a lively conversation ensued. When the symposium was over, we opted to keep the discussion going by sharing and revising essays for this book. We then expanded the scope of the volume to include colleagues engaged in similar programmes of teaching and study in different parts of the world, including the United Kingdom, Norway, South Africa, and Thailand. This volume represents the work of an international group of scholars who teach in a diversity of degree programmes, ranging from the Master of Divinity (MDiv) and the Doctor of Ministry (DMin), which focus on preparing students for ministry and enhancing their competence for religious leadership, to the Doctor of Philosophy (PhD), which emphasizes research and teaching, to the Professional Doctorate in Practical Theology (DProf), established in the United Kingdom and described here as a programme for the 'researching professional' rather than the 'professional researcher'. The 17 of us contributing to the book hail from varied institutions, including both free-standing seminaries and major public and private universities, and represent diverse theological disciplines. Our disciplinary orientations include practical theology and its subfields of pastoral theology and religious education, theological ethics, systematic and constructive theology, sociology of religion, and anthropology. Seasoned scholars as well as fresh younger voices weigh in.

The theologically based teaching of qualitative research principles and practices is a hardy and growing phenomenon in seminaries, theological schools, and university-based programmes. We assert that such teaching is critical to the enterprise of theological education, for the scholarly, moral, and pastoral formation of scholars and religious leaders. Practical and pastoral theologians have long emphasized the importance of the embodied and contextual dimensions of faith. In the broad field of practical theology, Don Browning's foundational text emphasizes the importance of description to practical theology's prescriptive work.[3] Elaine Graham later suggests a shift in the theological task toward interpretation of a community's faith in action.[4] In the last 30 years, the field of pastoral theology has been 'widening the horizons', from Anton Boisen's concept of the 'living human document' to

Bonnie Miller-McLemore's broader focus on the 'living human web', recovering the communal and prophetic strands in the care of souls of tradition.[5] Seeking to understand practices of faith in diverse cultural contexts and influenced by liberation theologies and calls for social justice related to race, gender, age, dis/ability, sexual orientation, and gender identity, practical and pastoral theologians have increasingly turned to qualitative research methods.[6] Similarly, religious educators, in part due to the influence of Thomas Groome and his work on shared Christian praxis, have emphasized the importance of embodied expressions of faith.[7] Educator and participatory action researcher Elizabeth Conde-Frazier notes that 'orality does not permit the academy to abstract and dilute the power of narrative. It fosters knowledge that comes from passion and experience and expands the space of the academic world.'[8] These shifts have rendered evident the dual need for interdisciplinary engagement with the social sciences and expanded repertoires of research methodologies.

A number of ethicists and constructive theologians, too, have adopted the methods of qualitative research, particularly anthropology, out of a concern for 'the moral and theological formation of persons and communities', asserting that 'in o. der to do theology and ethics well, scholars need to explore them through visceral ways, within embodied communities, and in particular contexts'.[9] In a volume that inaugurated this discussion, Christian Scharen and Aana Marie Vigen go so far as to describe the practice of ethnography *as* Christian theology and ethics.[10] Theologian Mary McClintock Fulkerson notes that the incarnational nature of Christianity almost requires this kind of investigation: 'There is . . . no other place to look for God than as mediated through the messy place that is the world.'[11] Similarly, Charles Marsh, Peter Slade, Sarah Azaransky, and their colleagues are developing the concept of 'lived theology', and are adopting research methods that include ethnography and new practice-based pedagogical strategies as well.[12]

This wealth of intellectual and pedagogical ferment in our disciplines confirms the concern that Susan Willhauck and I share for the formation of religious leaders and scholars whose theology is discerned not only in wrestling with ancient and contemporary texts, but also through face-to-face encounters with living human beings engaged in their complex and varied practices of faith. We also note that the educational impact upon theological students who design and carry out qualitative research projects is significant. While the research does not always go smoothly, students themselves often describe how their research experiences have changed them.[13] In engaging in fieldwork, students are confronted with various kinds of challenges, at once ethical, intellectual, practical, and vocational. These challenges may include forming respectful relationships with diverse persons and groups, honouring ethical guidelines, learning to read interpersonal interactions, analysing the role of social factors in religious practices, and composing nuanced corporate narratives. Tasked with observing faith in action, student-researchers are challenged to discern the complex interplay of history, culture, and theology in people's lives. This is difficult and decentring work.[14] The de-centring of the self may be the key to the sense of transformation that some students as well as senior scholars report: the illuminating, moving, or humbling aspects of the work. Fieldwork requires openness to others' lives and faith, and such openness and curiosity often lead to compassion and/or connection with research partners.[15]

Students and others who conduct research studies of religious practices also often arrive at conclusions that call for social and political change. Some forms of research (such as standpoint and participatory action) are more consciously aimed at promoting change from the start. Yet even in the case of studies undertaken without such an agenda, theological or ethical reflection upon the research findings tends to evoke some kind of a response. Scharen and Vigen point out that theology and ethics concern descriptions not only of what is, but also of what should be.[16] Theologically motivated researchers may therefore perceive a need for change in themselves and/or the situations they study. Such changes might be personal, ecclesial, cultural, or political. For example, Brett Hoover's sociological research on shared Catholic parishes in the United States, which is described in this volume, led him to the recognition that racist cultural formations are embedded in Church structures and practices. When researchers articulate both the limiting and life-giving aspects of the situations they study, they are in fact engaged in practical theology, in interpreting situations.[17] A combination of humility and courage is needed. So much is at stake.

While the teaching and learning of qualitative research in theological fields can be transformative, as educators we are also aware of numerous potentially serious pitfalls in attempting to teach qualitative approaches. Postcolonial and decolonial insights raise critical questions and remind us of the danger of objectifying research partners. Researchers need to be accountable to people's struggles to name their own identities and to represent themselves.[18] These challenges are inherent in every phase of research, from designing protocols to defining the research questions, to strategies for analysis and interpretive frameworks, to writing and visual forms of representation. For whom is this research being done? Who will benefit from it? Will it lead to the construction of challenging new knowledge? Or will it support the status quo?

## Part 1: Exemplary Research Essays

### Representation

The first two chapters presented in this volume reflect on exemplary research projects that carefully attend to the questions above. Anthropological theologian and ethicist Todd Whitmore conducted research in a war zone in northern Uganda over a period of nine years. Whitmore worked in the local languages and adopted a form of open-ended interviewing designed to attend to the focus on orality in many regions of sub-Saharan Africa. The 350 hours of recorded interviewing included songs, cosmological origin stories, and more, in addition to life narratives. Whitmore's careful research practices brought him into close communion with his research partners, whose faith he describes with enormous respect. In his first essay in this volume, 'Theology as Playbook and

Gamefilm: Explaining an Ethnographic Approach to Theology to a Sports-Centred Culture', Whitmore artfully presents the comments of one of his research partners, a member of the Little Sisters of Mary Immaculate in Gulu who suffered a traumatic abduction 'into the bush', on the left side of each page. The Sister describes how she is able to help other women and girls in the area who have suffered from similarly horrific experiences by relying on 'the whole of God who is in me' to protect and sustain her. Here Whitmore allows his research partner to speak for herself, and to speak to his readers, of her life and faith. Juxtaposed to the Sister's raw story of embodied faith is, on the right side of the page, Whitmore's explanation, by way of sports analogies (that have particular resonance at the University of Notre Dame), of the inseparable nature of theology and practice. For him, the work of writing and teaching theological anthropology constitutes nothing less than the proclamation of the Gospel.

In the second essay, 'Qualitative Methodology and Critical Pedagogy: A Study of the Lived Experiences of Thai Peasants within the Context of Western Development Ideology', pastoral theologian Siroj Sorajjakool and education specialist Apipa Prachyapruit describe extensive interviews conducted in twenty provinces in Thailand with peasant farmers and their children. Both Thai nationals, these authors conducted their study in the local language, going out to meet the farmers on their own turf. The authors are careful to foreground the views of the local farmers, whose experiences offer a cultural critique of Western concepts of modernity. Sorajjakool and Prachyapruit highlight the practical knowledge of local farmers who have based their approach to farming on two key principles: strong communities and the principle of sufficiency (multi-crop farming that provides the farmers with the food that they need, as opposed to mono-cultural farming that grows one crop at a time). These two key principles, the authors assert, have been delegitimized by the imposition of Western farming models. Additionally, the farmers' pursuit of tertiary education for their children incurs great expense and yields mixed or questionable benefits. This study describes the marginalization and impoverishment of farmers by global markets that disregard the wisdom and welfare of the Thai people and offers a counter-story that highlights the voices of the people as they grapple with changed conditions.

We include this essay for many reasons, not least the way in which it embraces a broader view of practical theological research, one that is not limited in focus to exploring Christian faith practices. The exigencies of farming discovered in these remote communities are compelling. It is a situation that calls for a response, and thus it makes a claim on people of faith.[19] As a theological educator, Sorajjakool claims that the experiential dimensions of qualitative research are critical to students' formation in that they ground students in the everyday existential struggles of the people they serve (instead of in theoretical texts). This experience, he finds, moves students beyond the descriptive limits of words to the language of the heart, while it promotes a form of decolonization and brings an awareness of God to the complex reality of everyday living.

## Part 2: Issues in Education and the Practice of Research

### Ethical Considerations

In 'Promoting the Good: Ethical and Methodological Considerations in Practical Theological Research', distinguished practical theologians Elaine Graham and Dawn Llewellyn describe their innovative Professional Doctorate in Practical Theology (DProf) programme at the University of Chester in the United Kingdom. They helpfully articulate the distinctions between this and other degree programmes, noting the goal of educating 'researching professionals', whose rigorous scholarship will serve practical theology as it seeks to 'transform the researcher's practice, their institution, and the academy'. After reviewing a diversity of forms of research in practical theology, these authors focus on qualitative methodologies and some of the ethical challenges that their students' work highlights. Navigating the complexities of the British Sociological Organization, comparable to the

Institutional Review Board in the United States, students learn to attempt to avoid doing harm. Yet Graham and Llewellyn suggest a higher standard, that of promoting the good, which means both striving for excellence in research practices and promoting the well-being of participants. The authors offer three illustrations of their students' work in this programme that complicate established ethical principles such as informed consent, anonymity, and disclosure.

Evident in this essay is the authors' profound respect for both their doctoral student-researchers and their research partners. Ethical research procedures require ongoing consideration, especially when circumstances change and understandings of the good evolve in the course of the research. Teaching at this level requires sensitivity to student-researchers' dilemmas and awareness of the possible challenges to existing review board standards. 'Promoting the good' suggests a standard that is at once more ethically rigorous and more humane than simply attempting to avoid harm.

A good example of ethical challenges that emerge in the course of qualitative research is offered in David Csinos's fresh and candid essay, 'Between Yes and No: The Inner Journey of Qualitative Research'. Csinos shares the story of his interior growth through his doctoral research in small Aboriginal congregations of the United Church of Canada's All Native Circle Conference. When he first met with the church's minister to request permission to do research in these congregations, he was not told yes, and he was not told no. He notes that Aboriginal communities in Canada have been heavily researched in the past and meagrely rewarded; systemic injustices continue to do them harm. Nevertheless, Csinos was invited to keep talking, to stay in conversation, and to get to know the people over time. As he accepted the pace and continued the relationship for a full year before he could begin his fieldwork, there began what Csinos calls 'an inner journey of transformation'. He experienced personal growth and an increase in his practical understanding of the people's situation and the research process. He notes, 'I noticed ways that my university's research ethics guidelines were actually inappropriate and even downright unethical in some of the non-dominant, oppressed groups with which I was working.' Though navigating these dilemmas proved demanding, Csinos believes that this process helped form him as researcher and a person. He describes changes he has made in the way he orders his thoughts and performs actions in the world. His non-traditional essay, written in clear and accessible language that his research partners can understand, exemplifies such a change. This piece illustrates the potential for research journeys to open and transform researchers who are willing to learn *from* their research partners and to do the hard work of personal reflexivity along the way, before, during, and after the outer journey of research.

Todd David Whitmore's second essay, 'The *Askēsis* of Fieldwork: Practices for a Way of Inquiry, a Way of Life', continues to address the ethical and formational features of fieldwork. Ethnography, Whitmore claims, can best be understood as both a distinctive mode of enquiry and a way of being. Whitmore suggests the Greek and Roman term *askēsis*, rather than science or art, to name this work. He understands *askēsis* not as self-denial (as the term asceticism might suggest), but as something more like training or discipline, pointing to the rigour of research and its capacity to shape one's disposition. He describes two research practices as illustration: *originating hospitality* and *approaching softly*. Referring to his research in an Internally Displaced Persons camp in northern Uganda during the Lord's Resistance Army conflict, Whitmore details his experience of *originating hospitality* offered him by his hosts, who welcomed him – the researcher, the stranger – into their midst. His recognition that he is in their debt prioritizes the people's originating practice. *Approaching softly* designates a way of being that involves learning to sit and listen with people on their own terms, a practice that one friend calls 'deep hanging out'. Like Dave Csinos, Whitmore learns the power of patience in the work of establishing trust. Even so, the ethical challenge to honour the stories shared and offer something in return remains. Whitmore calls on researchers to consider 'the practice of love and solidarity' with research partners, so that research does not become 'mere plunder'. *Askēsis* requires the work of reflexivity, which, like spiritual reflection, involves researchers in disciplined contemplation of their impact on the communities they study.

## *Reflexivity*

Reflexivity is a theme in almost all of these essays; it is key to the practice and teaching of qualitative research. Aware that there is no one metanarrative that tells an 'objective' truth, qualitative researchers accept the burden of acknowledging and tracking their role in the research field, noting their impact on the study and the impact of the research on them. In teaching theologically grounded qualitative research, reflexivity is *always* required. Christian Scharen, following Pierre Bourdieu, comments on the dual types of reflexivity that are needed: 'The focus here is not simply the individual observer but the social world inhabited by the observer and the analytic tools marshalled for the work as part of the collective enterprise of science.'[20] Teaching students to note and track their influence upon a qualitative study is difficult, though students who discuss their research regularly in classrooms often hold each other – and sometimes their teachers – accountable in this regard. But the broader form of reflexivity, the sort that plumbs the depths of the assumptions and motivations animating both our research and the practices of the academy, is more complicated to understand, more difficult to own up to, and more challenging to communicate to students. Finally, it seems to be the responsibility of those who would teach reflexivity to model it in the classroom.

Ethnographic theologian Natalie Wigg-Stevenson, in her essay, 'Just Don't Call It "Ethnography": A Critical Ethnographic Pedagogy for Transformative Theological Education', describes a pedagogical practice through which she models the second, broader form of reflexivity, the form that John Swinton and Harriet Mowat call 'epistemological reflexivity'.[21] She begins by describing the challenge of moving beyond what Paulo Freire called 'banking' models of education when attempting 'to teach ethnographically' toward liberation and transformation in her privileged North American context, in Toronto, Canada.[22] In order to consciously work against 'a pedagogical agenda that trains producers for the globalized marketplace', Wigg-Stevenson has students write brief autobiographical vignettes that provoke awareness of their social locations as researchers. In her classrooms, both students and teacher analyse the ways in which colonial influences have shaped their lives and invariably appear in objectifying research relationships and traditional modes of theological education. She calls this approach 'transformative education for oppressors – of which I am one'. In her interactions with students and particularly in her willingness to be called out by them for her own forms of privilege, Wigg-Stevenson models a way to teach justice through relationships in the classroom. Through the different levels of reflexivity involved, she keeps this teaching grounded in the ethnographic principles of curiosity, openness, and attentiveness to human interactions.

## *Embodied Research and Teaching*

British practical theologian and educator Anthony Reddie, whose research base is in South Africa, similarly relies on the work of Paulo Freire in his 'performative action' approach to pedagogy. In 'Teaching and Researching Practical Theology – A Liberative Participative Approach to Pedagogy and Qualitative Research', Reddie notes the radical and revolutionary intent of education that seeks to conscientize participants in order to foster social change. He describes exercises he uses in classrooms and workshops that involve participants in interaction and reflection upon the meaning of Christian discipleship 'in contexts where white nationalism and racism are on the rise'. Also employing the work of Augusto Boal and the theatre of the oppressed, Reddie's pedagogy aims to create new knowledge in practical theology through 'personal, subjective, and affective learning experiences as a conduit for transformative, anti-racist practices of Christian discipleship'. The qualitative research embedded in this pedagogy involves both participants and teacher in reflecting on what is said and what is left unsaid in the course of the interactive exercises; this often reveals a degree of obliviousness to white privilege and/or other forms of injustice. The reflexive exercise he describes involves raising awareness of intersectional social realities, including race, gender, dis/abilities, and sexual orientation. Students are then encouraged to bring their awareness into the qualitative research projects that they themselves undertake. Reddie sees this as a 'bottom up, transgressive mode of critical pedagogy' that empowers students, through experiential learning, to know themselves better and thus to be able to engage in more informed ways with the Other.

Power dynamics and race are also very much at the centre of Catholic pastoral theologian Brett Hoover's essay, 'I Am Not a Sociologist: Reflections on Sociological Research in Theology'. Hoover helpfully clarifies the distinctions between the role of sociology of religion in his work and the role of pastoral theology. Hoover employs the tools of sociological theory and methods in order to understand the 'historical reality' in which the Church is embedded. In the discipline of sociology of religion, where both quantitative and qualitative methods are employed, he finds the frameworks and methods needed to interpret the social realities of congregational and social life. Aware of social power asymmetries in cultural formations in the wider society, he is dismayed, although not surprised, to discover these same asymmetries operating in the shared parishes he studies. Among the various ethnic and racial groups that share the space and resources in these parishes, inequalities persist. Hoover writes, 'It may seem difficult to reconcile the things we say about the Church – that it is the Body of Christ, a Trinitarian communion, a sacrament of divine unity – with the reality of societal injustice as embedded in the local faith community.' When discovering such dissonances, Hoover avoids pitting theology against empiricism. Instead, he asserts that theological reflection is vital in this situation. It is theology, not sociology, that challenges the Church not only to rebalance power inequities, but also to reform its organizational culture, so that it might more aptly reflect 'a theological vision of the Church rooted in the revelation of Jesus Christ'.

Practical theologian Boyung Lee, a religious educator and the current Dean of Iliff Theological Seminary in Denver, Colorado, teaches reflexivity in the realm of spirituality. Like Natalie Wigg-Stevenson, she employs a Freirean model. She uses it to teach 'engaged spirituality', which is defined as spiritual awareness that is nurtured and practised in the midst of social activism, rather than through withdrawal to monastic settings for contemplative prayer in silence. In this course from the Master's degree programme, qualitative research methods are employed as pedagogical strategy, rather than as the main content or substance of the course. Lee developed the course to address the high levels of burn-out in religious vocations and her students' own burn-out from working on the front lines in various social change movements. Lee's teaching is aimed at helping students sketch out a path toward spiritual renewal. It should be noted that the students include leaders in diverse religious traditions, racial/ethnic minority contexts, and LGBTQ communities. After students have read about diverse theological traditions of spirituality, Lee describes Paulo Freire's four-phase model of participant observation, which becomes the pedagogical frame of the course. The four phases – description, analysis, evaluation, and response – are used throughout the course as students examine their own and others' leadership practices. Students go on site visits to four diverse religious settings, where they also employ methods such as open-ended interviews and focus groups, in order to listen deeply and work together to understand their experiences.

Lee describes how students have gained appreciation for the spiritual wisdom of diverse religious groups and their approaches to social justice work. This course exemplifies Tom Beaudoin's challenge to move 'beyond Christianicity in practical theology' in that the pedagogy includes but is not limited to the study of ecclesial practices.[23] The Freirean model that Lee employs keeps epistemological reflexivity in the forefront, since students are required to reflect on social and cultural power dynamics throughout the course.

## Normativity

New definitions of spirituality also attract the attention of practical theologian Tone Stangeland Kaufman. In 'The Researcher as Gamemaker: Teaching Normative Dimensions in Various Phases of Empirical Practical Theological Research', Kaufman describes teaching reflexivity in relation to normative dimensions of research to students in both Masters and PhD programmes at MF Norwegian School of Theology, Religion and Society, in Oslo, Norway. Using the metaphor of the researcher as Gamemaker, Kaufman illustrates the need for this particular kind of reflexivity by referring to her own doctoral study of spirituality with Norwegian pastors. In the course of her investigation, Kaufman discovered that the normative concept of Christian spirituality with which she had been working was insufficient to account for her research findings. She made a normative decision when she shifted her concept of spirituality away from monastic understandings and toward 'everyday' notions of spirituality, and correspondingly shifted the list of authors whose work she would engage in the discussion. Kaufman explains how normativity – here defined as an explicitly evaluative position making truth claims – can be either a pitfall or an ally for researchers, depending upon whether they are conscious of the assumptions they are making and transparent about their trail of decision-making in their written accounts. In order to encourage this awareness and transparency, Kaufman requires students to write papers identifying their motivations for research, their preliminary assumptions and hunches, and how they position themselves theologically in relation to the field of research they are undertaking. Kaufman describes three different kinds of normativity – evaluative, rescriptive, and prescriptive – and encourages students to be clear about the choices they are making at every stage of the game.

The issue of normativity in both theology and research practices also figures prominently in sociologist of religion Nichole Renée Phillips' account of a robust tradition of teaching qualitative research at Candler School of Theology at Emory University in Atlanta, Georgia. A history of strong scholarship in the sociology of religion, established by luminaries such as Nancy Ammerman, Nancy Eiesland, and Steven Tipton, has contributed to Emory's status as a centre for teaching and learning qualitative research methodologies in diverse fields including Christian social ethics, cultural studies, and practical theology. Here Phillips concentrates on her teaching of ethnography, in both theological and religious studies programmes. She notes the power of students' fieldwork experiences of cultural immersion in religious worlds to inform theology and practice and to expand cultural knowledge. Phillips requires all of her students to read exemplary ethnographies (whether grounded in theology, anthropology, or sociology), particularly those that 'are marked by the distinctions of gender, ethnicity, class, race, religion, and region'. She contends that normative rules in both fields of study need to be challenged, so that theology can open up new vistas of understanding for sociologists and so that social science can help theologians and religious leaders see more clearly the social dynamics and 'partial truths' that ethnography reveals.

## Research and Pastoral Formation

The reflections of Bernardine Ketelaars, Director of Pastoral Formation at St Peter's Seminary in London, Ontario, lift up another theme running through many of these essays: the pastoral value of qualitative research. Ketelaars begins by describing her own doctoral research, which involved a series of open-ended interviews with 18 men and women who had been away from the Catholic Church for more than three years. She wanted to find out why they had absented themselves. Using a deep listening approach inspired by Henri Nouwen's concept of 'spiritual hospitality', as well as Max van Manen's notion of 'research as caring act', she allowed the interviews to unfold. After her research partners had listed the typical reasons for leaving the Church, such the Church's stand on the ordination of women or on homosexuality, they began to speak of 'more intimate and personal' reasons. Moved by their explanations, Ketelaars began to consider her research a 'holy conversation' with 'the dispersed children of God'. This work and the pastoral moments and insights it afforded have motivated her to teach the skills of qualitative research and theological reflection to Catholic seminarians and lay students who are preparing for the priesthood or various other forms of ministry. She asserts that rather than seeking power and authority over others, seminarians must model themselves after Jesus and 'learn to go to the peripheries, to seek out those who are wandering, to be a voice of hope'. Ketelaars challenges students in their supervised ministry settings to engage in intentional listening and observation as well as in outreach and dialogue. Students have later reported that this practice of research has been invaluable to them in their ministries.

## Part 3: Integrating Qualitative Research into Theological Education

Given the strength and scope of the qualitative research trajectory in theological education, academic administrators are called upon to provide key support and encouragement of this teaching at the programmatic level. In this section, two theological school deans, David Mellott of Lancaster Theological Seminary in Lancaster, Pennsylvania, and Jody Clarke of Atlantic School of Theology, in Halifax, Nova Scotia, describe their approaches to the work of integrating qualitative research principles and practices into the mission and curricula of their respective academic institutions. While not all academic institutions will be willing or able to revise their programmes so thoroughly, there is much value in considering such possibilities for integrative teaching and learning.[24]

David Mellott, a scholar of ethnography and liturgy, describes how he has integrated qualitative research methods into both Master of Divinity (MDiv) and Doctor of Ministry (DMin) programmes at Lancaster Theological Seminary, a free-standing seminary of the United Church of Christ. Because learning these research methods changed him as a scholar, Mellott believes it is important to introduce them to students at the beginning of their degree programmes. He asserts that qualitative research methods 'have the potential to fundamentally shape the ways in which our students think about the world, create knowledge, and theologize'. Even though some students are uncomfortable in the face of religious difference, all MDiv students are required to visit four particular congregations, and then debrief about these visits in class. The faculty strive to communicate that one can listen to and understand a faith perspective with which one does not agree. In DMin programmes, where students are typically professional ministers who know little about qualitative research methods, students are required to read ethnographies and also to engage in five pastoral visits in the homes of their parishioners. While this exercise is not a formal research study, students are taught to ask a few well-honed, open-ended questions during these visits and to look around at art and artefacts and try to take in a sense of their parishioners' lives. Students who engage in this assignment report surprising experiences of getting to know and understand people in their churches at a new level. Mellott notes that by learning qualitative research methods, students in both programmes expand their epistemic frameworks, learn to interpret contexts, and discover how to stand non-judgementally before the practices and beliefs of others. Students also become skilled at balancing the voices of religious practitioners with the voices of Scripture and the voices of scholars, even as they entertain the question 'Who am I in relation to others?' This integrative process contributes to students' spiritual formation and their theological wisdom.

In 'Wonder and the Divine Dance: The Lived Reality of Qualitative Research within a Master of Divinity Curriculum', Joseph (Jody) Clarke describes the process of intentional institutional discernment that the faculty, students, and administration of Atlantic School of Theology (AST), an ecumenical school of theology, undertook before deciding 'to weave qualitative research into the fabric of its MDiv curriculum'. This discernment process itself employed some of the principles and practices of qualitative research: it involved a combination of seminars, where participants read educational theory, as well as a series of field visits and interviews with artists, musicians, and community leaders who live in neighbouring communities along Canada's eastern coast. Those who participated included coal miners, a fishing community, people of Canada's First Nations, and a community of African Nova Scotians. These conversations revealed a depth of stories, insight, and emotion that brought AST into closer communion with its neighbours. Clarke notes that 'the experience of the AST community as it stood in close proximity to the Other is that our appreciation of the world, and our place in it, was increasing'. During the months that these interviews were taking place, participants in the seminars were also reading Canadian philosopher Charles Taylor's work on social fragmentation. Reflecting on both their field visits and their reading, AST leaders decided to embrace qualitative research in the MDiv curriculum, concluding that such research is a tool for understanding and constructing a more relational way of being.

## Valediction

Co-editor Susan Willhauck brings this work to completion with her essay 'The Gift and Challenge of Qualitative Methods for Pastoral Formation'. Here she reflects on her rationale for teaching qualitative methods in theology, noting that qualitative research is both a gift – 'a gift of profound encounter with others, a gift that leads to one's own self-giving in response to the Gospel call' – and an enormous challenge to both students and faculty. Drawing upon her research and teaching at Atlantic School of Theology, and her Wabash Research Grant project, which provided the impetus for this book, she also includes the challenges of research from the point of view of her students. The hurdles they face include anxiety at the thought of designing and implementing a research project, resentment of the amount of time the research takes, and difficulties with ethical review boards. Interestingly, faculty frequently complain about similar challenges: a lack of recognition of the extra time it takes to do rigorous qualitative studies on the part of administrators and tenure committees and a lack of integration of contextual approaches into theological schools' larger curricula. Yet the most significant pedagogical challenge is one that many of the other authors in this book have alluded to: the promotion of transformative learning that is not reducible to acquiring a new set of skills to be 'applied' in ministry. The quest is to effect formational growth in student-researchers who learn how to analyse social settings and how to imagine, with their research partners, what might be changed, what might be different. Willhauck notes that the gift of teaching qualitative research in its various forms is realized when, through what Rowan Williams has called the practice of dispossession,[25] the giving away of oneself to the needs of the world and the call of God, students 'come to a deeper understanding of their call and role in relationship to those whom they will serve'.

\* \* \*

This volume reflects a wide scope and variety of theological, pedagogical, and programmatic approaches to the teaching of qualitative research methods and methodologies. In the mix of the diverse experiences and strategies described here, there is a consistent focus on major themes, including ethics in teaching and research, representation, reflexivity, normativity, and the pastoral and professional formation of scholars. In addition, many of the contributors are teaching toward justice and working at understanding what it means to construct, in Jody Clarke's words, 'a more relational way of being'. Because these themes and goals involve questions that evolve and shift in diverse settings and situations and therefore cannot be settled once and for all, it is critical to continue this kind of thoughtful reflection and conversation across geographic and disciplinary boundaries. As researchers and teachers, we must continually consider the well-being of students, research partners, educational institutions, congregations, communities, and all of creation. The research and teaching projects and programmes shared here are offered in the hope of enriching current thinking and practice, as well as stimulating further reflection on the role of qualitative research in theological education.

## Notes

1 The 2016 symposium, 'Teaching Qualitative Research in Theological Education to Enhance Leadership in the Church', was funded by a 2014–15 Wabash Grant. Eight scholars from theological schools in the United States and Canada were invited to join the Atlantic School of Theology faculty in deliberating on a series of questions related to the rationale and practice of teaching qualitative research. Willhauck concludes that learning qualitative methods can enhance the practice of leadership for change as students are taught and embrace the arts of listening, attending to people, holding back judgement, observing and analysing to get at the meanings of things in order to disrupt the status quo. See Willhauck's essay in this volume.

2 Charles Marsh, 'Introduction', in *Lived Theology: New Perspectives on Method, Style, and Pedagogy*, eds Charles Marsh, Peter Slade, and Sarah Azaransky (New York: Oxford, 2017), 9.

3 Don Browning, *Fundamental Practical Theology: Descriptive and Strategic Proposals* (Minneapolis, MN: Augsburg-Fortress, 1991).

4 Elaine Graham, *Transforming Practice: Pastoral Theology in an Age of Uncertainty* (Eugene, OR: Wipf & Stock, 2002).

5 Charles Gerkin, *Widening the Horizons: Pastoral Responses to a Fragmented Society* (Louisville, KY: Westminster John Knox, 1986); Glenn H. Asquith, Jr., 'Anton T. Boisen and the Study of "Living Human Documents"', *Journal of Presbyterian History* 60, 3 (1982), 244–65; Bonnie J. Miller-McLemore, 'The Living Human Web: Pastoral Theology at the Turn of the Century', in *Through the Eyes of Women: Insights for Pastoral Care*, ed. Jeanne Stevenson-Moessner (Minneapolis, MN: Fortress, 1996), 9–26.

6 For a brief historiographical essay on pastoral theology and qualitative research, see Mary Clark Moschella, 'Practice Matters', in *Pastoral Theology and Care: Critical Trajectories in Theory and Practice*, ed. Nancy J. Ramsay (Chichester: John Wiley and Sons, 2018), 5–29.

7 Thomas Groome, *Sharing Faith: A Comprehensive Approach to Religious Education and Pastoral Ministry. The Way of Shared Praxis* (San Francisco, CA: Harper, 1991).

8 Elizabeth Conde-Frazier, 'Participatory Action Research: Practical Theology for Social Justice', *Religious Education* 101, 3 (2006), 327.

9 Christian Scharen and Aana Marie Vigen, eds., *Ethnography as Christian Theology and Ethics* (New York: Continuum, 2011), xviii.

10 Scharen and Vigen, *Ethnography*.

11 Mary McClintock Fulkerson, 'Foreword', in Scharen and Vigen, *Ethnography*, xi.

12 Marsh, Slade, and Azaransky, *Lived Theology*. See especially the last section on pedagogy, which incorporates various forms of activism in concert with theological classes.

13 See examples of students' remarks in Mary Clark Moschella, 'Enlivening Local Stories Through Pastoral Ethnography', in *Teaching Our Story: Narrative Leadership and Pastoral Formation*, ed. Larry A. Goleman (Herndon, VA: Alban, 2010), 67–86.

14 For a discussion of the phenomena of displacement and de-centring in fieldwork, see Scharen and Vigen, *Ethnography*, xviii.

15 The term 'research partners' is used in this Introduction as a general term referencing the participants in qualitative research projects. While the authors in this volume, coming from different disciplinary traditions, use a variety of terms, such as 'informants' or 'research subjects', here 'research partners' is used to convey more fully the contributions of participants.

16 Scharen and Vigen, *Ethnography*, 3.

17 Edward Farley, *Practicing Gospel: Unconventional Thoughts on the Church's Ministry* (Louisville, KY: Westminster John Knox, 2003), 29–43.

18 Norman K. Denzin and Yvonna S. Lincoln, eds, *The Sage Handbook of Qualitative Research* (4th edn; Thousand Oaks, CA: Sage, 2011), 123.

19 Farley, *Practicing Gospel*, 39–40.

20 Christian Scharen, *Fieldwork in Theology: Exploring the Social Context of God's Work in the World* (Grand Rapids, MI: Baker Academic, 2015), 22.

21 Swinton and Mowat helpfully distinguish between the two forms, calling them *personal* reflexivity and *epistemological* reflexivity (italics original); see John Swinton and Harriett Mowat, *Practical Theology and Qualitative Research* (2nd edn; London: SCM Press, 2015), 57.

22 Paulo Freire, *Pedagogy of the Oppressed*, trans. Myra Bergman Ramos (4th edn; New York: Bloomsbury Academic, 2018).

23 Tom Beaudoin, 'Why Does Practice Matter Theologically?' in *Conundrums in Practical Theology*, eds Joyce Ann Mercer and Bonnie J. Miller-McLemore (Leiden: Brill, 2016), 8–31, esp. 24–27.

24 See Kathleen Cahalan, Edward Foley, and Gordon S. Mikoski, eds, *Integrating Work in Theological Education* (Eugene, OR: Pickwick, 2017).

25 Rowan Williams, *A Ray of Darkness: Sermons and Reflections* (Cambridge, MA: Cowley, 1995), 231.

# PART I

# Exemplary Research Essays

# Theology as Playbook and Gamefilm: Explaining an Ethnographic Approach to Theology to a Sports-Centred Culture

## TODD DAVID WHITMORE

The use of ethnographic methods of research and modes of writing in the doing of theology is relatively rare, so presenting such methods and modes requires some extra explaining when introducing them in the classroom.[1] For this, I draw upon one of Jesus' rhetorical strategies: utilizing images from the common life of his audience – planting mustard seeds, fishing with nets – to convey both the glory and the demands of the Gospel. Given that over 114 million people in the United States – the largest audience in US television history – watched the 2015 Super Bowl, the example of sports perhaps works best for contemporary American culture for providing images from common life.[2] And sports are central to identity at the University of Notre Dame, where I teach. The most dramatic recent instance of institutional expansion on campus on the part of the university – its central importance underscored by its official title as the 'Campus Crossroads Project' – is a $400 million bid to involve academic space in a plan to expand the football stadium with luxury seating. The monetary numbers serve as rough indices of institutional value: buy-in for the most exclusive seating is a $1 million opening donation plus annual $120,000 gifts over the ensuing

20 years for a total payment of $3.4 million for a pod of eight seats.[3] To put the monetary valuation a different way, the university's nine-year buyout agreement with a former head coach fired for poor performance, Charlie Weis, amounted to almost $2.1 million per year, or approximately 27 times what a newly tenured – and thus successful – professor in the humanities earns.[4] Given their centrality in popular culture in general and at Notre Dame in particular, then, sports and images from sports appear to be the best way to teach anthropological theology. So I will take precisely this tack.

I grew up in Kitgum mission.[5]

I studied my primary in Kitgum girls primary school.

As I was living with the Sisters, the Little Sisters of Mary Immaculate of Gulu. I started to admire them. Yeah, their way of life actually, struck me and I started to share with them what I feel.

I wanted to become like one of them, the kind of life the Sisters were living. Community life.

And they were so lovable, charitable, they could move around the community.

The way they were also caring for the girls. Really I feel that it was . . . I don't know how to say it because the Sisters were living very very close, directing them to do this and that, both spiritual and physical.

Perhaps the single most significant intellectual error in the history of theology is its appropriation of philosophy's separation of theoretical and practical reason, and its own frequent self-categorization as a mode of the former.[6] Once they separate the two, thinkers of all sorts must design ways in which they come back together – or at least relate to each other – and theologians feel compelled to identify their project as first and foremost one or the other. This kind of taxonomization has been less than helpful for doing theology. Typically, it has led to the elevation of the theoretical over the practical, a hierarchization that has given rise to mistakes like the idea of there being 'applied' areas of theology and ethics as a distinct thing that we do after we do theology or ethics proper. Pierre Bourdieu's attempt to discern

They train us how to work in the field, how to cook, how to knit and all this.

And the kind of love they were showing us . . . That is what I really admired.

And the prayer life of course. The best prayer was rosary. They taught how to say the rosary, you know how to lead the rosary in the church and every evening when the bell goes we run to the church, each one of us wants to what? to lead the prayer . . .

After completing P7, we were invited in the convent. That was completely prayer life. They were now training us in prayer life and also to know more about the congregation . . .

You could go to school and then you come back in the convent . . .

During the school you do the academic work.

When you come to the convent you are being formed spiritually.

It was a very nice thing because we were really taught deep in the spiritual life, deep in the spiritual life. More even the social life.

the 'logic' and develop a 'theory' of practice is a significant relatively contemporary non-theological attempt to bridge the two while protecting practice's autonomy from the tendency to reduce it to what can be explained by theory. Showing the shortcomings of his approach helps to limn what a theology looks like for which the theory/practice separation is a non-factor. This is the kind of theology that, if we can pull it off, can be a proclamation of the Gospel.

Though Bourdieu stakes out his 'theory of practice' over against both subjectivism and objectivism, it is the latter that he develops most fully as a threat both to the development of an accurate theory of practice and to practices themselves.[7] Objectivism attempts to isolate the object of inquiry from the investigator so as to bring the former under the rational control of theory. Objectivist theory is totalizing in that it presumes to explain and anticipate everything about a practice, and it presupposes that correct practice follows logically, even mechanistically, from the application of the theory.[8] Bourdieu finds the social presuppositions of objectivism in the Greek word *skholé*, which originally meant 'leisure' or 'free time' – that is, time away from activity – and, while maintaining this

How when you become a Sister how you behave outside there with the what? With the community. How do you do your work.

So they prepare us actually how to interact with the people.

After novitiate I took my first vows. My first work was teaching.

We were brought in 1987 to Kitgum . . . From Kitgum we stayed some three days, and we were asked to go to Padibe.

In Padibe there was nobody. The missionaries were in Kitgum. All of them were in Kitgum . . .

In Padibe, things were not easy. Things were not easy.

Many of the people around were living in the mission, so all of us were in the mission . . .

I cannot remember the number because all those buildings in Padibe, they were filled up.

In the hospital, the health centre, people were there in the school, and then at the Sisters'.

You find people really suffered. And you could not eat twice a day.

During the evening they come. We eat once a day.

Because the people are there we said, 'Now we are sent there', which means the congregation wants us to die together with

meaning, came also to indicate 'time for intellectual discussion' and ultimately intellectual discussion itself. The problem with the split between the *theoria* which takes place in *skholé* and the *praxis* which takes place everywhere else, according to Bourdieu, is that it has from the beginning been articulated as a valuation of the former over the latter.[9]

Bourdieu cites Plato, but it is also evident in Aristotle, who mounts multiple arguments, each of which reinforces the others, that *theoria* is better than *praxis*: *theoria* pertains to *nous* (the intellect), the best part of us; it is self-sufficient and carried out for its own sake; and it takes place during leisure, upon which our happiness depends.[10] Bourdieu also emphasizes that, historically, writing both facilitates the development of *theoria* and has served as a crucial mechanism by which literate cultures (those that value *theoria* over *praxis* dominate predominantly oral cultures. He warns of the 'total or partial monopolizing of the [previously oral] society's symbolic resources in religion, philosophy, art and science, through the monopolization of the instruments for appropriation of these resources (writing, reading and other decoding techniques), henceforward preserved not in memories but in texts'.[11]

I share Bourdieu's concern about the

the people. We are not going to leave them.

In Padibe at least we have one hour Adoration. We used to do one hour Adoration before the Blessed Sacrament. We would close all the doors so people don't know where we are.

Just once they wake. But we do as a group . . . When we were going for prayers we tell our people.

Because there was no – you could not predict when things may not be okay at that particular moment . . . Because there was no communication outside.

Padibe was very risky. So we were confined in Padibe.

And once in a while, maybe twice in the month, we footed from Padibe to Kitgum together with the catechumens.

We come Kitgum to get the what? The Blessed Sacrament.

When it was consecrated then we carry together, we move on foot with the children in back.

That was the Sacrament we put in the tabernacle for daily Holy Communion.

Sometimes we were scared. But knowing we were going back with the Blessed Sacrament we keep on praying praying praying . . .

oppressive uses to which writing has been put, and I agree that, historically, writing has arisen in the context of, and in turn has reinforced, presuppositions about the primacy of the intellect understood as a kind of disembodied aspect of ourselves.

The problem is that in accepting the *theoria/praxis* separation to begin with, even as he tries to relate the two, he, in an act that he would term a 'misrecognition', reinforces both the presuppositions and, in the end, the value system of that split. As *theoria* is opposed to *praxis*, writing, according to Bourdieu, is opposed to mimesis. Whereas particularly oral societies engage in learning by mimesis, a kind of 'practical reactivation which is *opposed* to both memory and knowledge' and is 'never detached from the body', all theoretical schemes, particularly where writing is involved, 'intervene between the individual and his/her body'. Bourdieu draws from Weber in calling writing a tool of 'disincarnation'. The theoretical models that arise through writing therefore have '*nothing* in common with participation in practical experience'. In fact, trying to teach about practice in schools – the etymology of the latter is traceable to the idea of *skholé* – directly and conclusively interferes with practice. 'Excellence (that is, practical mastery in its accomplished form) has

We were just praying, 'O Sacrament Most Holy, O Sacrament Divine, all praise and all thanksgiving be every morning thine. O Blessed Sacrament.' Just like that.

So when we reached somewhere in the middle we were almost approaching Kitgum mission. That is when we met the rebels.

For the first time . . . They took us and moved in the bush . . . We moved throughout the night until the next morning throughout the day and then at six o'clock that is when they release us.

And we came back . . .

. . . What we were usually – when we were coming to Kitgum we would keep on saying rosary.

At that time we were also saying rosary, we had not yet finished the what? The decades.

So as soon as the rebels stopped us, I jumped out and I raise my arm and the rosary was there . . . They came and snatched it, you know, picked away the rosary.

Say 'Bring it here'. So as we were moving, going, I was not even scared. I don't know why. I was not scared because I say,

*ceased to exist* once people start asking whether it can be taught, as soon as they seek to base "correct" practice on rules extracted, for the purposes of transmission.'[12] This outright separation of theory and practice (which Bourdieu then tries to overcome) carries with it an exoticization of the practitioner over against the theorist whereby the former becomes a re-creation of early twentieth-century anthropology's 'noble savage'. This is most evident in Bourdieu's insistence that the practitioner is not consciously aware of the true rules of their actions. Learning and re-creation of correct practice 'tend to take place below the level of consciousness' and have 'nothing in common with an imitation that would presuppose a conscious effort to reproduce a gesture'. In an act of what Bourdieu calls 'learned ignorance', participants 'conceal, even from themselves, the true nature of their practical mastery'. Such *docta ignorantia* 'does not contain knowledge of its own principles'. The only time that there is reference to any explicit rules is 'in cases of misfiring or failure' in the practice itself.[13]

I understand and share Bourdieu's concern with the *ideology* of theory and writing that separates both from the body, but the fact of the matter is, as Ecclesiastes tells us, conscious intellectual activity and the body are deeply intertwined: 'The sayings of the

'Now Jesus we have not done anything wrong' . . .

I was the first Sister for the first time to be taken in the bush by these people.

So now when they took us in the bush I just moved with them . . .

One time when the rebels entered in the convent the Sisters were beaten.

I had come to Kitgum town. I was preparing myself to go to school now, in '88 September.

But now when I heard that they have entered the convent, I took my motorcycle.

I told the Sisters in Kitgum I'm going back . . .

We had been so close together all along, suffering together and now I am away from them. I felt that I should go again, we be together . . . I was praying, 'God allow me, let nothing happen to me, let nothing happen to me. Just let nothing happen to me' . . .

When I went back to Padibe, I did not even feel bad because I know my Sisters are there, and they are those who I have been working with.

They are there. So if they are suffering, why can't I suffer together with them?

wise are like goads, and like nails firmly fixed are the collected sayings that are given by one shepherd. Of anything beyond these, my child, beware. Of making many books there is no end, and much study is a weariness of the flesh' (Eccles. 12.11–12). Recent studies tell us what all scholars know: writing contributes to back pain, eye strain, and carpal tunnel syndrome. In short, writing and theorizing *are* bodily practices. The question for Christian theologians is not how we can relate them to practice, but how to practise them so that they can be taken up as integral parts of proclaiming the Gospel.

Bourdieu himself gives us an avenue for doing so by describing practice as 'practical participation in a game'.[14] He draws upon the game analogy precisely to distinguish practice from objectivist theories about practice, and it is here (and elsewhere) that he stresses the lack of practitioners' consciousness about their practices. However, if we look at actual games, we can see that writing and other techniques that abstract from on-field action are very much a part of the practice. During timeouts in basketball, the coach typically crouches with a dry-erase clipboard to diagram the next play for the team huddled around him. When the players return to the court, they are *consciously* aware of what they are trying to do. In baseball,

So I did not feel actually so bad, and I did not even complain, 'Now why are you taking me back where I've been suffering?' and the rest of it. But I knew those are the people; I have been suffering with them; I think that is where my happiness also will come.

That trauma is still disturbing me.

And sometimes because, now as I talk, I move to Padibe every week.

Whenever I reach that spot where the rebel picked me and went with me to the bush, that thing always come back in my mind, much as I was not hurt.

I was not even beaten by them. They did not even use any bad words on me.

But still I think, 'Why?'

. . . And going to Padibe and now I'm living, I'm going, I sleep in the same room where they broke the door.

Sometimes it all comes back as a sort of dream, like where somebody says, a day-dream.

You can dream when your eyes are open.

So that is still a fight. That is still a fight . . . In fact the most help that I'm getting is being close to the Sacrament,

the third-base coach sends plays to the batter and runners through a series of abstracted signals – touching their nose or cap, brushing their sleeve – for such plays as the 'squeeze bunt' and the 'hit and run'. Again, the players are very conscious of what they are trying to do. And all of these explicit plays take place not 'in cases of misfire or failure' in the practice, as Bourdieu would have it, but precisely to increase the likelihood of performative success. If the practice of abstracting from practice to improve practice did not work in practice much of the time, there would be no courtside dry-erase boards or third-base line signals. Instead, we find that the condensed abstractions constitute, to use Alasdair MacIntyre's phrase, 'internal goods' for the practice of the sport.[15]

The role of abstraction through writing and other means for enhancing the practice of a sport is perhaps most thoroughly developed in American football. When a new player arrives at pre-season camp, one of the first things he receives is a thick 'playbook', which he is required to 'study' and memorize. Though, technically, what is called the 'game' takes place later, the practice of football for a new arrival begins with study of the playbook. When the quarterback or the defensive captain calls out a play on the field through coded names – say, 'wing right, 23 dive' – the player is supposed to know what to do from the Eucharist, the Body of Christ.

I know that that one is the one that sincerely is helping me to push ahead.

Because I meet Christ and he is always in me.

I never – I used to say 'Communion'; I say now, 'You are with me. Everywhere I go. Whatever I do. You are here within me. I'm not praying, but the whole of you is in me. I move with you.'

. . . And I say that it is really very very important that we unite with Jesus in the Blessed Sacrament.

The whole of Jesus is in me. 'I'm moving with you.'

Whenever I receive the Holy Sacrament, the Holy Communion, I feel protected. I feel protected.

Much as those things – because it was really something that has touched our lives directly.

And it is not easy because we need to be full in order to make others also keep hope.

Without which, things will not be easy . . .

. . . Then the Sisters decided to bring me back to Kitgum. They didn't tell me anywhere but they from having studied the playbook. The conscious practice of abstracting gameplay and memorizing the abstracted text are *assumed as part of the game*. To be sure, the player is to memorize the play so that he does not have to think consciously much at all about it, and playbooks without on-the-field experience are next to useless, but the movement during this segment of activity is clearly from explicit symbolic practice (which still very much involves the body; players will say how playbook study is tiring) to on-field practice in order to raise the excellence of the latter.

It is also true that much of what occurs on the playing field takes place, as Bourdieu stresses, below the threshold of consciousness, and that there are virtuoso players who cannot fully articulate the 'logic' of their play. For both better and worse, far from all of what goes on on the field goes according to explicit plan. The on-the-field practice is not reducible to the practice of abstracting from that in order to improve it in the future. Yet the on-field and off-field practices are deeply interrelated – not as practice and theory, but as two moments in the overall practice of the game, as is evident when the quarterback calls out the abstracted signals *on the field*. Study of the playbook is part of the larger field of the sport. Practitioners of American brought me to a school, and this school had just started.

And the school was started for abductees. The girls who had come back from the bush.

Secondly, girls who were living in the camp around here. IDP camp.

Then the priest collected these girls and brought them here.

And says, 'Sister come and help.' . . .

I sit down and make tea for the priest. He says, 'God has something for you.'

Much as I've been traumatized with this war, he wants me again to help the traumatized . . .

So we started this school with the twenty-one girls.

There were bush mothers. Very young girls, like this, and this girl having a child with her.

Others are big, big, but because they went in the bush, and they remained there, they came back with kids.

And it is not easy: this is a woman, this is a girl who is completely traumatized.

You need to mould them, talk to them, show them the way how to behave and the rest of it . . .

And I was thinking, I said 'I think God has something for me.'

football account for and bridge the gap between what is usually recognized as on-field play and the playbook by watching – players refer to it as 'studying' – gamefilm. Someone who watches a lot of gamefilm is called a good 'student of the game'. What the gamefilms provide are the designed plays in action so that the observer can diagnose what makes the play work or not work on the field more narrowly conceived.

The practice of theology, when it works, is Gospel playbook and gamefilm. The more abstracted sections – like the one that I am writing right now – are like a playbook. They present in schematic form the outlines of what a good 'play' (or a bad play) in the game of the Good News looks like. It can be difficult for the reader to integrate the schematic presentation with the broader practice of the Gospel, and for this the theologian draws upon a more time-sensed, narrative mode of presentation, like that on the left side of these pages – our version of gamefilm. The Gospels themselves tack back and forth between playbook and gamefilm when they move from Jesus' sayings to his parables/stories and back again. Erich Auerbach notes in *Mimesis: The Representation of Reality in Western Literature* that the biblical narratives are 'visually concrete', even though they do not provide much in the way of descriptive detail. Such fine detail was not initially necessary because the

Because I would have said no, I would have said no to the what?

To my superiors: 'Please you take me somewhere else. Because I am also traumatized, and I have to come and help the traumatized.'

[But] I say, 'No, He has something for me' . . .

And the first group went out and now some of them are becoming nurses. One already a qualified nurse.

And I think that is something God has spoken to me . . . But out of 21, only seven succeeded with life.

The rest are now there in the villages.

And I said, 'No, I think God will work a miracle.'

I want to call those very good who come back from the what? From the bush.

I want them by next year. I want them to come back so that we train them how to do tailoring. Because with the tailoring you can sit with your machine somewhere, even in the village.

She can get some one hundred, two hundred, even more . . .

A woman can have something if every day she is having two

original hearers of the message to a large extent had a fund of shared cultural experiences, so the language of the stories could be metonymic and therefore still be, as Auerbach says, 'fraught with background'.[16] The hearers could fill in the details themselves. Globalization and the fragmentation and hybridization of cultures mean that we can no longer rely on such metonymic communication in the same way, and therefore must employ what Clifford Geertz calls 'thick description'.[17] The role of ethnography in theology, then, is that of helping to provide a particularly rich, fine-grained account of God's actions and of Christian practices (and of practices that are otherwise) in response for consideration for re-enactment or rejection.[18]

Describing theology as playbook and gamefilm is also to suggest that the theologian is analogous to the coach of a sports team. To the extent that this is true, we can learn from the case of sports. For instance, in almost every case of professional and collegiate sport, the coaches, particularly head coaches, were, at least at one point in their lives, players of the sport at a relatively high level, whether in high school, college, or even professionally. This suggests that to understand how to abstract the rules of practice so that they can in turn enhance the practice itself requires some degree of on-the-field familiarity with the hundred shillings, which she made with the dress, she is able to buy salt in her house.

She's able to buy the soap for the washing.

So this is the thing that has been, you know, disturbing me . . .

. . . Sometimes I ask 'Why, why God again, why? I am traumatized. And you want me again to work with the traumatized. Am I going to help them anyway?' . . .

But I've seen that I am helping them. So I praise the Lord for that.

And that's why I told you my experience.

What is helping me is Holy Communion. Because I know that Jesus is in me whole, not part of him.

Maybe if I am the one who, you know, stops my work, my heart falls to the side . . .

But He is whole. With him, and him now, I have become one at my working place.

practice. It also suggests that one reason why Charlie Weis – the fired Notre Dame football coach mentioned earlier – has failed as a head coach at Notre Dame and elsewhere is that he lacks that on-the-field experience.[19] The other lesson to be drawn from the world of sport and the coaching analogy is that while coaches typically have played at a relatively high level, it is almost never the case that good coaches were on-the-field *virtuosi* in the sport. Magic Johnson and Isiah Thomas were failures as coaches; Michael Jordan knew not to try. Most good coaches were 'role players' as athletes.[20] Doc Rivers, Phil Jackson, and Steve Kerr come to mind. Exceptions would have to include Larry Bird (who found coaching so frustrating that he had to stop after three seasons) and Bill Russell (and whether he was a good coach can be debated). Joe Torre might be an example. If the analogy from sports holds, then it appears that most good theologians have some significant on-the-field experience, but are not among the saints.

Theology as Gospel mimesis rejects the idea of theological knowledge for its own sake both because Jesus of Nazareth, the one whom we are to imitate, was not, whatever else he was, a gnostic,[21] and because of the problematic implications – the denigration of the body, of everyday practice, and of cultures deemed 'backward' – that inevitably operate under the knowledge-for-its-own-sake model. Still, the aim of writing anthropological theology is not simply (though it includes) the defence of the cultures encountered against the onslaughts of modernity and post-modernity; it is also, through vivid mimetic re-presentation of what it looks like,[22] to prompt you, the reader, to step onto the 'field' of the Gospel, first through allowing you to enter into the lives of the people in these pages, and then through inviting you to put this book down and to enter the Gospel game, again, yourself.

## Notes

1 Some notable exceptions to this lack of ethnographic method include, for instance, Mary McClintock Fulkerson, *Places of Redemption: Theology for a Worldly Church* (Oxford: Oxford University Press, 2007); Christian Scharen and Aana Marie Vigen, eds, *Ethnography as Christian Theology and Ethics* (London and New York: Continuum, 2011); Michael Banner, *Ethics of Everyday Life: Moral Theology, Social Anthropology, and the Imagination of the Human* (Oxford: Oxford University Press, 2014); Natalie Wigg-Stevenson, *Ethnographic Theology: An Inquiry into the Production of Theological Knowledge* (New York: Palgrave Macmillan, 2014); Siobhán Garrigan, *The Real Peace Process: Worship, Politics, and the End of Sectarianism* (London: Equinox, 2010); Luke Bretherton, *Christianity and Contemporary Politics: The Conditions and Possibilities of Faithful Witness* (Malden, MA, and Oxford: Wiley-Blackwell, 2010); Luke Bretherton, *Resurrecting Democracy: Faith, Citizenship, and the Politics of a Common Life* (New York: Cambridge University Press, 2015). There are others.

2 Frank Pallotta, 'Super Bowl XLIX Posts the Largest Audience in TV History', *CNN Money* (2 February 2015), http://money.cnn.com/2015/02/02/media/super-bowl-ratings/. The number does not reflect those who watched the game in sports bars or at viewing parties. Including these populations would increase the figure dramatically. Mark Lazarus, the chairman of NBC Sports, which broadcast the game, called the Super Bowl 'the most dominant and consistent property on television'; see Pallotta, 'Super Bowl XLIX'.

3 *Campus Crossroads* (brochure sent to major university donors; the PDF copy I obtained listed no specific author or publisher information, and contains no date of publication). For the official promotional video see http://crossroads.nd.edu/. For critiques of the project see, for instance, Nathaniel Gotcher, 'An Ill-conceived Bragging Point', *The Observer* (30 January 2014), at http://ndsmcobserver.com/2014/01/ill-conceived-bragging-point/; Colin Fleming, 'Redirect Crossroads', *The Observer* (13 February 2014), at http://ndsmcobserver.com/2014/02/redirect-crossroads/; Robert Alvarez, 'Beyond the Crossroads', *The Observer* (25 February 2014), at http://ndsmcobserver.com/2014/02/beyond-crossroads/, and Fr. Bill Miscamble, CSC, 'Notre Dame at a Crossroads: Misplaced Priorities and a Flawed Vision', *The Irish Rover* (23 February 2014), https://irishrover.net/2014/02/notre-dame-at-a-crossroads-misplaced-priorities-and-a-flawed-vision/.

4 On the Charlie Weis buyout, see Matt Fortuna, 'Charlie Weis Still Paid \$2 million Annually from Notre Dame', *ESPN* (18 May 2015), http://espn.go.com/college-football/story/_/id/12910308/charlie-weis-cashing-big-paychecks-via-notre-dame-fighting-irish. The starting salary for departmental office staff is as low as \$20,837. See http://hr.nd.edu/compensation/overview/#/general-administration/department-administration. The 2016 poverty line for a family of four is \$24,250 (for a family of three it is \$20,090). For poverty levels, see https://www.parkviewmc.com/app/files/public/1484/2016-Poverty-Level-Chart.pdf. The starting salary for some custodial workers at Notre Dame is even lower (\$17,539). See http://hr.nd.edu/compensation/overview/#/facilities/custodial.

5 What follows in this left-hand column is the testimony of one of the nuns I interviewed during my fieldwork in northern Uganda and South Sudan.

6 An exception, of course, would be the minority sub-discipline calling itself 'practical theology'. Here, the exception proves the rule, as the felt need to use the qualifier 'practical' affirms both its minority status and the theoretical/practical split.

7 Bourdieu, *The Logic of Practice* (Stanford, CA: Stanford University Press, 1990), 1–51.

8 Bourdieu, *Logic of Practice*, 105, 107.

9 Bourdieu, *Logic of Practice*, 27–28, 31.

10 Aristotle, *Nicomachean Ethics*, 1177a11–b26. I am aware of the interpretation that this passage in Book X conflicts with passages elsewhere in the text, but find Arthur Adkins' argument to be convincing that, in the end, Aristotle is consistent and that Book X is the controlling view. Adkins is also helpful in noting that *theoria* is not research, but contemplation of knowledge that we already have. See A.W.H. Adkins, '*Theoria* versus *Praxis* in the *Nicomachean Ethics* and the *Republic*', *Classical Philology*, 73, 4 *(1978)*, 297–313.

11 Bourdieu, *Logic of Practice*, 125.

12 Bourdieu, *Logic of Practice*, 73, 104, 103; emphases added.

13 Bourdieu, *Logic of Practice*, 73, 102, 103–4.

14 Bourdieu, *Logic of Practice*, 104.

15 Alasdair MacIntyre, *After Virtue: A Study in Moral Theory* (London and New York: Bloomsbury Academic, 2013), 228.

16 Erich Auerbach, *Mimesis: The Representation of Reality in Western Literature* (Princeton, NJ and Oxford: Princeton University Press, 2003), 47–48, 11–12.

17 Clifford Geertz, *The Interpretation of Cultures* (New York: Basic Books, 1973), 3–31.

18 As indicated earlier, the practitioners of the desired practices need not be people regarded as Christian; in fact, Jesus regularly featured protagonists not from the people of Israel in his stories as a means of both pointing to a reality and giving the accounts a particular rhetorical edge.

19 Weis could still be (and has been) successful as an assistant coach, where he is more responsible for the abstract xs and os of the playbook than for embodied practice.

20 See, for instance, Ray Fitipaldo, 'Hall of Fame Players as NFL Coaches Are a Rare Breed'. *Pittsburgh Post-Gazette* (6 September 2013), at http://www.post-gazette.com/sports/steelers/2013/09/06/Hall-of-Fame-players-as-NFL-coaches-a-rare-breed/stories/201309060129.

21 It is generally agreed that the 'gnostic gospels' were written between the second and fourth centuries. The Gospel of John, the most gnostic-like of the canonical gospels, was written last and is the least historical of the gospels.

22 Michael Taussig is clear regarding the mimetic potential of ethnographic writing. Writing about the work of Stephanie Kane, he says, 'I want to emphasize that unlike most ethnographic modes of representation . . . Stephanie Kame's mode relies not on abstract general locutions as "among the Emberá it is believed that . . .," but instead concentrates on image-ful particularity in such a way that . . . she creates a magical reproduction itself, a sensuous sense of the real, mimetically at one with what it attempts to represent. In other words, can't we say that *to give an example, to instantiate, to be concrete*, are all examples of the magic of mimesis wherein the replication, the copy, acquires the power of the represented? And does not the magical power of this embodying inhere in the fact that in reading such examples we are thereby lifted out of ourselves into those images? Just as the shaman captures and creates power by making a model of the gringo-spirit-ship and its crew, so here the ethnographer is making her model. If I am correct in making this analogy with what I take to be the magician's art of reproduction, then the model, if it works, gains through its sensuous fidelity something of the power and personality of that which it is a model', Michael Taussig, *Mimesis and Alterity: A Particular History of the Senses* (New York and London: Routledge, 1993), 16.

## 2

# Qualitative Methodology and Critical Pedagogy: A Study of the Lived Experiences of Thai Peasants within the Context of Western Development Ideology

SIROJ SORAJJAKOOL
AND APIPA PRACHYAPRUIT

Western-influenced educational systems often view pedagogy as an art or as a set of skills or techniques for the transmission of knowledge. Proponents of critical pedagogy argue, however, that pedagogy is political and that the uncritical application of pedagogic tools can result in the reproduction of a social system that privileges a certain demographic, particularly the elites. In *Ideology and Curriculum*, Michael Apple insisted:

> The structuring of knowledge and symbol in our educational institutions is intimately related to the principles of social and cultural control in a society . . . our basic problems as educators and as political beings, then, is to begin to grapple with ways of understanding how the kinds of cultural resources and symbols schools select and organize are dialectically related to the kinds of normative and conceptual consciousness 'required' by a stratified society.[1]

In a similar vein Henry Giroux has stated, 'Teaching for many conservatives is often treated simply as a set of strategies and skills.' However, he argues, 'pedagogy is always political because it is connected to the acquisition of agency'.[2] At a time when we witness both intense inequality within our society and the power of knowledge to control a society, pedagogy has to take a different approach. Giroux encourages education to become critical pedagogy, noting:

> As a political project, critical pedagogy illuminates the relationships among knowledge, authority, and power. It draws attention to questions concerning who has control over the conditions for the production of knowledge, values, and skills and it illuminates how knowledge, identities and authority are constructed within particular sets of social relations.[3]

This article explores the relationship between power, knowledge, and politics in the lives of Thai peasants as we seek to understand the impact of a dominant discourse on the lives of local farmers and their ways of living, both existentially and philosophically. Additionally, it seeks to show how qualitative methodology can act as a tool of critical pedagogy. This article explores how qualitative research can engage the everyday experiences of the people to reveal a hidden political agenda, identify the relationship between knowledge and power, and generate awareness of the dominant societal discourse for the purpose of emancipation.

## The Project

The project presented here was carried out among Thai farmers who are among the poorest in the country. It seeks qualitative data that can inform theological reflections on appropriate ways to address the needs of such local Thai farmers. Methodologically, it intends a dialogue between lived experiences and theological perspectives so that theological constructs can find grounding in shared narratives of the farmers.

The study explores what higher education has done to facilitate social mobility, what the current status of local Thai farmers is, what farmers think of higher education, and what the role and function of education are in the context of the lived experience of local farmers. The specific research questions were: What do farmers have to say about the ways in which a dominant discourse has impacted their ways of living? What role did knowledge play during the past 60 years of rural development? How can we understand the current situation for Thai farmers whose debts increase even as they are forced to sell their land just so they can manage their lives? To answer these questions, we draw on historical texts and other documents to help determine the role of higher education in facilitating social mobility, but our data is primarily qualitative in nature, and we use qualitative methods and grounded theory in our interpretation.

Snowball and convenience sampling methods were used to select participants. The qualitative data is based on three groups of participants: the first group consisted of 67 farmers from nineteen provinces in the north and the north-eastern parts of Thailand; in the second group there were eight participants, children of farmers, who have been through higher education; the third group had six participants, children of farmers, who are currently pursuing higher education. The interviews took place between January and August 2015. Six trips were made, covering 19 provinces in the north and north-east of Thailand.

'Coding', according to Kathy Charmaz, 'means naming segments of data with a label that simultaneously categorizes, summarizes, and accounts for each piece of data.'[4] Coding of the interviews was done in two stages. The first stage was carried out line by line, identifying participants' ideas and opinions. In the second stage, main ideas were grouped together to form concepts while at the same time they were organized into categories and subcategories. As the researchers worked on emerging themes a question was posed consistently: What do the participants really wish to convey, beyond our interpretation of the scripts? When themes became stable, subsequent interviews were carried out to identify the point of saturation. The organizing themes and categories were further analysed to make certain that process and concepts were aligned. As a final step, other scholars with a research focus on higher education, the lived experiences of farmers, and Foucault's archaeology and genealogy were consulted, to make certain the concepts that had been identified were represented accurately.[5]

The results of this qualitative study fall into two main categories. The first category describes the current situation for farmers after 60 years of development, with higher education as a primary variable. The themes that have emerged from the data are: changes related to modernization; limited access to resources; increasing costs of farming; poor return on investment; and increased living expenses. The second category looks at farmers' experiences of and perspectives on higher education, specifically in relation to its role in social mobility. Here the themes that have emerged from the qualitative data are: modernity makes the pursuit of higher education necessary; higher education does not support the lived experiences of farmers; and social mobility is not a part of farmers' cultural practices.

Conceptually this research explores the relationship of knowledge and power with reference to Foucault's genealogy concept, which is used as an analytic tool for tracing genealogies of knowledge in order to differentiate between traditional and modern world-views that guide very different approaches to reality. A preliminary survey of the struggle of Thai peasants raises awareness of the need to explore the place of modernity within the socio-economic reality of Thai communities. As the primary philosophical assumption, modernity plays a significant role in determining social status, defining social hierarchy, legitimizing knowledge, and stipulating social norms. These norms are sanctioned by formal education, which can facilitate social mobility. Formal education gives access to the industrialized world. Not only is industrialization about job security but also, directly and indirectly, it is an endorsement of a world-view that dictates cultural values. How do these factors impact the lives of local Thai peasants? What is the pastoral theological implication for those wishing to address the local needs and struggles of this population?

How does one translate theological education into everyday living for the marginalized? Perhaps this is where qualitative research can inform theological education, by grounding students' perspectives in the everyday struggle of the poor and the oppressed.

## The Context

In the late 1950s and early 1960s communism made rapid headway into Southeast Asia with the fight for independence from the French in Vietnam and the spread of communism to Cambodia and subsequently to the Lao People's Democratic Republic. The domino theory was widely discussed within the political arena with reference to various regions, with rural areas deemed vulnerable. For the United States government, Thailand was geographically strategic, a location where ideological struggles were being played out and with the potential to be dominated.[6] The instability caused by the transition from absolute monarchy to constitutional monarchy left Thailand vulnerable. Against the background of calls for geo-political security and national development, Field Marshal Sarit Thanarat came to power through a coup d'état.[7] The World Bank played an important role in the pursuit of such an agenda in Thailand, in conjunction with the International Monetary Fund, the World Trade Organization, and the Asian Development Bank. The World Bank stepped in to help draft the economic plan that saw the creation of the First National Economic and Development Plan. Financial resources entered the country in various forms, from development aid to military support.[8] Infrastructure building reached the most remote areas of the country in an attempt to deter rural Thais from adopting communism.

One of the most important developments during this period was in education. Forces, both internal and external, were gathering to make sure that Thailand invested in development, in modernization. To be a part of the modern world was to be a part of the global industrial community and the world economy. Knowledge was a prerequisite for such involvement. Development requires a pool of knowledge. Human resources were viewed as necessary capital. Many Thais travelled to the United States to further their studies. Numerous scholarships were offered through Fulbright programmes. Local training brought Western scientific approaches to farming. Universities were established across the country. Modernity became the primary form of knowledge dispensed through regional universities, and even, for a long period, the only legitimate form of knowledge. To develop was to modernize through the acquisition of knowledge especially in science and engineering. Modernization has been the sole episteme guiding the dominant discourse in Thailand for generations right up to today. Social mobility has been viewed as the most viable form of economic growth within the poorer population. And education became a vehicle for the acquisition of wealth and upward mobility.

However, the status of local farmers is not in accord with the picture associated with the rapid expansion of higher education in Thailand. According to the Agriculture Census of 2013, approximately a quarter of the population in Thailand works as farmers, 28 per cent of 5.9 million farmers' income level is at 100,001 baht and over, while 28 per cent had an income between 50,001 and 100,000 baht and 24 per cent had an income between 20,001 and 50,000 baht, and the remainder an income of 20,000 baht or below. Poor farmers are categorized among the lowest 20 per cent in income level in relation to the national population. The average income per farm household was 50,656 baht or 11,125 baht per person with average land sizes of seven acres.[9] The apparent incongruence between what the government hoped to achieve and the reality of the lived experience of local farmers raises a significant theological question.

## Problematizing Everyday Experience

In *Ideology and Curriculum*, Apple argues that it is essential to begin by problematizing the everyday experience of the people, by taking the lived experience seriously. At times our pedagogy is limited to available texts in the discipline, but qualitative skills and methodologies open up access to further information and often lead to new perspectives not available through traditional texts. In our experience, we have found that the themes and outcomes that have emerged from qualitative studies were far beyond anything we could have predicted or might have anticipated in light of the existing literature. Listening to lived experiences through qualitative studies has reinforced the importance of experience as an alternate text. This alternate text is considerably more than words on a page. This text breathes. And it sweats, feels, knows hardship and pain, conveys sensation, and speaks expressively. Here learning takes on an existential dimension, with knowledge derived from the reality of everyday living and conviction that lies beyond the intellect.

## Modernization

Almost all the farmers mourned the loss of their way of living prior to the government's implementation of modernization. They reminisced about the easy, simple living that had made it possible for them to remain independent: holding on to traditional family values, fishing from the ponds, gathering food from the fields, and spending time supporting each other during planting and harvesting seasons. Their farming methods have been altered significantly by modernization, creating dependency on monetary systems and technology. Credit loans became a part of the community because of the need to borrow money to implement modern methods of farming. Farmers started getting into debt and many lost their rice fields. Life changed when monoculture farming was introduced. The dependency on cash instead of crops transformed their society. Now food has to be acquired beyond the farmers' own fields through monetary exchange. Migration became necessary for survival, creating a generational gap within the community. Young people migrated to cities for financial reasons, leaving the older generation to care for young children.

Participants recognized that the downsizing of farmland, access to water, and soil type imposed limitations on their output as the rural population was gradually growing.[10] Local farmers also reported an annual increase in fertilizer use. What was sufficient one year is no longer sufficient the following year.[11] Farmers consistently complained of the high investment required for the production of rice and the consequentially poor return. The average cost of production per rai (1 rai = 40m × 40m = 0.16 hectare) among participants was approximately 3000–4000 baht while the gross income is only 6000–6500 per rai. Returns, according to participants, were better under former Prime Minister Yingluck Shinawatra, thanks to her rice subsidy scheme. Expenses include labour, seeds, fertilizers, pesticides, fuel, transportation, and the use of machinery.

Farming is not what it used to be and the changes to the farmers' lifestyle are significant. Crops are no longer regional, and farmers no longer have control over their product because the outcome of their labour is determined by market mechanisms regulated, and perhaps manipulated, at a distance. Production mechanisms are currently connected to fuel transportation, credits, loans, currency exchange, outlets, advertising, packaging, chemical factories, legal contracts, and market systems. These factors impose restrictions on farmers. Farmers have become merely providers of labour, often on their own land. 'Yet farmers are willing to subject themselves to these new farming arrangements because they have so little choice. With banks wielding the threat of foreclosure, any kind of farming, even the kind of farming that asset-strips the soil, is preferable to no farming at all.'[12]

## The Dominant Discourse and Higher Education

A dominant discourse in modern society holds that higher education facilitates social mobility, that knowledge is essential for personal growth and development. This attitude has determined the rhetoric of most government policies globally promoting meritocracy in education. In our study, the children of farmers who had earned academic degrees or were pursuing higher education acknowledged the positive contributions of higher education when it came to social status within the community and financial stability. At the same time they displayed a deep respect for farmers' cultural practices and values that were leading them to maintain their identity as farmers' children. 'Once a farmer, always a farmer' was a comment made by the daughter of an elderly farmer during an interview. They pointed out that knowledge acquired through higher education does not contribute to the lives of farmers. These participants no longer engage in rice farming although some still help their parents on occasion or employ others to plant and harvest for them. Three farmers with undergraduate degrees did express appreciation for what they learned. The head of a village in Roi Et Province discussed ways in which the knowledge he had acquired helped him better manage his rice production. Another farmer, who had earned a degree in development, expressed her appreciation for the programme's focus on self-sufficiency.

Most farmers said of higher education only that is expensive, and yet such farmers, especially those within the younger age group, were determined to send their children to pursue higher education. Pessimism about the future of rice farming was given as their primary reason for this commitment. A farmer from Khon Kaen stated,

> Everything costs money. It is becoming a part of the global economy that makes the transition into the industrial world a necessity for farmers as they envision the future of their children. It is no longer subsistence and the communal support no longer exists. It is about generating income and one of the most viable ways is through employment. And for the most part when it comes to employment, tertiary education is a basic requirement.

In recent decades, life has become harder for farmers, and hence they see a college degree as a path to employment and a more secure future for their children. Securing a job as a civil servant has broad benefits, often enhancing a family's stability. However, farmers do not see college degrees as benefitting their everyday life. The holder of a college degree will likely migrate out of the village and enter a career other than farming. Most farmers interviewed admitted that higher education was one of their most expensive investments. A teacher from Ku Ka Sing sub-district related that by the time she graduated from her undergraduate programme, all the cows that her parents raised were gone. Some farmers sell their lands, while other take out loans. Families without children have a much easier time. Life is very manageable when they do not have children to send to college or university.

Additional to the expense, getting admitted into a good programme is a real challenge. Three students currently pursuing undergraduate degrees at Rajabhat University Loei explained that they were among the very few students from their villages to be admitted to universities. Two major challenges were distance and time. For many students, the farther their homes are from the district with strong academic institutions, the smaller their chance of getting into a good university. Another major challenge is the need to help parents with farming. These students had neither the time nor the money for private tutoring, unlike students in the city. So, while taking on loans, they end up in regional universities of lesser reputation with a reduced chance of a good job upon graduation. Further, education does not always translate into employment. In some cases, graduates return home to farm, but still carry the obligation to repay their student loans.

## Established Cultural Practice

Thai farmers see higher education as a path toward a career other than farming (horizontal mobility). And this career path is at the same time a promise of a better future economically (vertical mobility), which will enhance the degree holder's social status. However, most participants prefer to remain farmers, work in the fields, and live self-sufficiently. They prefer their occupation to allow them to remain independent. Hence if mobility implies success, how farmers define success is an ironic twist in higher education's facilitating of social mobility. While higher education prepares students for employment within industrial society, farmers, if given a choice, prefer to stay on their farms and work the fields. For farmers, success is connected to independence, hard work, self-sufficiency, and the ability to take care of one's family. Success is not defined by the acquisition and accumulation of wealth. While social status may have some appeal for the younger generation of farmers, the concept of sufficiency remains because it implies freedom and the ability to be independent.

A farmer in Srisaket lives in a small wooden shack with a rusted zinc roof on a small piece of farmland off the main highway. He refused to hire labourers or pay for tractors, choosing instead to sweat year after year saving money and working the field. Two of his children are completing undergraduate degrees. When asked how he managed to support his family and afford higher education, his response was succinct: 'simplicity'. It seems that in such an act of resistance farmers find a way of retaining their identity and their independence by disengaging from the social norms established by industrial society. They must disavow social mobility in order to live a meaningful agrarian life. Farming and living sufficiently are their ways of being in the world. Success is about aligning themselves with the seasons of life and nature, living in simplicity. Wendell Berry has written,

> A good farmer . . . is a cultural product; he is made by a sort of training, certainly, in what his time imposes or demands, but he is also made by generations of experience. This essential experience can only be accumulated, tested, preserved, handed down in settled households, friendships, and communities that are deliberately and carefully native to their own ground, in which the past has prepared the present and the present safeguards the future.[13]

Berry captures for us the essence of an agrarian lifestyle, living always in alignment with nature, adjusting and adapting to the natural cycle of the environment. With this lifestyle, the immediate environment is of great significance.

## Knowledge, Power, and Politics

How are we to understand the rapid expansion of higher education as essential to national development when the status of farmers is declining? Sixty years after this push was initiated, they struggle even harder to make ends meet. Yet within this constraint, most invest heavily in their children's education, from primary to tertiary levels.

Utilizing Foucault's genealogy as the tool for analysis, this study asks how farmers came to find themselves where they are today.[14] His concept of genealogy explores changes over time, the episteme of a particular time that guides the formation of the dominant discourse, the place of power, the identification of the subject and object of socialization, the mechanism that generates norms, and finally the disciplinary process.

Genealogical analysis shows the gradual shift from agrarian society to industrial through the process of modernization, guided by modernity as the episteme of the era. Modernity exerts itself as the only viable form of reliable knowledge that has the potential to transform the world into a new utopia through science and technology and within a new democratic (modern) society. From emerging capitalist economic theories intensified by neoliberal economic policy comes the drive toward maximum productivity and therefore the unrestrained exploitation of natural resources. This method of quantifying success permeates modern society. It promotes accumulation and the search for higher social status.

Within this context, higher education plays an important role in facilitating social mobility and enhancing economic growth and social standing through career choice and career change. Here productivity has become the condition for 'success', with a university degree the path to this possibility. Those who have undertaken no higher education find the options for employment that promises high salaries limited. Higher education plays a dual role in nurturing the dominant discourse: it endorses modernity as the primary viable and reliable source of knowledge, and it is the primary gatekeeper to the knowledge needed to acquire employment in modern society. As such, education exerts its disciplinary power.

Within this dominant discourse, farmers' world-views and knowledge are delegitimized. During the interviews references were made to a particular form of knowledge, transmitted informally, which enabled families to sustain themselves from generation to generation. Many farmers talked about local wisdom and knowledge that had been passed on by their parents and by elders in the community, such as how to read the weather, how to identify the type of soil, how to get rid of insects, and efficient ways to harvest. Some identified the importance of the sacred realm in the practice of farming that helps to restore and retain the cycle of food production. This knowledge is rooted in their discursive practices and is based on their understanding of community culture, involving beliefs and practices that have shaped and formed their agrarian society for generations. This knowledge is, in the farmers' opinion, slowly being replaced by modern science.

An agrarian society operates on the principle of sufficiency. Farmers practice subsistence farming. Simplicity is the norm. Success for them is defined within this different cultural framework. Since the implementation of the First National Economic and Social Development Plan, however, development ideology based on modernity has exerted its domination over knowledge and its culture of high yield.

Higher education seeks to facilitate social mobility for farmers within the conceptual framework of the global economy. Yet it is this global economy that has removed farmers from the core of their community culture. Their labour and their production are regulated by market mechanisms from across the world, mechanisms that they know nothing about. In the language of genealogy, they have been disciplined into the industrial world, into the global economy. And education is an important part of the disciplinary process. However, the principles of sufficient economy and community culture do survive on occasion within various academic institutions and among local farmers. Here is a hopeful sign that remnants of the farmer's identity and the discursive practices of farmers can remain a force of resistance against the mainstream trend that promotes higher education.

What might be an appropriate response to this domination of knowledge? In *The History of Sexuality*, Foucault introduced the concepts of 'aesthetic existence' and the 'history of the present' as natural outcomes of his idea of genealogy.[15] His history of the present refers to the ability to come into the moment, to live in the present. This capacity stems from an appreciation of the history that has led one to a particular location, sociologically, economically, philosophically, and ideologically, for example. It is the realization that the process that leads to the slow disappearance of subjects is based on historically imposed social constructions and not on the linear progressive development of truth. Such awareness liberates one from limits imposed by normalization. Foucault's aesthetic existence is now possible because in this place the self can return as subject and make decisions that are not constrained by the dominant discourse.[16]

## Reflection

The perspectives and lives of local Thai peasants challenge the trend that sees education as the way out of poverty. The qualitative data questions that fundamental assumption while exploring the genealogy of knowledge. Modernity has transformed ways of farming by promoting maximum production (with chemical fertilizers, pesticides, machinery, for example) and dependency on the world market. Monoculture left farmers with no alternative to the monetization of crops, in contrast to the polyculture of subsistence farming. Neoliberal policies, less capital, and less opportunity to compete mean that for the majority of local farmers their lives have become much harder. At the same time, with education as an avenue for mobility, urban migration and movement toward industrial society require the agrarian lifestyle to be abandoned. At a deeper level, this transition is the result of the delegitimization of agrarian knowledge and the dominance of the modernist world-view. Farmers are viewed as poor and uneducated, but in reality their knowledge is derived from a different genealogy, that of the agrarian world-view. Within that agrarian world-view, subsistence farming is considered normative, and knowledge is rooted in everyday living transmitted through traditions, cultural practices, and methods of food production.

The agrarian world-view shares common values in simplicity, sufficiency, and sustainability with the Hebrew Scriptures. Walter Kaiser has noted that

> in an ultimate sense, in Israel all property belonged to the Lord, as Leviticus 25.23 (NIV, 1984) made clear: 'the land is mine and you are but aliens and my tenants.' Because Yahweh is the one and only Lord and ultimate king over Israel, he was also Lord of the soil and its products. Accordingly, the Holy Land was God's domain (Josh. 22.19) and that land was the land of Yahweh (Hos. 9.3; Ps. 85.1 [2]; Jer. 16.18). Indeed, this was the very land that had been promised to the Patriarchs – Abraham, Isaac, and Jacob (Gen. 12.7; 13.15; 15.18; 26.4; Ex. 32.13; Deut. 1.35–36).[17]

Listening to narratives of local Thai farmers helps us recognize that a tool that we are endorsing as a means to assist the poor may be the very thing that further marginalizes this population. Modernity, the episteme of development ideology, has made everyday living for Thai farmers more complex and more challenging. Western education has delegitimized local learning. The creation of an industrial social hierarchy shifts farmers from the centre to the periphery. Within the context of ministry to farmers, theology becomes a critique of modernity and its episteme while promoting the year of the Jubilee and the metaphorical redistribution of land.

This qualitative research has also raised awareness of the impact of neo-colonialism (through globalization) on the current Thai educational system. Such qualitative research can thus contribute significantly to critical pedagogy by problematizing the everyday experience of people on the margins, by identifying the relationship between knowledge and power, and by raising awareness of the hegemony of the dominant discourse. In this case, the discourse of modernity, deeply imbedded in the Western educational system, has marginalized all other forms of knowledge. Dip Kappor writes:

> [Frantz] Fanon suggests that colonial relationships did not restrict themselves to appropriating the labour of colonized peoples but through the 'burial of their local cultural originality' created people with an 'inferiority complex which rested in their souls'. The attempt to reshape the structures of knowledge and the active subjugation and de-valuation of local knowledges . . . meant that several branches of learning were touched by the colonial experience . . . as an exercise toward the colonization of the mind, a process marked by the cultural arrogance of a Macaulay who once said that 'a single shelf of European literature was worth all the books of India and Arabia'.[18]

Most essential for critical pedagogy is emancipation. How do we move forward? Here again a qualitative method can provide resources. Our theological reflection is limited by the lack of local resources that might provide alternative lenses for viewing the world. Take the discipline of psychology as an example. Our texts in the field of pastoral theology find their roots mostly in Western psychology, which is rooted in Western epistemology and the scientific study of Western populations. Hence it reflects a particular type of knowledge that draws on a particular form of epistemic metaphysics within a particular form of cultural expression applied globally. This perspective categorizes local and ethnic approaches to the issues of mental health as unscientific and primitive.

How might we decode other practices through the lens of other cultural and religious world-views? The restoration of local wisdom and knowledge may well depend on skills, methods, and philosophical assumptions made available through qualitative methodologies.

## Notes

1 Michael Apple, *Ideology and Curriculum* (New York: Routledge, 1990), 2.

2 'Henry Giroux: The Necessity of Critical Pedagogy in Dark Times', interview by Jose Maria Barroso Tristan, *truthout*, 6 Feb. 2013, http://www.truth-out.org/news/item/14331-a-critical-interview-with-henry-giroux.

3 'Henry Giroux'.

4 Kathy Charmaz, *Constructing Grounded Theory: A Practical Guide through Qualitative Analysis* (New York: Sage, 2006), 43.

5 'Genealogy' can be defined as a methodology used to uncover power domination through the creation of public discourse. It searches for fragmentation and discontinuity in historical development and studies the voices of the marginalized to gain insight into the interplay of power and cultural movement. It looks for periods within history and the discourse that guides the movement. It traces changes within history and how these changes are closely related to power and domination. Archaeology, on the other hand, explores changes in discourse over a period of time that has implications for the socialization and normalization of that particular society. Gary Gutting, 'Michel Foucault', *The Stanford Encyclopedia of Philosophy*, ed. Edward N. Zalta (2014), https://plato.stanford.edu/archives/win2014/entries/foucault/.

6 After the Second World War and with the onset of the Cold War in the 1940s, the domino theory emerged to address the potential fall of countries in Southeast Asia to communism. Intervention in a country to ensure it could withstand the pressure was deemed the best way of preventing such a chain reaction. Thailand was identified as a strategic location. In 1949 the US Ambassador to Thailand, Edwin Stanton, wrote to the Secretary of State: 'I do not need to emphasize the advisability and timeliness of establishing and implementing an affirmative policy regarding Siam in view of developments in China and the certainty that communist activities and pressure will be greatly intensified throughout Southeast Asia and this country. It is not argued that this area is equally as important as Europe, but communism being a global problem it appears to us here to be both wise statesmanship and good strategy to take steps now before this area is completely dominated by communism, to contain this threat and give support and encouragement to such countries as Siam which are not yet seriously infected', cited by Sean Randolph, *The United States and Thailand: Alliance Dynamics, 1950–1985* (Berkeley, CA: Institute of East Asian Studies, 1986), 11.

7 Thitinan Pongsudhirak, 'Learning from a Long History of Coups', *Bangkok Post*, 6 June 2014, https://www.bangkokpost.com/print/413829/.

8 See also Leon P. Tikly, 'Education and the New Imperialism', in *Postcolonial Challenges in Education*, ed. Roland Sintos Coloma (New York: Peter Lang, 2009), 23–45; Fazal Rizvi and Bob Lingard, *Globalizing Education Policy* (London: Routledge, 2010).

9 National Statistic Office, *Agricultural Census: Whole Kingdom* (Bangkok, Ministry of Information and Communication Technology, 2013).

10 In 1954, the average agricultural land parcel was 8.36 rai (2.5 rai to one acre) per person. In 1960 it decreased to 6.42 rai per person. By 2007 the average land size for agriculture was 2.67 per rai per person. From 1987 to 1993 approximately 18,000 rai of agricultural land were converted to residential estates, resorts, golf courses, and factories; cited by S. Chomchan, 'Kwam luem lum lae kwam mai pen tum dan ti din lae pa mai' (Inequality in the use of land and forest), in *Kwam luem lum lae kwam mai pen tum nai karn kao tung suphayakorn lae borikarn puentan kong prated Thai* (Inequality in the use of resources and basic services in Thailand), ed. A. Ratanawaraha (Bangkok: Chulalongkorn University Press, 2013). Phasuk Pngpaijit has estimated that approximately 800,000 agricultural households or almost 20 per cent of the agricultural population are landless, while 1 million to 1.5 million households rent land or have insufficient land for cultivation; cited in J. Kiengthong, Kwam sumkan kong rang ngan kaset radub klang lae rang ngan rai ti din nair abop phalit chueng panit (The importance of production within the commercial system among landless agricultural labour at the medium and lower levels), in *Chonabod Thai: kasetthakorn radub klang lae rang ngan raiti din* (Rural Thailand: Landless labor and agricultural production at the medium level), ed. J. Kiengthong et al. (Chiang Mai: Chiang Mai University Press, 2013), 9–25.

11 Chemical fertilizers account for 18 per cent of the costs related to rice production. In 2009 Thailand imported 3.8 million tons of chemical fertilizers worth 42 billion baht. In 2013, imports of chemical fertilizers went up to 5.6 million tons worth 72 billion baht, an increase of 47 per cent. Chemical fertilizers within the country come under the monopoly of five major agrobusiness companies which control 90 per cent of the fertilizer market and play a significant role in determining prices. See Areewan Koosanteeya, *Pui Chami Kumrai Kong Thurakit Muen Lan Kub Ton Toon Kong Kasetakorn* (Chemical fertilizer, multi-million business enterprise and investment cost for agriculturists), *The Nation* (16 April 2015), http://landactionthai.org/land/index.php/content/kwan/937-ปุ๋ยเคมี-กำไรของธุรกิจหมื่นล้าน-กับต้นทุนของเกษตรกร.html.

12 Raj Patel, *Stuffed & Starved: The Hidden Battle for the World Food System* (New York: Melville House, 2007), 7.

13 Wendell Berry, *The Unsettling of America: Culture and Agriculture* (Berkeley, CA: Counterpoint Press, 1996), 44–45.

14 On Foucault's genealogy, see note 7.

15 Michel Foucault, *History of Sexuality*, vol. 2: *The Use of Pleasure* (New York: Vintage, 1990).

16 Foucault writes of 'aesthetic existence': 'An analysis that relates to what we are willing to accept in our world, to accept, to refuse, to change, both in ourselves and in our circumstances. In sum, it is a question of searching for another kind of critical philosophy. Not a critical philosophy that seeks to determine the conditions and the limits of our possible knowledge of the object, but a critical philosophy that seeks the conditions and the indefinite possibilities of transforming the subject, of transforming ourselves', Michel Foucault, 'Subjectivity and Truth', in *The Politics of Truth* (New York: Semiotext, 1997), 179.

17 Walter Kaiser, 'Ownership and Property in the Old Testament Economy', *Institute for Faith, Work and Economics*, 12 Sept. 2012, https://tifwe.org/resource/ownership-and-property-in-the-old-testament-economy/.

18 Dip Kapoor, 'Editorial Introduction: International Perspectives on Education and Decolonization', *International Education* 37, 1 (2007), 4, http://trace.tennessee.edu/cgi/viewcontent.cgi?article=1029&context=internationaleducation.

# PART 2

# Issues in Education
# and the Practice of Research

# 3

# Promoting the Good: Ethical and Methodological Considerations in Practical Theological Research

## ELAINE GRAHAM AND DAWN LLEWELLYN

Over the past generation, practical theology has experienced unprecedented growth. The discipline has matured from a largely clerical pursuit, in which academic insights were 'applied' into ministerial practice, into a 'first order' theological field, which understands reflection on experience and practice as the wellspring of theological understanding. This has engendered a number of characteristic features: a renewed interest in and turn to 'practice', attention to the principles of theological reflection, and an emphasis on theology as practical wisdom (*phronēsis*) which originates in and is tested by lived experience.

However, practical theology has still to prove itself in the face of systematic and philosophical models which privilege abstract reasoning and deductive methodology at the expense of praxis-centred, empirically based, and inductive approaches. It still suffers from the appellation of 'applied' theology, and perspectives which insist that human or pastoral contexts are deviations from the integrity of the theological sciences as mediations of God's self-revelation. Yet for practical theologians, the purpose of theology is to meet the challenges of lived experience with the resources of faith and to express that faith in the practices of everyday life. Theological discourse emerges from the imperatives of discipleship and lived experience and finds its telos and purpose in guiding, disciplining, correcting, and nurturing the practices of faith.[1] Theology is the habitus of reflective disciples, prophetic communities, and prayerful action.

With this renewed attention to practice as the object and end of research comes a growing interest in how social scientific and practice-based enquiry might be harnessed for practical theological reflection. Practical theologians enquire into embodied expressions of situated knowledge. However, given the contextuality and complexity of such real-world research, no single methodology or interpretative framework is able to do such a process of enquiry justice. Furthermore, the researcher is embedded in and complicit with the field of activity to be studied.

In this chapter, we draw on our experiences as supervisors on the Professional Doctorate in Practical Theology (DProf) degree programme at the University of Chester, United Kingdom, to reflect on the ethical dimensions of undertaking research and offer examples, based on our students' work, of how practical theological research can trouble well-established practices. First, we contextualize the professional doctorate and introduce the 'researching professional', before suggesting that although practical theology is a broad discipline, it aims to transform the researcher's practice, their institution, and the academy. The chapter then outlines the part that qualitative methodologies play in the discipline, focusing on research as implicated and therefore an ethical project. Finally, we discuss three illustrations of recent doctoral work that raise issues of consent, privacy, anonymity, and avoiding harm. In doing so, we demonstrate how research methods used in practical theology strive to promote the 'good'.

## The 'Researching Professional' Doctorate

A number of higher education institutions in the United Kingdom have been offering a 'professional doctorate' in practical theology since 2006, and the shaping and delivery of this programme is integral to our understanding of the role of qualitative research methods within the discipline.

There is a distinction between research for the traditional PhD degree and professional practice-based enquiry. If the PhD is designed as a career entry for the 'professional researcher', then professional doctorates equip the 'researching professional'. Nevertheless, professional doctorates are fully comparable in ambition and scope, if not methodology and structure, to a PhD. As Tony Fell, Kevin Flint, and Ian Haines contend, quoting the European University Association, '[Professional doctorates] must meet the same core standards as "traditional" doctorates in order to ensure the same high level of quality.'[2] Furthermore, the Professional Doctorate in Practical Theology is not solely intended for those entering the Christian ordained ministry. Its curriculum, modes of delivery, and even nomenclature are designed to differentiate it from programmes such as the Doctor of Ministry, which often assumes that research is undertaken primarily to facilitate ministerial formation and competence.[3] By contrast, the professional doctoral programmes in the United Kingdom are all based in mainstream public universities – albeit with established traditions in academic study of theology and religious studies – which espouse a 'non-confessional' ethos in the selection and training of students.[4]

The constituency for the professional doctorate is also broad-based. While around half the students on the professional doctorate programmes will be ministers of religion (drawn from a wide range of Christian denominations and increasingly from Jewish and Muslim traditions), they will find themselves in a study cohort that also includes lay Christians, Buddhist practitioners, and others who profess no formal religious belief. In addition to congregational ministry, candidates work in chaplaincy, churches, youth work, secular or religious educational or administrative posts, non-governmental organizations, charities, counselling and psychotherapy, sports coaching, and teaching. This, together with its institutional setting in non-confessional universities rather than theological colleges, means that the professional doctorate has been free to identify more closely with other types of advanced research, designed for the researching professional in education, health care, counselling and psychotherapy, law, or engineering. There is close affinity, therefore, between models of practice-driven or enquiry-based research and an approach to theology which is epistemologically committed to viewing practice as disclosive of understanding and truth, which works from practice to theory to practice, and is methodologically committed to a dialectic of reflection and action.[5]

This practice-based approach means there is no singular way to undertake research. Sociology, psychology, cultural studies, feminist and women's studies, biblical studies, education studies, geography, counselling studies, creative arts, and business and management studies have featured in work that identifies as practical theology.[6] In some ways, though, the question of adopting an interdisciplinary canon of research methods and methodologies remains work in progress.[7]

Professional doctorates are understood as contributing to advanced knowledge and practice in three domains: the academy, the organization in which the candidate is embedded, and the student's personal or professional development. Echoing David Tracy's elaboration of the 'three publics' of Christian theology and definitions of doctoral degrees constituting 'a contribution to academic knowledge', this characterizes the professional doctorate not only as furthering academic excellence, but as enhancing candidates' skills, understanding, and personal and professional maturation, and as potentially generative of new knowledge and practical wisdom that may lead to changes in professional or organizational practice, policy, or protocol.[8]

## Research Approaches in Practical Theology

Given that researching professionals in practical theology are engaged in an interdisciplinary undertaking across many fields of study and impact, it is unsurprising that a range of methods are used to examine faith lives and transform practice. For example, quantitative approaches deductively examine religious phenomenon, behaviours, trends, and patterns through statistical, experimental, or mathematical information. They use numerical data, gathered through surveys and questionnaires, for example, to measure frequency or to explore relationships between variable indicators of the research. Rooted in a positivist ontology and objectivist epistemology, practical theologians have examined attendance at cathedrals, personality types in relation to biblical beliefs, and religious attitudes and opinions.[9]

Taking a different approach, and one more commonly adopted by DProf students, qualitative work is 'usually used when the object of study is some form of social process or meaning or experience which needs to be understood and explained in a rounded way'.[10] It follows inductive reasoning to access how people construe and produce their intimate, social, and institutional worlds, using a range of flexible methods that are receptive to the situations in which the phenomena being researched occurs. Qualitative methods – interviews, focus groups, ethnography, autoethnography, visual methodologies, questionnaires, narrative, critical discourse approaches, digital methodologies, documentary, action research, oral approaches, poetry, life writing – generate conclusions that are understood to be partial and constructed representations that give detailed and nuanced insights. Therefore qualitative approaches are highly suitable for researching the fluid and multi-layered experiences that go into Christian lives, communities, and organizations to assess, transform, and challenge practice and scholarship.[11]

When objective, positivistic paradigms favoured the 'neutral' researcher, there was also a suspicion that researching one's community or oneself would result in 'biased' findings. This assumed that the production, analysis and dissemination of data was untainted by the values of the researcher and devoid of social, historical, and political motives, while concurrently failing to discern that striving for objectivity is itself a subjective and self-interested claim. Sandra Harding explains:

The conception of value-free, impartial, dispassionate research is supposed to direct the identification of all social values and their elimination for the results of research yet it has been operationalized to identify and eliminate only those social values and interests that differ among researcher and critics who are regarded by the scientific community as competent to make such judgments.[12]

However, since the poststructuralist challenge to metanarratives and the acknowledgement that no research is conducted 'objectively', research practices have evolved to acknowledge that the researcher changes and is changed through the process.

Reflexivity is a device that assesses how research is implicated, while also refuting the myths of 'objective' and 'hygienic' research.[13] It exposes how personal and interpersonal factors influence the research processes, demanding that the researcher is self-critical and able to show that 'our research . . . will have our own thumbprints all over it'.[14] Reflexivity attempts to avoid the tyranny of our own experience via an analytical subjectivity, where the researcher defines and renders transparent, where possible, their positionality and interests. Increasingly, then, reflexivity, with corresponding attention to autoethnography, life writing and narrative, has become fundamental to the epistemology of practical theology, and is embedded in the methodological and pedagogical architecture of the professional doctorate.

## Research Ethics and Promoting 'the Good'

In practical theology, research is relational. This is immediately identifiable through action research or other forms of participant observation. It may also be manifest in less explicit ways, such as the researcher's deep investment in their work and its outcomes as promoting, however indirectly, the well-being of their informants. Given that these can provoke feelings of vulnerability and accountability (central to forms of qualitative research that aim to make a difference), combined with the unavoidable complicity of the researcher with their wider research environment, it is inevitable that research will carry ethical and moral implications.

Ethics are central to any research that relies on the involvement of human (and non-human) participants, and the onus is on the researcher to behave ethically, from the project's inception through execution, analysis, and dissemination. This is often regarded as a matter of minimizing risk and avoiding harm, of observing the right protocols, and it might mean adhering to codes of conduct laid out by the professional bodies researchers belong to and the ethical approval applications they have to make. In the UK context, DProf students regularly navigate the procedures of the National Health Service, Prison Service, sports associations, charities, and academic organizations like the British Sociological Association (BSA). It involves consent and maintaining privacy and anonymity, or refusing to act in ways that violate ethical, academic, or legal standards, for example by deliberately misrepresenting data, breaking data protection laws, rejecting coercive recruitment strategies, or exposing private information without permission.[15] However, research ethics is more than that which complies with acceptable practice. It can also be thought of as that which promotes 'the good': in terms of excellence in research – of rigour, innovation and communicability – and as an activity devoted to the pursuit and realization of social goods by contributing constructively to participants' welfare.

Trust is at the heart of this paradigm.[16] If 'good' research is persuasive, then those to whom it is directed must trust the probity of the evidence, the arguments, and the conclusions. Qualitative research must abide by received principles of reliability, rigour, and responsibility. Researchers have to assess not only whether they have avoided harm but also whether they have modelled best practice. Have they been transparent about the reasoning that underpins their approach? Is there continuity between problematic, objective, and design? How do the stages of their strategy reflect core understandings about the nature of reality (ontology) and how we know what we know (epistemology)?

As supervisors, we find that often the challenges faced by our students prompt critical reflections on research ethics, especially when their work runs counter to the academic literature, appears anomalous to the parameters in which we usually practise, and, therefore, challenges extant research methodologies and methods. Here we highlight three ethical issues that have emerged in the work of candidates on the DProf in practical theology programme at the University of Chester: informed consent, anonymity, and disclosure. These are often understood as pivotal to research ethics, but they can sometimes seem fragile and can undermine the knowledge generated in the field.

## Informed Consent: An Insufficient Principle?

Informed consent is one primary way respect is upheld and requires that researchers explicitly explain what the research is for and describe the expectations, roles, and responsibilities of the researcher (or the research team). According to the BSA's Statement of Ethical Practice:

> As far as possible participation in sociological research should be based on the freely given informed consent of those studied. This implies a responsibility on the sociologist to explain in appropriate detail, and in terms meaningful to participants, what the research is about, who is undertaking and financing it, why it is being undertaken, and how it is to be disseminated and used.[17]

Through informed consent, participants are given the information they need before they can agree to participate, so that volunteering can be made without undue pressure, understanding the commitments, any benefits and risks, and what will happen to the research. In addition to informed consent, the BSA states: 'Research participants should be made aware of their right to refuse participation whenever and for whatever reason they wish.'[18] Recognizing that participants have individual agency and choice means researchers 'are obligated to fully . . . inform them with respect to our research and allow them the opportunity voluntarily to choose whether or not to participate'.[19] Informed consent is based on recognizing respect, dignity, and the individual human right to exercise autonomy.

There are instances where it is not always possible or appropriate to seek written consent from participants: research on crowd behaviour, studying public events, in covert research when important matters of social significance are unlikely to be revealed through overt approaches, or with communities and groups who might find it difficult to sign official documents.[20] However, historically, there are acute dangers when consent is not obtained, perhaps the most terrifying example being the medical experiments conducted under the Nazi regime.[21] Therefore, the impetus and obligation to gain consent emerge from a need to protect participants, and they should be made aware of what they 'are letting themselves in for' when taking part.

However, this response supposes that a researcher is omniscient, able to anticipate the possible permutations and directions the research might take, and is in a position to lay out exactly what impact the research might have, or what might happen to the researcher, participants, or the data. As researchers, we can only attempt to be transparent about the process and what we need and want from the individuals, communities, and the organizations we work with.

Informed consent also assumes that consent is a unique event occurring at the beginning of recruitment and that it is an unconditional, static, transactional agreement between researcher and participants. Interviewees, gatekeepers, and informants sign forms and tick boxes, once they have read through the blurb, and it is the researcher who ensures consent has been secured. Yet, consent is often more unstable than the way institutional ethics processes allow, and can fail to acknowledge that qualitative research is contextual, situated, and responds to the field.

One strategy, as Heather Piper and Helen Simons have suggested, is to conceive of 'rolling informed consent' that admits agreement is a constant process and pragmatically leaves room for renegotiation if circumstances alter.[22] Yet even rolling consent

47

can be inadequate. Most understandings of consent assume that the agreement and any concessions are between the researcher and the participant – but occasionally, experiences in the field question the strength of consent, particularly when events dictate that consent has to be renegotiated.

In Martin McAlinden's professional doctoral project, informed consent presented an impossible concept and practice. Martin, a Roman Catholic priest, conducted interviews with his fellow Irish clergy and drew on his own experiences to examine the theological implications of *acedia*, or the malaise of spiritual burn-out.[23] Martin wanted to use his research in his practice as Director of Pastoral Theology at St Patrick's Seminary, Maynooth, to prepare priests in his care for their ministry and develop resources to confront *acedia*. When designing his project and applying for approval to his University's ethics committee, Martin followed the usual orthodoxies for consent: he produced letters inviting clergy and spiritual directors working with clergy to take part, advertised that he was looking for volunteers at clergy conferences, wrote a detailed Participant Information Sheet outlining what the research entails, why, and how, completed a consent form that detailed the voluntary nature of the project, and emphasized participants' right to refuse questions and to withdraw at any time.

Consent, as Paul Spicker argues, is paramount because 'research is liable to be intrusive, and intrusion is only legitimate if consent is obtained'. Obtaining consent acknowledges that 'people have a sphere of action that is private, and theirs to control'.[24] Producing data can threaten the rights of individuals, communities, and organizations to decide, control, and resolve on their own terms whether to be researched, and the extent that information about them is shared with another or others (and that includes how, when, and why).[25]

However, the grounds on which consent was initially negotiated were confounded when, in June 2016, before completing his thesis, Martin died of cancer. His participants – his fellow clergy, his professional and faith community – had agreed to take part in the interviews based on the understanding that his analysis of their experiences would feature in his thesis and in presentations of work in progress to his peers, or at conferences, or in publications.[26] Usually, the researcher is the custodian of the data, and the experiences gathered through qualitative work, and the knowledge it creates only exists – and perhaps should only exist – between the researcher and participants. The research is premised on the promises enacted by that initial process of consent. Therefore, if a researcher dies, the project is likely to come to an untimely and premature, but understandable, conclusion.

During Martin's illness, he often discussed the grief caused by not completing his doctoral work. However, Martin's primary concern was not missing out on a qualification, but that his research would not contribute to the academy or to practice. For Martin, not naming the painful, sensitive, and hitherto silenced experiences that cause spiritual burn-out in priests meant a missed opportunity to construct a meaningful theological response, including raising the Church's awareness of the condition to facilitate an appropriate course of prevention and action. Driven by these deeply held commitments, Martin arranged that on his death his thesis notes and interview transcripts were to be given to his primary supervisor to keep and, at some point in the future, to be disseminated.

## From Consent to Privacy

In Martin's research the overriding concern was not the breach of consent *per se* but working to protect the participants' privacy. He followed the usual strategies to keep confidentiality intact, and since Martin's death the original interview recordings have been destroyed (even though the British Data Protection Act states that data can be kept for ten years). We do not know, however, how Martin corresponded with actual and potential participants, and he did not pass on participants' email, postal addresses, or telephone numbers for subsequent contact. In short, it would be incredibly difficult to establish who took part in the project. If the golden rule of research is that participants are not be deceived or put knowingly at risk, and that public and private good are to be maximized while harm is minimized, then *privacy* might have been a more satisfactory principle in Martin's case, when procedures of informed consent were insufficient.[27]

## Anonymity

Anonymity is another staple of research ethics. It protects research participants against being identified in any specific fashion, for example, by age, gender, sexuality, or political or religious affiliation. Most ethics protocols require the researcher to provide a statement indicating how anonymity will be guaranteed, such as use of pseudonyms for personal names, places or organizations.

When discussing data storage and archiving, the British Sociological Association offers the following guidelines:

> Appropriate measures should be taken to store research data in a secure manner . . . Where appropriate and practicable, methods for preserving anonymity should be used including the removal of identifiers, the use of pseudonyms and other technical means for breaking the link between data and identifiable individuals. Members should also take care to prevent data being published or released in a form that would permit the actual or potential identification of research participants without prior written consent of the participants.[28]

This blanket notion of anonymity may be challenged on at least two counts. In some cases, participants may actually want to be publicly identified, particularly in the case of an issue they feel needs to be brought to wider attention or where experiences have not been sufficiently acknowledged. Sometimes, participants simply want their stories to be told and to see their names attached to their narratives.[29] As Anne Grinyer notes, such considerations lie at the heart of much oral and social history, which insists on valuing perspectives not normally given credence.[30]

Although anonymity is considered paramount, Grinyer's work with young adults aged between 18 and 25 who had been diagnosed with cancer, and with their parents, suggests that sometimes a more pragmatic approach is required. Grinyer and her co-researcher began to question their own strategy of renaming participants and the resulting impact on parents of reading their own offspring's words under a pseudonym – especially when the young person concerned had subsequently died. When consulted, nearly three-quarters of their sample requested that their own names or those of their child be used. However well-intentioned, the decision not to use real names somehow deprived informants of a sense of ownership of their own words. For the researcher to allocate a new name to a participant is an ethical issue in its own right.[31] The major consideration is agency and control: wherever possible, participants should have the final word on whether or not their identities are disclosed.

It is also difficult to ensure absolute anonymity, especially if those reading the research are actively engaged in the issue under investigation or are located within a relatively small organization or culture in which networks of association and acquaintance go beyond anything a researcher might be able to anticipate. This is particularly relevant for practice-based researchers conducting a project within their own professional networks, or where research submitted to decision-makers or managers may expose those under their jurisdiction.

The BSA guidelines continue:

> Potential informants and research participants, especially those possessing a combination of attributes that make them readily identifiable, may need to be reminded that it can be difficult to disguise their identity without introducing an unacceptably large measure of distortion into the data. In some situations, presenting findings by way of hypothetical composite and/or partially fictionalised case studies can address this issue.[32]

One solution might lie in presenting participants' perspectives through what Christine Bold terms 'representative constructions'. When researching undergraduates, Bold surveyed their use of reflective diaries. Rather than depicting their findings through themes, percentages, or codes, she created two fictional narratives to express the students' responses – for 'Una' who found the diaries useful and for 'Duet' who found the diaries unhelpful.

For Bold, representative constructions 'suggest the story is constructed to represent a particular type of person or set of events'.[33]

If researching human life is an attempt to understand the complexity of individuals, groups, organizations, and systems – including the meanings, beliefs, and values that motivate them – then narrative is an ideal medium. The interpretative nature of qualitative research is premised on writers working with people's stories, listening to the narratives of those around them, understanding that they are already a representation and interpretation of experience, and placing social phenomena in a wider network of meanings, contexts, and relationships.[34] Since qualitative data usually draws on narratives, Bold argues that it is appropriate to represent the resulting analysis in similar form.[35] Narrative research offers 'a rendition of how life is perceived', serving as 'a way of creating order and security out of a chaotic world'.[36] These are fictional narratives which are nevertheless derived from and convey biographical truths. Developing interpretative themes that represent raw data can produce 'overlapping stories' and a 'convincing set of evidence to support understanding'.[37] Constructing narrative accounts also requires a high level of reflexivity by the researcher, as they are constantly making judgements that balance the specificities of accounts with their capacity to fulfil the criteria of trustworthy, plausible, and applicable conclusions. Since perspective and interpretation are crucial to narrative, they are never a 'view from nowhere' and already reflect the understanding 'that truth and certainty are unstable', but always rooted in context and subjectivity.[38]

Researching the concept and practice of equal marriage (the possibility of recognizing same-sex partnerships as of equal validity to heterosexual marital relationships) within the Church of England, professional doctoral student Gill Henwood decided to use representative narrative constructions.[39] This was, partly, to avoid informants being recognized by colleagues or senior clergy, when maintaining confidentiality by anonymity alone might not have provided sufficient protection, but where changing personal details could have 'flattened out' aspects of the stories. Gill interwove different narratives into representative constructions as a means of interpreting and analysing the realities behind the information conveyed in data. This aids readability and communication of the diversity of findings and provides a level of confidentiality for participants in sensitive research.[40]

## Disclosure

Even though, as we have suggested, researchers take steps to avoid harm by making agreements with participants to protect their privacy, either through anonymizing or producing composite narratives, identification is still possible. In practice-based research this risk is especially acute because researchers are often insiders investigating a problem in their practice, in their own communities. Practical theologians on doctoral programmes are usually working professionals in an institution – teachers, clerics, administrators, managers, sports coaches, counsellors, social workers, managers, priests – and their position is often public (particularly as organizations increasingly have some web presence that profiles employees, stakeholders, and users). In addition, if the aim is not only to contribute to the academy but also to enrich practitioners' skills and to challenge and augment institutional cultures through *phronēsis*, then at some point, and in some form, the research may well be presented back to the community that is the primary site of study.[41]

In feeding back to communities or in publications there is the potential to do harm. There is often a concern, particularly if the conclusions question deeply held beliefs, assumptions, and practices or if the topic is sensitive and potentially stigmatized, that the research will expose those taking part to criticism or hostility, or place them in a hazardous position in relation to their family, friends, acquaintances, faith community, or work. In addition, under-researched topics tend to rely on recruiting through pre-existing networks, which means participants are likely to know each other. In these situations, there is the potential for others to recognize a turn of phrase or an experience that is recounted in the research, even if careful measures are in place.

For Paul Howell, another professional doctorate candidate at the University of Chester, these concerns are pressing. A pastor in an evangelical congregation, Paul's primary motivation for his project is his role as a church leader and father of three, with one adult child having a long-standing diagnosis of Autistic Spectrum Disorder (ASD).[42] His thesis explores the intersection of these experiences – as a father, minister, and researching professional – to interrogate how his community's reliance on biblical understandings of discipleship can marginalize his family as they wrestle with issues of disability. Paul's dilemma is that his research draws on very personal and painful dilemmas centring on his son with ASD, who is unable to consent through the usual means to being discussed as part of a research project. Moreover, his research troubles the lived hermeneutics of the conservative evangelical congregation to whom he ministers. When we write research, as Anna Fisk comments,

> our stories are never just our own: they are also part of the stories of those others whose lives intersect with ours. In putting experience into the public domain of academic discourse, respect for the feelings and privacy of partners, family, and friends will often require that only certain stories are told, in a very certain way.[43]

To protect himself, his partner, his children, and his congregation, Paul has adopted autoethnography, a technique where the researcher's experiences are a site of reflection and knowledge-making. Carolyn Ellis, a pioneer of this method, describes it as 'research, writing, story, and method that connect the autobiographical and personal to the cultural, social, and political ... [its] forms feature concrete action, emotion, embodiment, self-consciousness, and introspection portrayed in dialogue, scenes, characterization, and plot'.[44] Autoethnography can be framed as a theological enterprise because it is a form of attentiveness that can 'pave the way for spiritual growth and transformation' and establishes a literary, critical vantage point from which the researcher can critically probe their own, and their participants', assumptions and experiences.[45]

## Conclusion: Promoting the Good

We want our research to be, as feminist ethnographer Kamala Visweswaran argues, 'believable', but we have to listen to the narratives our participants share, understanding that any research is already a representation and interpretation of experience. Qualitative research with human subjects is the product of a conversation, in which participants emphasize, minimize, leave out, and edit in their exchanges with the researcher. This does not mean that qualitative data is 'not true', but it is always 'partial, incomplete, and detached from the realms to which it points'.[46] Similarly 'consent' is fragile. It is not a one-off, never-to-be-repeated event, but should be extended as an ongoing negotiation as the research process evolves – sometimes beyond the researcher's involvement. Research rarely goes to plan, for it is 'organic'.[47] We are working with people's anxieties and concerns, their lives and their deaths, and all we can hope to do is honour the fragments of the stories we are given to curate.

### Notes

1 Elaine Graham, Heather Walton, and Frances Ward, *Theological Reflection: Methods* (London: SCM Press, 2005).

2 Tony Fell, Kevin Flint, and Ian Haines, *Professional Doctorates in the UK 2011* (Lichfield: UK Council for Graduate Education, 2011), 13.

3 Zoë Bennett and David Lyall, 'The Professional Doctorate in Practical Theology: A New Model of Doctoral Research in the UK', *Reflective Practice: Formation and Supervision in Ministry* 34 (2014), 190–203.

4 Katja Stuerzenhofecker, 'Transforming Practical Theological Education in the Changing Context of Non-confessional Higher Education' (Doctor of Professional Studies dissertation, University of Chester, 2016), http://chesterrep.openrepository.com/cdr/handle/10034/620544#.

5 On models of practice-driven or enquiry-based research, see Carol Costley, Geoffrey C. Elliott, and Paul Gibbs, *Doing Work-based Research: Approaches to Enquiry for Insider-researchers* (London: Sage, 2010); Liz Bondi, David Carr, Chris Clark, and Cecelia Clegg, eds, *Towards Professional Wisdom: Practical Deliberation in the People Professions* (Farnham: Ashgate, 2011); on an approach to theology that sees practice as revealing understanding and truth, see Elaine L. Graham, *Transforming*

*Practice: Pastoral Theology in an Age of Uncertainty* (Eugene, OR: Wipf & Stock, 2002); Dorothy C. Bass, Kathleen A. Cahalan, Bonnie J. Miller-McLemore, James R. Nieman, and Christian B. Scharen, *Christian Practical Wisdom: What It Is and Why It Matters* (Grand Rapids, MI: Eerdmans, 2016); on works from practice to theory to practice see Don S. Browning, *A Fundamental Practical Theology: Descriptive and Strategic Proposals* (Minneapolis, MN: Fortress Press, 1991).

6 Sociology: Nicola Slee, Fran Porter, and Anne Phillips, eds, *Researching Female Faith: Qualitative Research Methods* (London: Routledge, 2018); John Swinton and Harriet Mowat, *Practical Theology and Qualitative Research* (London: SCM Press, 2006); psychology: Mandy Robbins, 'A Matter of Age or Experience? Parishioners' Attitude toward Women Vicars in the Church in Wales', in *Honouring the Past and Shaping the Future: Religious and Biblical Studies in Wales*, ed. Robert Pope (Leominster: Gracewing, 2003), 253–64; cultural studies: Tom Beaudoin, 'Why Does Practice Matter Theologically?' in *Conundrums in Practical Theology*, eds Joyce Ann Mercer and Bonnie J. Miller-McLemore (Leuven: Brill, 2016), 8–32; feminist and women's studies: Elaine Graham, 'Feminist Theory', in *The Wiley-Blackwell Companion to Practical Theology*, ed. Bonnie J. Miller-McLemore (Malden, MA: Wiley-Blackwell, 2011), 193–203; Nicola Slee, *Women's Faith Development: Patterns and Processes* (Aldershot: Ashgate, 2004); biblical studies: Zoë Bennett, *Using the Bible in Practical Theology: Historical and Contemporary Perspectives* (Abingdon: Ashgate, 2013); education studies: John M. Hull, *God-Talk with Young Children: Notes for Parents and Teachers* (Derby: CEM; Valley Forge, PA: Trinity Press International, 1991); geography: Christopher R. Baker, *The Hybrid Church in the City: Third Space Thinking* (2nd edn; London: SCM Press, 2009); counselling studies: Peter Madsen Gubi, 'Assessing the Perceived Value of Reflexive Groups for Supporting Clergy in the Church of England', *Journal of Mental Health, Religion and Culture* 19, 4 (2016), 350–61; phenomenology: R. Ruard Ganzevoort and Johan Roeland, 'Lived Religion: The Praxis of Practical Theology', *International Journal of Practical Theology* 18, 1 (2014), 91–101; creative arts: Heather Walton, ed., *Literature and Theology: New Interdisciplinary Spaces* (Aldershot: Ashgate, 2011); and business and management studies: Stephen Pattison, *The Faith of the Managers* (London: Cassell, 1997).

7 'Methodology' and 'method' are connected, and often used synonymously, but there is a distinction, albeit contested. Methodology is the study of research methods (a discipline in its own right) and also refers to the philosophical and theoretical commitments underlying the research. Methodology reflects the ontological and epistemological position of the researcher, which tends to shape the research question and subsequently informs the choice of methods. Methods are the specific techniques used

to conduct the research – interviewing, focus groups, ethnography, sampling strategies, data analysis. See Sandra Harding, ed., *Feminism and Methodology: Social Science Issues* (Bloomington and Indianapolis, IN: Indiana University Press, 1987); Slee, Porter, and Phillips, *Researching Female Faith*; Joey Sprague, *Feminist Methodologies for Critical Researchers: Bridging Differences* (Walnut Creek, CA: Rowman & Littlefield, 2016); Liz Stanley, ed., *Knowing Feminisms: On Academic Borders, Territories and Tribes* (London: Sage, 1997); Swinton and Mowat, *Practical Theology*. On work in progress see Zoë Bennett, Elaine Graham, Stephen Pattison, and Heather Walton, *Invitation to Research in Practical Theology* (London: Routledge, 2018).

8 David Tracy, *The Analogical Imagination: Christian Theology and the Culture of Pluralism* (New York: Crossroad, 1981).

9 Cathedrals: Leslie J. Francis, ed., *Anglican Cathedrals in Modern Life: The Science of Cathedral Studies* (Basingstoke: Palgrave Macmillan, 2015); personality types in relation to biblical beliefs: Andrew Village, *The Bible and Lay People: An Empirical Approach to Ordinary Hermeneutics* (Aldershot: Ashgate, 2007); and religious attitudes and opinions: Robbins, 'A Matter of Age or Experience?' These scholars sometimes identify as empirical theologians; for more examples see the *Journal of Empirical Theology*.

10 Jennifer Mason, *Qualitative Researching* (London: Sage, 2002), 134.

11 While there used to be a rigid, often contented distinction between the two strategies, many researchers use methodologies and methods from both approaches to research religious belief and experiences.

12 Sandra Harding, 'Rethinking Standpoint Epistemology: What Is "Strong Objectivity"?' *Centennial Review* 36, 3 (1992), 437–70, at 458.

13 Liz Stanley and Sue Wise, 'Feminist Research, Feminist Consciousness and Experiences of Sexism', *Women's Studies International Quarterly* 2, 3 (1979), 359–74.

14 Jane Ribbens, 'Interviewing: An "Unnatural Situation"?' *Women's Studies International Forum* 12, 6 (1989), 579–92, at 591. See Linda Finlay, 'Negotiating the Swamp: The Opportunity and Challenge of Reflexivity in Research Practice', *Qualitative Research* 2, 2 (2002), 209–30.

15 Frederick Bird and Laurie Lamoureux Scholes, 'Research Ethics', in *The Routledge Handbook of Research Methods in the Study of Religion*, ed. Michael Stausberg and Steven Engler (London: Routledge, 2013), 81–105.

16 Bennett, Graham, Pattison, and Walton, *Invitation*, 97–98, 143–44, 159–66, 171–74.

17 British Sociological Association, *Statement of Ethical Practice* (Durham: BSA Publications, 2017), paragraph 18.

18 British Sociological Association, *Statement of Ethical Practice*, paragraph 22.

19 Bird and Scholes, 'Research Ethics', 87.

20 Alan Bryman, *Social Research Methods* (2nd edn; Oxford: Oxford University Press, 2004).

21 The Nuremberg Code (1947), developed in the aftermath of the Second World War, placed ethics at the heart of research practice and also informed the Universal Declaration of Human Rights (1948) and the Declaration of Helsinki (1964), which made consent mandatory for human experimentation in medical research.

22 Heather Piper and Helen Simons, 'Ethical Responsibility in Social Research', in *Research Methods in the Social Sciences*, ed. Bridget Somekh and Cathy Lewin (London: Sage, 2005), 56–64, at 56.

23 Martin McAlinden, 'Living Baptismally: Nurturing a Spirituality for Priestly Wellbeing', *Practical Theology* 7, 4 (2014), 268–79.

24 Paul Spicker, 'Research without Consent', *Social Research Update* 51 (Winter 2007), 1, http://sru.soc.surrey.ac.uk/SRU51.pdf.

25 In social research, the debate about privacy often refers to the 'ethics of deceptive research' (see Charlotte Allen, 'Spies Like Us: When Sociologists Deceive Their Subjects', *Lingua Franca* 7, 9 [1997], 31–39, http://lingua-franca.mirror.theinfo.org/9711/9711.allen.html), in discussing cases such as Laud Humphreys' covert research in public toilets that focused on gay men's sexual behaviour (Laud Humphreys, *Tearoom Trade: A Study of Homosexual Encounters in Public Places* [London: Duckworth, 1970]) and Cornell University's study of the pseudonymous town 'Springdale' (Arthur J. Vidich and Joseph Bensman, *Small Town in Mass Society: Class, Power and Religion in a Rural Community* [Princeton, NJ: Princeton University Press, 1958]). In such examples, participants were unaware they were being researched and how the information gathered about them would be used. Recently, Internet research has questioned what constitutes public and private information; see David M. Berry, 'Internet Research: Privacy, Ethics and Alienation: An Open Source Approach', *Internet Research* 14, 4 (2004), 323–32.

26 Martin has been awarded a posthumous honorary Doctor of Professional Studies in practical theology by the University of Chester. The ceremony included a symposium with papers from staff and DProf students reflecting on Martin's work. See Wayne Morris, ed., *Acedia and the Transformation of Spiritual Malaise: Essays in Honour of Fr Martin McAlinden* (Chester: Chester University Press, forthcoming).

27 On the 'golden rule': Christina Allen, 'What's Wrong with the Golden Rule? Conundrums of Conducting Ethical Research in Cyberspace', *Information Society* 12, 2 (1996), 175–88; Jim Thomas, 'When Cyberresearch Goes Awry: The Ethics of the Rimm "Cyberporn" Study', *Information Society* 12, 2 (1996), 189–97, at 197.

28 British Sociological Association, *Statement of Ethical Practice*, paragraph 31.

29 Dawn Llewellyn, *Reading, Feminism, and Spirituality: Troubling the Waves* (London: Palgrave, 2015). ¶

30 Anne Grinyer, 'The Anonymity of Research Participants: Assumptions, Ethics, and Practicalities', *Pan-Pacific Management Review* 12, 1 (2009), 49–58.

31 Grinyer, 'Anonymity', 55.

32 British Sociological Association, *Statement of Ethical Practice*, paragraph 31.

33 Christine Bold, *Using Narrative in Research* (London: Sage, 2011), 145–46.

34 For further consideration of qualitative data as representations and interpretations of experience, see Angela McRobbie, 'The Politics of Feminist Research: Between Talk, Text and Action', *Feminist Review* 12, 1 (1982), 46–57.

35 As another example, in feminist practical theology, Nicola Slee has presented interview transcripts as poetry; see Slee, *Researching Female Faith*.

36 Bold, *Using Narrative*, 17.

37 Bold, *Using Narrative*, 13.

38 Bold, *Using Narrative*, 13.

39 Gill Henwood, 'Is Equal Marriage an Anglican Ideal?' *Journal of Anglican Studies* 13, 1 (2015), 92–113.

40 On the question of confidentiality in representative constructions, see Bold, *Using Narrative*, 145–46.

41 Albeit the presentation to the community is not in the form of the thesis, which is primarily submitted to fulfil a university's criteria for an advanced level postgraduate qualification. In addition to papers for academic audiences (including a mandatory publishable article), DProf students offer workshops, reports, training, and consultations to their organizations. This is not to dislocate the academic from the practical but to acknowledge there are potentially diverse audiences that research can reach, which may require different modes of dissemination.

42 Paul Howell, 'From *Rain Man* to *Sherlock*: Theological Reflections on Metaphor and ASD', *Practical Theology*, 8, 2 (2015), 143–53.

43 Anna Fisk, *Sex, Sin, and Ourselves: Encounters in Feminist Theology and Contemporary Women's Literature* (Eugene, OR: Pickwick, 2014), 10.

44 Carolyn Ellis, *The Ethnographic I: A Methodological Novel about Autoethnography* (Walnut Creek, CA: AltaMira Press, 2004), xix.

45 Citation: McAlinden, 'Living Baptismally', 13.

46 Kamala Visweswaran, *Fictions of Feminist Ethnography* (Minneapolis, MN: University of Minnesota Press, 1994), 1.

47 Mason, *Qualitative Researching*.

# 4

# Between Yes and No:
# The Inner Journey of
# Qualitative Research

## DAVID M. CSINOS

It was a good thing that I had grabbed my gloves on the way out the door. It was the kind of February day when the air bites at every bit of skin that peers out from under layers of wool, cotton, and polyester. The sun may have been shining, but as snow blew from one side of the road to the other, it gave the illusion of fresh flakes falling from the sky.

My mind raced and my heart rate increased as I drove down the highway to meet the leaders of Colkirk United Church, a small Aboriginal congregation of the United Church of Canada's All Native Circle Conference.[1] The minister of this church had agreed to speak with me about being part of the dissertation research I was hoping to conduct over the next few years. Only a couple of weeks earlier I had been heading down the same road to attend a continuing-education event hosted by this faith community and the local Aboriginal cultural centre. The leaders of this event graciously invited students to learn about the Church's past role in the exploitation of Canada's Indigenous people and its potential future role in healing this broken relationship.

With stories of abuse in Church-run residential schools and the ways in which the 'good intentions' of the Church continue to do harm to communities such as this fresh in my mind, I knew that there were difficult conversations awaiting me at my destination. I was excited by the possibility of joining with this community to embark on my research, research that I hoped would be fuelled by mutual partnership, support, and accountability. Yet at the same time a fearful anxiety at having to face difficult facts and uncomfortable situations swept through my body. What if I say something that offends them? What if I'm just another white person using Aboriginal communities for my own benefit? I was afraid of the truths about myself that I would learn in our conversation that afternoon.

I turned off the road and drove up a gravel path that was just as wide as my car. Ever since my family vacationed in a small campground in northern Ontario, I have loved the sound of gravel shifting under tires and occasionally being thrown up toward the underbelly of the car. I drove up the laneway slowly, savouring the sounds my car was making. Eventually I pulled around to the side of the church and put the car in park. The car had gradually warmed up on the long drive, so at some point on the trip I had taken my gloves off and thrown them on the seat behind me. As soon as hot air stopped blowing through the vents, I was reminded of how cold it was outside and I reached to the back seat to find my gloves. As I put them on, I heard myself utter a profanity. These weren't just any gloves. With a white maple leaf adorning each of the red knitted mittens, they were a symbol of Canada. These patriotic mittens may have warmed my heart as well as my hands, but could they be offensive to members of this community, who have been the victims of injustices perpetrated by this country? How many other things will I do, I wondered, that – unaware to me – offend and disrespect this community? I shoved this question deep inside my mind as I left the gloves in the car. Then I walked to the church, worried that those extra few seconds I'd spent in the car might have given away the fact that I was nervous about this meeting.

I hurried through the chilly air toward the side door of the church and stepped inside a brightly lit fellowship hall. I was greeted by the caring smile of Martha, the Church's minister. As we shook hands, I couldn't help but notice that her palm and fingers felt so warm against mine, which had come into the church unprotected against the Canadian winter. Martha offered me a cup of tea and invited me to join her in her office to talk about the project I was proposing. For the next few hours, we sipped our tea while chatting about what exactly I hoped to do and addressing the challenges – even dangers – of allowing a settler like me to conduct research in an Aboriginal community.

I was certainly not the first white person to have approached her to undertake research in their community. Martha shared that Aboriginal communities are the most heavily researched communities in Canada but receive the least in return for their involvement in research. We talked (I did more listening than talking) about some of the systemic injustices that continually do harm to this community and how the path to reconciliation – with the Church and with the nation as a whole – was long and strewn with roadblocks. She said, with good reason, she was sceptical about how we might ever find a way to work together. 'But let's keep talking about it', she kept repeating.

As our conversation was coming to an end, a look of serious thought crossed Martha's face. She peered up toward the ceiling as though she had just been hit by an idea, and she said to me, 'If we can't find a way to make it work for you to engage our community, how can we ever expect to reach some sort of reconciliation on a large scale?' She continued, 'I'm not saying *yes* to your request. But I'm not saying *no* either.' We agreed that the best way forward would be to take small steps together, one of which would be to have me visit the congregation a few times so they could get to know me. We didn't know what exactly it might take for us to work together, but we knew that moving forward in a way we could all feel good about meant that we would have to address some deep-rooted challenges.

After a long conversation filled with intense questions, awkward silences, and some hearty laughter, we hugged goodbye and I drove away. With the sun setting behind me, I smiled with anticipation of the possibilities before us.

## Qualitative Research and Theological Education

This story recounts a moment during a multi-year qualitative research study that I undertook for my doctoral dissertation. It attests to the formational nature of qualitative research. This story is a glimpse into the profound process of inner transformation that was engendered in me as I pursued qualitative research in a mode that Natalie Wigg-Stevenson refers to as ethnographic theology.[2] What began as a question about how children generate theological meaning in diverse cultural contexts morphed into a very personal journey that fundamentally changed who I am as a scholar and researcher, as a pastoral practitioner, and ultimately as a person of faith.

There's something about qualitative research (many things, actually) that have led researchers and clergy to investigate it as a form of pastoral practice. Mary Clark Moschella, in the introduction to *Ethnography as a Pastoral Practice*, makes the connection between such research methods and pastoral ministry explicit: 'when conducted and shared as a form of pastoral practice, ethnography can enable religious leaders to hear the theological wisdom of the people, wisdom that is spoken right in the midst of the nitty-gritty mundane realities of group life'.[3] Throughout this book, Moschella explores how the rhythms of ethnography – which is one form of qualitative research – allow researchers to embark on a journey that can bring about social change and spiritual transformation as it uncovers nuances and hidden meaning within faith communities.

But this is only one way that qualitative research can be seen as possessing pastoral dimensions. Yes, pursuing such research certainly aids religious leaders in becoming more aware of and thus better equipped to transform the faith communities and wider contexts in which they minister. We might refer to this as the *outer* journey of qualitative research. But there is an *inner* journey as well. As qualitative researchers explore the details of a circumstance, community, or set of individuals, they are often confronted with realities and knowledge their research generates that challenge their ways of thinking and being in the world. In this way, such research can involve a deeply personal sojourn into the hidden realities of one's inner life, calling the researcher to give themselves over to a process of personal transformation.

Herein lies one of the core benefits of including qualitative research within theological education programmes – it can arouse within oneself profound processes of inner change through confronting realities and spawning ideas that shake up our pre-existing understanding of the world – and of ourselves. Yes, qualitative research has the potential to allow those of us who pursue it to be stretched and to be shaped and, ultimately, to better know ourselves, which is crucial to healthy pastoral leadership. This is not to say that qualitative research inevitably engenders such a transformative inner journey. But when undertaken with particular assumptions and an openness to change, such research can be a deeply formational experience for those pursuing it.

What are these assumptions? For the rest of this chapter, I'll explore three broad qualities of qualitative research that impregnate it with potential to arouse inner transformation in the researcher. This list is far from exhaustive, and each quality is intimately connected to one another. I include these aspects because they are those that became central to my most recent experience of qualitative research. And because they are embedded in such a profoundly personal experience of transformation, it only seems appropriate for me to explore them in light of my own journey.

## Qualitative Research Cultivates Deep Listening

Our hyper-paced, social-media-driven world is shaping us into people who value being heard. Through Facebook, YouTube, Instagram, and countless other social-media platforms, we are able to speak into the world what we wish others to hear. And after we have cast our voices into cyberspace, we can scan through news feeds that give us quick glimpses into the information that others have placed before the world. The more we engage in these sorts of practices, the more we become a people shaped by a desire to be heard and a need to scan a mass of soundbites at breakneck speeds.

Both of these practices – being heard and glancing at great amounts of information – are counter to those necessary for qualitative research. Rather, what is vital for good research is the ability to listen deeply, to pay close attention to the individuals who participate in the research projects one is undertaking. This listening goes beyond using our ears: it is a process of opening oneself to gaining as much information about a person, place, or situation as possible. It involves paying attention to what others are conveying through body language, taking note of the feel of a space, and even getting a sense of what smells are in the air. When we engage in such a multifaceted deep form of listening, as I did when I met Revd Martha on that blustery winter day, we are better able to generate a full sense of a situation and we become attuned to others in a manner that values them as full and complex human beings, made in God's image. Moschella names this sort of listening as deep because it 'validates and honors another person's experience, insight, and soul'.[4]

I remember how excited and anxious I was to hold my first interview with children for my doctoral dissertation research. After three years of coursework, comprehensive exams, and proposal writing, I was finally beginning the research I'd been preparing for all this time. I had just completed a pilot study in which I field tested my research methods, but this was the first time I got to sit down with some children on record and begin to talk to them about their theologies. Three girls on the cusp of adolescence – Grace, Angela, and Lizzy – met me in the fellowship hall at their diverse and eclectic church. For about an hour I listened as they explained their ideas about God, reminisced about past events in their congregation, and shared a moment of sadness for a well-loved congregant who had died recently.

At the time I thought I knew how to listen with depth. After all, this wasn't my first qualitative research study and my pilot project had prepared me for how to catch as full a picture as I could during these sorts of interviews.[5] It wasn't until I began listening to the recording of this interview and going over my notes in order to transcribe this session that I realized how much I had missed in the moment. I began playing close attention to the words these girls were saying, to their intonation, to the way they'd finish each other's sentences, and even to the times of silence around the table. And the more I paid attention, the more I noticed that something was going on here that I would have completely missed without practices of deep listening.

During the interview, these three young theologians had tended to finish each other's thoughts and give answers to questions that I had directed to one of their peers. At times one girl would respond to my question first and the others would say 'Yeah' or 'What she said'. All this left me frustrated because I wanted to know what each one of them thought and these habits appeared to me to mean that some of them wouldn't share much beyond what one of the others in the group had already stated. How could I know what Grace really thought about Jesus if she keeps saying 'Yeah' to what Angela and Lizzy said?

Through deep listening, however, I realized that something else was going on here. Theology, for these children, was not a solo enterprise. They were actually formulating their theological views with one another right there before my eyes. As they drew pictures of God and spoke about their congregations, they were engaged in a process of theological reflection through which they shared ideas and challenged one another as they did theology in community. Theirs was a communal theology, one that wasn't just generated through conversations and experiences with others, but was held in common among the group.

This sort of communal approach to theology challenged the assumptions and values that I had brought with me into the fellowship hall on that cold January day. Before that moment I had been operating under the assumption that theology was largely an individualistic and personal phenomenon. But by deeply listening to these children, I had my views of theology challenged and expanded to include communal theologies as well. The lenses through which I saw theology were transformed and I perceived theology in ways that I could not have conceived of before. And perhaps this is just the beginning. Maybe there are countless other ways that people generate and hold to theologies as they make meaning of their lives. By listening deeply I can continue to be transformed as I encounter new approaches to generating theologies.

## Qualitative Research Fosters Self-Awareness

Qualitative research is often an exercise in portraiture. Rather than using a wide-angle lens to capture a panoramic view of a landscape, this sort of research is about getting up close and personal with a very particular set of participants or scenarios. It sacrifices sweeping breadth for intricate details. Good qualitative research offers a snapshot of a specific group of individuals at a defined moment.

Yet as in all photographs, the subjects captured in the shot are only part of the photographic experience. Yes, qualitative research certainly seeks to look at what, metaphorically speaking, is imprinted in the image. But as with fully interpreting a photograph, qualitative research challenges us to peer behind the camera and examine the one who is taking the picture. It calls us to develop a more profound self-awareness as we keep ourselves in check and even write ourselves into our research. Every stage of my research – from the questions I sought to explore to the methodologies I used, from my use of institutional ethics guidelines to my intentions for making the knowledge generated from the research available – was shaped by my location and biases. All of these (and much more) had a role to play as I peered through the metaphorical camera looking to capture snapshots.

Ethnographers call this practice of critical self-awareness *reflexivity*. Rather than taking up the mantle of objectivity, many contemporary ethnographers admit clearly that theirs is a subjective position. As human beings none of us are capable of stepping fully outside our positions, the embodied realities of our social locations, our theological assumptions, and the whole range of biases we bring with us into the research project. Thus, good qualitative research demands critical self-awareness at every stage if we are to accurately represent ourselves and our participants in our work. Wigg-Stevenson argues, 'if I am not reflexive about myself in relation to the field, my descriptive analysis of it will be shaped unconsciously and thus distorted by my own biases'.[6] In fact, she holds that without reflexivity not only do we risk inaccuracy in our research, but we also risk causing harm to those individuals and communities who participate in our work.

This sort of reflexivity is apparent in the vignette with which I opened this chapter. The anticipation and anxieties that were bubbling inside me as I made the journey to Colkirk United Church on that particular day – almost a year before my formal field research would begin – were realities of which I needed to be aware. The questions that were floating around inside my head, the fear that I would do something to offend my gracious hosts, and the reflections I wrote down as I spoke with Revd Martha – all of these are tied to the biases and assumptions that I had carried with me into that conversation. If left unchecked, they could have caused me to mishear and misunderstand all that was happening during that visit. Thus, I built particular practices of reflexivity into my research, such as keeping a research journal in which I wrote questions and reflections on each step of the journey and using a voice recorder to capture my immediate reactions to interviews as I drove home afterwards. These sorts of reflexive practices helped me become better attuned to myself and develop a sharper critical self-awareness. In so doing I noticed particular edges that I needed to soften, gaps in my thinking that warranted further knowledge, and – perhaps the most difficult of all – prejudices that I was unaware I carried with me as I marched through life. The reflexive nature of qualitative research allowed me to use this growing self-awareness to become a better version of myself and to develop deeper sensitivities to human experiences that are unlike my own.

As conversations at the intersection of theology and ethnography continue to develop, theologians like Timothy Snyder are bringing to light the tendency of 'conventional theological methodologies' to overlook the importance of critical self-reflexivity.[7]

Theology is too often undertaken from an assumed objective perspective, one that is abstract and removed from the realities of concrete life, including the life of the theologian. Thus, by engaging in qualitative research that takes seriously practices of reflexivity, those pursuing theology can become more critically aware of their own biases, baggage, and assumptions. Especially for ministers-in-training who are undertaking theological studies, qualitative research can in this way become a critical formational practice that allows one to better know oneself, to peer behind the camera and see how we are implicated in all we do.

## Qualitative Research Demands Action

As those of us engaged in qualitative research learn to listen deeply to the individuals, communities, and circumstances involved in our projects, we can find ourselves bumping up against ideas and beliefs that challenge our preconceptions. This can in turn lead to processes of critical self-awareness as we become better attuned to our own biases and assumptions, especially as they collide with ones encountered along the research journey.

But the formational power of qualitative research – that inner journey of growing awareness and change – contains an outer component as well. The author of the epistle of James knows that internal change is manifested in external action:

> What good is it, my brothers and sisters, if you say you have faith but do not have works? Can faith save you? If a brother or sister is naked and lacks daily food, and one of you says to them, 'Go in peace; keep warm and eat your fill,' and yet you do not supply their bodily needs, what is the good of that? So faith by itself, if it has no works, is dead. (James 2.14–17)

So it is with the formational potential of qualitative research. Reflexive self-awareness that can be engendered by practices of deep listening is only fully actualized when it leads to changes in behaviour.

Based on René Descartes' famous statement 'I think therefore I am', Western philosophies in the modern era have focused on knowledge as primary for what it means to be human. This knowledge was largely understood as cognitive, involving those mental processes that are often seen as separate from the physicality of our bodies. Even today, as we continue to shed our modernist skin and grow into a new late-modern or postmodern era, this mind–body dualism continues to flourish, albeit in new manifestations.

Yet such epistemological and ontological assumptions are not the only way that human beings have understood themselves and their places within the world. Many indigenous communities perceive human knowledge as based on much more than abstract mental capacities. Rather, indigenous understanding sees knowledge in holistic ways, as undeniably connected to human experience.[8] It's inherently embodied, generated from and lived out in concrete ways in one's community and context. According to Margaret Kovach, indigenous ways of knowing 'are born of the necessity to feed, clothe, and transmit values. As such the method of knowing must be practical and purposeful.'[9] For knowledge to be real, it must result in practical, real-life action within the world.

According to this mode of thought, any true inner formation that occurs through engagement in qualitative research will be made manifest through changes in the way of life of the researcher. In my experiences of using ethnographic theology in my doctoral dissertation research, my critical self-awareness led to concrete action in at least four broad ways. There are several forms of action that can result from the inner journey of qualitative research. What I share are simply those that are most prominent in my own story.

First, action can occur before or during the research process. In the movie *Indiana Jones and the Last Crusade* (1989), the title character tells his students, 'Seventy percent of all archaeology is done in the library. Research. Reading.' Although almost every other scene in the franchise contradicts this statement, what this fictional archaeologist says contains an element of truth for qualitative research. A great deal of research occurs before fieldwork is even begun. In the three years that I spent preparing for my field-work, I expanded my views of ethnography by reading current analyses and studies that challenged conventional approaches to this sort of research, a practice that didn't end when I began interviewing participants. As I read the words of scholars and listened to individuals who participated in my study, I changed my research methods and tactics to better reflect what I was learning. For example, at one congregation it became apparent that, rather than my conducting one-on-one interviews with children, it was ethically appropriate for me to meet them in small groups. This action was a direct response to changes in my own assumptions and had a positive influence on the communities and children that participated in this way.

Second, inner transformation can be manifested through concrete action among those persons or communities that were involved. When we ask people to give of themselves for our projects, it's imperative that our work can have, even in some small way, a direct benefit for those involved. In my research with children's theologies, this action was different for each congregation that participated. In some churches, the knowledge I learned about the community allowed me to see a concrete need for assistance with leading their children's programmes, so I assisted with Sunday school in one church and with three week-long vacation Bible schools in another. At other congregations, the interviews I held with children were in themselves a benefit, for children told their parents and leaders that they appreciated the opportunity to share about their ideas openly with a non-judgemental, arm's-length adult. These are some of the more obvious ways that I was able to act out of the inner changes occurring within me throughout the research process.

A third form of action has to do with how the knowledge generated by qualitative research is shared after the study has ended. Does it remain among a small group of professors or an academic guild or is it – with proper permission, of course – made available to those who participated and other organizations and groups of practitioners that would benefit from it? Since completing my research and passing my dissertation defence, I have been challenged, in part by some participants, to share some of what I learned with broader groups of children's ministry leaders and theological educators so that they can adapt their work in light of the insight generated through the research. This chapter is one example of that process.

Finally, formational change that can result from qualitative research can occur in the personal life of the researcher. Once we are on the other side of a research project, the knowledge we learn through deep listening and the critical self-awareness that can come about as a result can cause inner transformation to be manifested in countless types of action we take in our personal lives. Four years after completing my field research, I still find myself pausing throughout my weeks and days, caught up short because the deep-seated assumptions I held before this study have been displaced by those that I developed along the way. And the results of these ongoing displacements are seen in my living my life differently now. For example, some of my research partic- ipants modelled the importance of time to relationships, and I am now much more likely to spend long amounts of time with those close to me and those who appear to need a friend at that moment. Rather than wondering how long this visit to a café might take and when I can get back to all the daily tasks that need accomplishing, I am more prone to allow myself to become immersed in conversation, for relationships require long bouts of deep listening and laughter and tears that can only come through dedicated time together.

## The Challenge of Qualitative Research

My experience with qualitative research has convinced me of the formational power it can have in the lives of those who pursue it. It has left indelible marks on my life, disrupting my patterns of thought and calling me to more faithful action in the world. My research has been a sacramental sojourn, one that has caused me to catch glimpses of God in the lives of the children and congregations that opened themselves to me. It has allowed Pierre Bourdieu's assertion to resonate with me, that 'the interview can be considered a sort of *spiritual exercise* that, through *forgetfulness of self*, aims at a true *conversion of the way we look at* other people in the ordinary circumstances of life'.[10]

But like all growth, the changes toward which this research has called me have come with pain and struggle and disequilibrium. To truly embrace the ways my participants and the broader research process were calling me to be transformed, I had to question conventional systems in which I lived and moved and had my being. For one thing, I noticed ways that my university's research ethics guidelines were inappropriate and even upheld expectations of research relationships that may have been downright unethical in some of the non-dominant, oppressed groups with which I was working. I had to navigate these waters carefully, and at times I had to swim against the tide of the university in order to remain true to the inner changes that my research participants were calling me to. Additionally, the style with which I communicated the knowledge I had learned transgressed academic writing conventions. I intentionally chose to begin with the stories of the participants, to allow these stories to critique scholarly theology and religious studies. And I did so in plain language (much like the style of this chapter, which in its own way counters norms of academic writing). After all, to not allow the voices of those who contributed to this study to have the most prominent place within it, and to write in a way that they would struggle to understand (i.e. with academic jargon and lengthy sentences that might make me sound more intelligent than I am) would be unethical. In my academic context, these choices – which come out of how I changed throughout the research process – are risky and are not always understood or appreciated. And these are just some of the surface-level struggles I faced. The deeper, more personal challenges upset the very assumptions and frameworks through which I live and give meaning to my life. But being formed by qualitative research sometimes calls us to transgress the norms and conventions of our communities, our contexts, and ourselves.

Qualitative research is so much more than a way of learning about a situation or a group of people. When pursued through a particular set of postures – such as a willingness to listen deeply, become more critically self-aware, and engage in consequential action – it can be a transformational process. It takes courage. It takes conviction and will. It takes humility to be willing to learn from others and to admit that we have been short-sighted, misinformed, and even harmful to others. It involves processes of confession and reconciliation as we realize our missteps, ask for forgiveness, and make new mistakes along the way. But we who take the journey from a theological standpoint know that God walks with us, convicting, supporting, and transforming if we remain open to taking up the challenges before us.

## Notes

1 To protect the identity of my research participants, I have assigned pseudonyms to all individuals and congregations.

2 Natalie Wigg-Stevenson, *Ethnographic Theology: An Inquiry into the Production of Theological Knowledge* (New York: Palgrave Macmillan, 2014).

3 Mary Clark Moschella, *Ethnography as a Pastoral Practice: An Introduction* (Cleveland, OH: Pilgrim, 2008), 4.

4 Moschella, *Ethnography*, 13.

5 For information about a previous qualitative study, see my book, David M. Csinos, *Children's Ministry that Fits: Beyond One-Size-Fits-All Approaches to Ministry with Children* (Eugene, OR: Wipf & Stock, 2011).

6 Natalie Wigg-Stevenson, 'Reflexive Theology: A Preliminary Proposal', *Practical Matters* 6 (2013), 2.

7 See Timothy K. Snyder, 'Theological Ethnography: Embodied,' *The Other Journal* 23, no. 5 (2014) Available from: https://theotherjournal. com/2014/05/27/theological-ethnography-embodied/ [17 November 2017].

8 See Marlene Brant Castellano's chapter, 'Updating Aboriginal Traditions of Knowledge', in *Indigenous Knowledges in Global Contexts: Multiple Readings of Our World*, eds George J. Sefa Dei, Budd L. Hall, and Dorothy Goldin Rosenberg (Toronto: University of Toronto Press, 2000), 21–36.

9 Margaret Kovach, 'Emerging from the Margins: Indigenous Methodologies', in *Research as Resistance: Critical, Indigenous, and Anti-Oppressive Approaches*, eds Leslie Brown and Susan Strega (Toronto: Canadian Scholars' Press, 2005), 28.

10 Pierre Bourdieu, 'Understanding', in *The Weight of the World: Social Suffering in Contemporary Society*, translated by Priscilla Pankhurst Ferguson (Stanford, CA: Stanford University Press, 1999), 614; italics as in original.

# 5

# The *Askēsis* of Fieldwork:
# Practices for a Way of Inquiry,
# a Way of Life

## TODD DAVID WHITMORE

There is ongoing debate among ethnographers about how best
to depict our mode of inquiry. The classic depiction, from the
early twentieth century, was in terms of the methods of ethnography constituting a scientific set of procedures. Beginning some-
time in the 1950s and reaching full voice in the 1980s, cultural
anthropologists, often borrowing from postmodern hermeneutics
and philosophy, began to identify ethnography as more an art or
literature than a science.[1] The language of science and/or/against
art and the humanities still dominates discussion of how to depict
the practice of ethnography.[2]

I would like to suggest that the term *askēsis* both articulates and
can foster an improved practice of ethnography more adequately
than either the rubric of science or that of art. The practice of
asceticism is often associated with specifically religious traditions
and acts of self-denial, but the ancient Greek and Roman concept
simply meant 'training' or 'exercise'. *Askēsis* is, in the words of
postmodern philosopher Michel Foucault, the 'set of necessary
and sufficient moves, of necessary and sufficient practices, which
will enable us to be stronger than anything that may happen in
our life'.[3] And what 'happens in life' in the doing of fieldwork
goes well beyond – and therefore is not a topic of – typical academic discussions of method. Hence the need for an *askēsis* specific to the practices of fieldwork. The aim of this article is to
articulate that need and specify some of the practices involved.

To fill out what I mean by fieldwork as *askēsis*, in what follows I first present some of the reasons for this rubric of interpreting fieldwork, and then describe, so as to illustrate, two practices that follow from this framing, what I call *originating hospitality* and *approaching softly*.

## The Case for *Askēsis* in Brief

There are a number of arguments for interpreting and practising fieldwork as *askēsis*. The first argument is that conceptualizing fieldwork as a form of *askēsis* foregrounds and allows recognition of the fact that fieldwork places the researcher's body in the middle of method. *Askēsis* highlights that the particular practice in question becomes, again in Foucault's words, 'integrated into the individual and control his action, becoming part, as it were, of his muscles and nerves'. In comparison to the usual forms of academic appropriation, *askēsis* involves 'a different form of *mnemē* [memory], a completely different ritual of verbal reactualization and implementation'.[4] Central to the scientific model, however, is the endeavour to keep the investigator and their body from entering into the methodological calculus; such an entrance is an intrusion and by definition taints the result. Even the art metaphor, which may recognize the role of the body in the moment of *poiesis* or production – *poiesis* meaning 'to make' – generally fails to account for the impact of fieldwork on the body of the researcher during research. Here Foucault cites the Stoic Marcus Aurelius in describing *askēsis* as 'more like wrestling than dancing, in that you must stay on your guard and steady your feet against the blows which rain down on you, and without warning'.[5]

The emphasis on the impact on and influence of the body leads to the second argument: *askēsis* recognizes the need for the researcher's (embodied) self to change, often dramatically, in order for them to understand the world of their subjects. Again Foucault: 'An act of knowledge could never give access to the truth unless it was prepared, accompanied, doubled, and completed by a certain transformation.'[6] Foucault does not hesitate to call this transformation 'conversion'.[7] First-person accounts of fieldwork often highlight the ways in which the researcher has to shift, alter, even fundamentally change their understanding of the world and themselves within it in order to 'get' what is going on among the people they are studying. Having removed the self from the investigative equation, the scientific model is incapable of accounting for this testified-to reality from the field. Even the art model, at least as it is commonly construed, stresses the way in which the artist's vision presents and thus alters the world, with less emphasis on how the world alters the artist.

Though interpreting fieldwork as *askēsis* presents these advantages over the science and art models, it also preserves what is helpful about these two approaches. The science model highlights specific techniques that offer the discipline of anthropology the promise of rigour. The ancient Greeks used the term *tekhnē*, which they distinguished from *phronēsis*, or 'practical wisdom'. Foucault translated *tekhnē* as 'technical procedure' and contrasted it with *ethos* or 'moral attitude'.[8] Fieldwork as *askēsis* incorporates *tekhnē* into a particular kind of practical wisdom, but the scientific – or perhaps more accurately scientistic – model rules out any kind of 'moral attitude' as a corruptive force in the investigative project. Fieldwork as *askēsis* can also facilitate the scope of interpretation and the innovation that the fieldwork-as-art rubric foregrounds. Such interpretation and innovation are evident in Foucault's insistence that *askēsis* 'must be training in some elementary moves which are sufficiently general and effective for them to be adapted to every circumstance and – on condition of their being sufficiently simple and well-learned – for one to be able to make immediate use of them when the need arises'.[9]

The deep suppleness of fieldwork practised as a form of *askēsis* points toward my last (for now) argument for so interpreting the ethnographic enterprise. For some time now, cultural anthropology has come under the criticism that while Christian concepts underwrote some of the founding ideas of the discipline, the discipline itself has remained for the far greater part staunchly secular in its self-understanding.[10] Even after its 'interpretive turn' in the 1980s, a turn that recognizes that it is impossible to carry out ethnographic research without deep value-laden pre-suppositions about how the world works – what anthropologist Henrietta Moore calls 'concept metaphors and pre-theoretical commitments'[11] – the discipline of anthropology as a whole still strongly resists religious modes of interpretation on the part of the researcher. In other words, the substance of the discipline of cultural anthropology has yet to be allowed to catch up with the dominant theoretical commitments it has held since the interpretive turn. This disjunction has been, and to a certain extent continues to be, largely a result of disciplinary boundary drawing. From the beginning of academic ethnography, anthropologists have encountered – and countered – Christian missionaries, competitors in the field who have drawn upon ethnographic methods for quite different purposes than the academic. It has been necessary, therefore, to distinguish the academic from the theological, and the scholar from the theologian.

This discomfort with and resistance to religious modes of reasoning runs up against one of the desiderata of anthropology: to understand the people and cultures studied as much as possible in their own terms. Many and perhaps most of those people and cultures have various kinds and degrees of religious orientation. The friction between cultural anthropology's secular intellectual habitus and its wish to provide at least partially emic – that is, internal to the community studied – interpretation has led some anthropologists to call for greater respect for their research subjects' world-views.[12] This has somewhat lowered the discomfort with and resistance to religious reasoning carried out by researchers.[13] The time would seem right, then, to widen this small opening to forms of anthropology being carried out from religious perspectives – or, to use Moore's terms, theological concept metaphors and pre-theoretical commitments. What this means in part is that the yeshiva, seminary, mosque, and temple can be sites *from* which (and not just *upon* which) scholars do fieldwork.

Although anthropologist Nancy Scheper-Hughes lost her Catholic Christian faith she nonetheless interprets ethnographic commitment in strongly analogous terms as a kind of *askēsis*:

> The secular humanism of anthropology offers an alternative form of discipleship, built around the practice of studied observation, contemplation and reflection. I know that anthropology is a powerful tool capable of taming unruly emotions, replacing disgust with respect, ignorance with understanding, hatred with empathy, and a practice of compassionate and modest witnessing to human sorrows.[14]

Given the analogy between anthropological and religious forms of 'discipleship', it is perhaps not too much to suggest that we can illuminate aspects of the latter in light of the former, and vice versa. That is the wager of this article and my larger project. In setting out the various practices of the *askēsis* of fieldwork below, I draw upon Daoist, Stoic, and Christian as well as anthropological sources to interpret, critique, and expand each other for the sake of a richer practice of fieldwork.

Together, the practices of fieldwork *askēsis* cultivate what a number of anthropologists and other qualitative researchers call an 'ethnographic sensibility', that is, a particular kind of *phronēsis*, 'a way of being in the world'.[15] An ethnographic sensibility is, in Carole McGranahan's words, 'a sense of the ethnographic as the lived expectations, complexities, contradictions, possibilities, and ground of any given cultural group'. It is 'experiential, embodied, and empathetic', and developing it involves 'listening, participating, witnessing, and reflecting, in ways both actual and approximate'.[16] The fact that scholars from other disciplines and methodologies call for the appropriation of an 'ethnographic sensibility' is evidence that even other academics consider it a distinctive mode of inquiry and being.[17]

The broad genre into which this kind of project fits is that of the enchiridion, or 'handbook' or 'manual', with its frequently direct form of address to the reader. It is meant to provide insights for those of you just beginning – or even just beginning to consider – fieldwork as well as for seasoned ethnographers who appreciate alternative ways of understanding anthropological practices. The modern meaning of 'handbook' and 'manual' can be misleading, however. The classic enchiridion is also a theoretical work, or, to put it more accurately, the enchiridion is a genre to which any theory-practice bifurcation is foreign. For Epictetus, whose *Discourses* and *Enchiridion* are perhaps the most influential Stoic writings, philosophical inquiry, to use Pierre Hadot's phrase, is 'a way of life'.[18] Saint Augustine's *Enchiridion* is an instructional manual for Christian faith written in terms of the three theological virtues of faith, hope, and love as traced through, for instance, the Apostles' Creed and the Lord's Prayer – in other words, theology as a way of life. Presented through an enchiridion, ethnography, as a form of *askēsis*, interprets fieldwork as an embodied 'way of inquiry' with implications for a broader way of life where, to again use Scheper-Hughes's words, 'studied observation, contemplation and reflection' have the capacity for 'taming unruly emotions, replacing disgust with respect, ignorance with understanding, hatred with empathy, and a practice of compassionate and modest witnessing to human sorrows'. That is not a bad way to live.

## Originating Hospitality

I think it best to begin with a practice performed not by the researcher, but by their research subjects, something we can call *originating hospitality*, because without it the practice of fieldwork more generally would be impossible. For fieldwork to work at all, it needs research subjects who are willing to open up the intimate dimensions of their world, their cultural and often literal homes, as it were, to you the researcher. It is important to begin with this practice for at least two reasons. First, it is a reminder to the researcher that you are the one who is the stranger. Colonial (and neo-colonial) forms of ethnography can be traced to the presupposition that it is the research subject who is the Other, the foreigner whose life must be charted in order to be understood.

Recognition on your part of locals' originating hospitality is one way to remind yourself that you are the stranger, and that your presence requires locals to figure out how to interpret and place you within *their* scheme of things. You are always also the ethnograph*ee*. If you are fortunate, your research subjects will open their lives up to you. Hospitality is a fitting term here because the Latin *hospitale* originally meant a 'house for the reception and entertainment of pilgrims, travelers, or strangers'.[19] And Michael Agar gets it exactly right in the title of his introduction to ethnography with his recognition that the fieldworker is a 'professional stranger'.[20]

The second reason to begin with locals' originating hospitality is that it highlights that their practice of such puts you in their debt. To understand the nature and magnitude of the gesture of offering hospitality, imagine someone whom you do not know at all arriving on your doorstep representing an institution that you may or may not have heard of and asking if they can crash on your couch, observe your intimate daily interactions for an extended period of time, and then tell the world about it in detail in the ineradicable form of written publication. Do you allow them in? Even in 'native' or 'home' research, where the ethnographer studies what they consider their own culture, their approaching it as a researcher makes them still a 'professional stranger', using ways of constructing the world learned elsewhere to investigate friends and family, and those locals still must be willing to expose their lives for subsequent public presentation if the project is to work.[21] To be sure, more recent writing in anthropology questions any sharp distinction between 'field' and 'not-field'[22] and presses ethnographers to identify their own social location both to their research subjects and in publication, but still, for it to work, fieldwork requires hospitality on the part of the researched.

Those whom you plan to research may know full well that by extending their lives for your scrutiny they are putting you in their debt, and such an arrangement might be deliberate on their part. Christian theology from the New Testament to John Milbank and philosophy from the Stoic Seneca to Derrida consider the question of whether any gift – even the gift of hospitality – can be unconditional.[23] Anthropology since Bronislaw Malinowski's account of the Melanesian *kula* system (1922) and Marcel Mauss's work on gifting in traditional societies (1925) has interpreted gifts as a form of social *exchange*, with economic dimensions, that promotes communal solidarity.[24] Gift exchange is a way of negotiating one's place in the social order. Given that anthropology has traditionally studied persons and groups with less socioeconomic and political power than the researcher, the research subject in such a context might view the approach and request of the ethnographer to be an opportunity for social or economic benefit. Experimental science tends to work out the dynamics of hospitality and debt through a straightforward contractual mechanism of monetary exchange, as is evident with the posters found on college campuses calling for subjects to participate in research in exchange for a set amount of cash. Ethnography can operate in this way, but often the exchange is less defined and more complex.

When I wanted to research an outlying Internally Displaced Persons (IDP) camp in northern Uganda during the Lord's Resistance Army conflict, I reached out to a nun, who contacted a priest, who inquired with a lay catechist living in the camp if arrangements could be made for me to stay there. The lay catechist, Ojara, welcomed me in dramatic fashion, giving me his sleeping hut while his family of five slept on the floor of his cooking hut.[25] After about a week of this arrangement, I thought it was too much to ask of Ojara. I told him that I could move into his storage hut, which was only half full (with three huts, Ojara was one of the best-off people in the camp; most families had just one hut). He declined: the storage hut was not a satisfactory dwelling for a guest. I offered to pay him to have another hut built. Again he said no: the camp was desecrated land; when the conflict was over and he moved to his familial land, he would build me a hut then. Finally, I said that I could move in with his brother-in-law, who had a smaller family and thus more room. Ojara simply said no, with no explanation. The brother-in-law later filled me in: if I moved out, it would show to the community that Ojara was not practising adequate Acholi hospitality. Whereas I was concerned that I was taking advantage of too much hospitality, Ojara was concerned that his hospitality might appear inadequate. My staying with him had increased his already significant stature within the community, and my leaving would be a blow to his standing. Understanding the wider social dynamics, I stayed. The importance of the public perception of Ojara's standing was perhaps most stark on the last day of my first stay with him: he announced to the community that he would put on a fête celebrating my visit, and then asked me privately to pay for all of the food and drink. Still, I would argue that even when originating hospitality is part of a larger set of social exchanges such as I have described with Ojara, it remains a gift, because it is not strictly obligatory and is not always proffered.

## Approaching Softly

Whether the gift of hospitality is freely given or part of a socio-economic pattern of exchange, the fact remains that fieldwork is impossible without it. It is important that attention to this fact shape your initial moves into the field. Be patient. Relationships of gift, even as part of a larger exchange, cannot be forced. Perhaps the most underestimated aspect of fieldwork in terms of time commitment is how long it takes to develop initial relationships of trust. Writing of his life and work among the Songhay people of Niger, Paul Stoller recounts that at first they would lie to him when he asked them questions. Eventually an elder provided insight:

> Monsieur Paul, you will never learn about us if you go into people's compounds, ask personal questions, and write down the answers. Even if you remain here one year, or two years, and ask us questions in this manner, we would still lie to you. You must learn to sit with people, Monsieur Paul. You must learn to sit and listen.[26]

Even if your research subjects are talking to you, they will not extend hospitality until you approach them as a stranger so that, if you are fortunate, you are received as a guest.

The Daoist concept and practice of *wu-wei*, literally 'nondoing', provides a helpful context within which to consider how to approach someone as a stranger. At first *wu-wei* may seem paradoxical, even nonsensical. Laozi's *Daodejing*, a primary Daoist source text, states,

> The pursuit of learning results in daily increase,
> Hearing the Dao leads to daily decrease.
> Decrease and again decease,
> until you reach nonaction.
> Through nonaction,
> no action is left undone.[27]

How can nonaction operate such that 'no action is left undone'? 'The Dao makes no effort at all/yet there is nothing it doesn't do.'[28] Following the Dao, we are to

> Act without acting
> work without working
> Understand without understanding.[29]

How are we to do this? The closing lines of the *Daodejing* offer some clarity:

> The Way of the Sage
> is to act without struggling.[30]

Some translations have 'without competing' and 'without contention'.[31] So nonaction, it seems, is action without struggle, competitiveness, or contention.[32] Recent commentators suggest that *wu-wei* means 'a form of action that is free of any desires, intention or motivation', 'non-intervention in the natural course of things', 'letting things follow their natural course', 'the avoidance of an authoritarian posture', 'accomplishing what is necessary without ulterior motive', and 'not using force'.[33] In keeping with this last interpretation, the Daoist practice of *qigong* is informed by the saying *Yong yi, bu yong li* ('Use intent/concentration/mindfulness, not force').[34] *Qigong* literally means 'vital breath' (*qi*) 'work' (*gong*) – in short, it is a 'spiritual exercise' or *askēsis* made up of physical movements and meditation practices aimed at cultivating *qi* such that in your action you do not need or feel the need to resort to force.[35]

The *Daodejing* describes the old sages who were united with the Dao and were therefore vehicles of *qi* in terms relevant to the ethnographic posture of stranger/guest:

> They were careful as if crossing a river in winter
> cautious as if worried about neighbors
> reserved like a guest
> ephemeral like melting ice
> simple like uncarved wood
> open like a valley.[36]

Forcing the shape of fieldwork relationships, like all relationships, before they have a chance to develop at their own pace is bound to fail.

> To act [through force] is to fail
> to control is to lose
> sages therefore don't act [through force]
> thus they don't fail
> they don't control
> thus they don't lose.[37]

Elsewhere, Laozi puts the matter even more starkly:

> Daring to act [through force] means death
> daring not to act [through force] means life
> of these two
> one benefits
> the other harms.[38]

The *Daodejing* conveys the difference between life-giving mind-ful action and death-dealing forceful action through a contrast between the qualities of softness and hardness:

> When people are born
> they are soft and weak
> when they perish
> they are hard and stiff
> when plants shoot forth
> they are supple and tender
> when they die
> they are withered and dry
> thus it is said
> the hard and stiff are followers of death
> the soft and weak are followers of life
> when an army becomes stiff it suffers defeat
> when a plant becomes stiff it snaps.[39]

A Daoist approach to fieldwork, then, would recommend *approaching softly*. But what might this look like in practice?

When I began my fieldwork in northern Uganda, I, like Stoller in Niger, battered the locals with decontextualized (to them) questions. I was particularly insensitive to the charged political context within which they lived. The residents had been forcibly displaced by the government into IDP camps. Residents who travelled beyond the camps outside designated hours might be treated as rebels by soldiers. In such a situation, the camp residents were unable to articulate their displeasure with President Museveni, yet I would ask in large focus groups (themselves a form of forced relationship) what they thought of how Museveni was handling the war. Of course they prevaricated; of course they lied. I had not yet learned the lesson of the French ethnographer and filmographer Jean Roche, passed on to Stoller, that the ethnographer 'is not a policeman who extorts what one does not want to say or to reveal, and his elementary honesty consists exactly of respecting those he learns to know better, which is to say love better'.[40] I did not think of myself as extorting anything until confronted by Olum at Pabbo IDP camp: 'You come and steal our knowledge. You steal our culture. You come and talk to us about our knowledge and our culture and then take it all back with you. And we have nothing left.'

Stunned by Olum's bluntness, I changed my approach. I would stroll around the camp until someone waved me over and engaged me in conversation. In doing so, I had stumbled upon what Stoller refers to as the improvisational *pourquoi pas* ('why not') method. I dropped my original research topic – the possibilities and limits of microfinance in IDP camps – to listen to whatever people in the camp wanted to talk about. The Acholi have a phrase for it: *cito mato yamo*, to go drink the wind. It means to walk about, to meander, to greet whomever you happen to see and, if asked, to hang out a bit with them. Sometimes people just wanted money. Sometimes I obliged. Other times they were intrigued that a white person would voluntarily live in an IDP camp. Reports of my walkabouts would often reach the priest in the parish compound:

I heard you climbed the old water tower today.
Yes.
They say you walk fast for a white man.

Improvisational does not mean haphazard, however. Over time, specific relationships emerge and take direction. *Cito mato yamo* is how I met the people – the traditional anthropological word 'informants' is both far too reductionistic and, in the political situation, far too charged a term – who allowed me to be not only stranger and guest, but also, to echo the title of anthropologist Hortense Powdermaker's account of her work in the field, 'stranger and friend'.[41]

There are decided limits, however, to approaching softly in the field in a fully Daoist manner. First of all, as Laozi makes clear, few of us are sages. More, a soft approach involves 'non-intervention in the natural course of things'. It is far from clear what constitutes the 'natural course of things'. Even 'hard' sciences like physics recognize, when they are honest, the 'observer effect', that is, the fact that observation, even when carried out with an inanimate apparatus, changes the phenomenon observed; such change is much more diffuse and harder to specify in the case of a human observer with human research subjects. The closest analogy to non-intervention in the natural course of things in present-day English that I have been able to identify is the phrase, borrowed from woodworking and generalized to life, 'go with, not against the grain'.

There are also impediments to the development of open friendship structured into the situation of the *professional* stranger. Again, unadulterated soft approaches require 'a form of action that is free of any desires, intention or motivation', yet academic ethnography brings with it the intention to publish. This was the force of Olum of Pabbo's indictment, 'You come and talk to us about our knowledge and our culture and then take it all back with you.' His charge undercut any illusion I had that I was 'free of any desires, intention or motivation'. Time constraints complicate matters even more, particularly for graduate students and junior professors. Stoller emphasizes the necessity of long-term fieldwork for his *pourquois pas* approach to bear full fruit[42] – his own research among the Songhay both in Niger and in the United States has lasted decades – but that kind of time is precisely what the young scholar does not have. The socially structured tension for her is that of being caught between institutional demands for production and the fact that, again, to put it in terms of the *Daodejing*, 'To act [through force] is to fail', in this case, to fail to develop the kind of relationships that themselves make for the best research. You can try to exert more control over the field process, but here, in the same way, 'to control is to lose'.

Finally, complications affect the possibility of open friendship, particularly when the researcher has more wealth and power than the researched. I have already discussed the complexities of my relationship with Ojara, but I was first made aware of the way that asymmetrical power affects the possibility of friendship – at least as friendship is understood in American everyday discourse – while at Pabbo camp.

* * *

'Will you remember us?'

It is two weeks before I will be leaving Pabbo, so Justin's question at first seems odd to me. Then I figure that he has seen other whites go and not return, not keep up contact. They may not have told the whites back in America what they have seen and witnessed in northern Uganda. Maybe what he is asking me is less that I stay in contact than that I testify in the United States to what is going on here. Certainly the Acholi have suffered enormously since the war began.

Justin is a catechist. In a continent where there are 8000 people for every priest, lay persons are of necessity prime evangelists. The Lord's Resistance Army rebels have killed 75 catechists in the war. There is a lot to remember and a lot to tell.

'Yes. I will remember you. And I hope to come back next year.'

'Because we catechists have it very difficult.'

I nod. Yes. Yes. We are standing under a mango tree just outside the parish compound, on top of, I am later told, a mass grave of Acholi killed by the government army, the UPDF.

'We earn only 7800 for six months. That is not very much, is it?'

I hesitate, startled by what seems to be a new line of questioning. I do the computation anyway. It is about four US dollars.

'No.'

The conversation – or, more accurately, my perception of it – begins to shift.

'Can you find me a friend in America?'

His reaction prompts recollections from my previous trip to Uganda. An assertive young man extended a pad and pen toward me as I walked to Mass in Kyarusozi in western Uganda and asked to exchange addresses. 'I have always wanted a friend in America.' His letter arrived two months later with a request to sponsor his schooling. Conversation decoded: In discourse between blacks and whites in Uganda, to 'remember' is to fundraise, to 'befriend' is to become a benefactor, and to be white is to be constantly reminded that you are the promise of both.

I look up at the mango tree and then at Justin.

'I'll see what I can do.'

I do not have any ready answers for how to get rid of these obstacles to greater openness in the field because they *cannot* be eliminated. Here, though, it is helpful to return to Foucault's understanding of *askēsis* as constituted by a 'set of necessary and sufficient moves, of necessary and sufficient practices, which will enable us to be stronger than anything that may happen in our life', aware that, even at its best, such practice is 'more like wrestling than dancing'. I do think that attentive immersion in the classic texts of Daoism and engagement in *qigong* – or analogous texts and practices from other traditions[43] – can cultivate a sensibility in the researcher such that we can approximate the Daoist ideal of acting 'without struggling', 'without competing', or 'without contention'. Perhaps 'non-contentious wrestling' is about as apt a description of good fieldwork as there can be.

## Looking Forward: Other Practices

There are any number of practices that constitute good fieldwork and to delineate in detail more of them would require more space than this chapter allows. It is possible, however, to gesture in their direction. *Awakening the senses* is necessary because much modern research method has worked to suppress smell, touch, taste, hearing, and, other than in the act of reading, sight. Even the empirical sciences tend to reduce the senses to sight, in the form of observation, and in constructing the ideal of the god's-eye-view 'objective' observer they represent seeing as if the person doing the viewing is not really there in the scene. *Activating the affect* is important for much the same reason: much if not most modern research considers feelings or emotions to be simply subjective, and believes that they taint inquiry, whereas fieldwork as *askēsis* considers them crucial data.[44]

Awakening the senses and activating the affect allows a flood of new kinds of information into the researcher, a process which can and should be disorienting. Some kind of distance from what you are observing seems necessary. *Detachment* as a practice of *askēsis* is not like that of objectivism, where researchers cast themselves as if not in the world. Rather, it is the distance and equilibrium you gain by being *between* two (or more) worlds. In popular literature, being between two worlds is often described as being 'caught' and is interpreted as a source of disorientation (as it often is). However, you cannot gain distance and equilibrium, if they are to be had at all, by 'escaping' from one of the worlds into the other. 'Going native' in any sort of complete sense, on the one hand, and returning to your 'home' world to establish an utterly external god's-eye-view, on the other hand, may sound tempting, but both are impossible. In my reading, Daoist, Stoic, and Ignatian Christian interpretations of detachment are concerned with a suspension between two worlds that offers a perspective on both and, ultimately, not disequilibrium but rather resilience.[45]

*Listening* is a practice appropriate for a guest and takes on particular importance during the field interview. It is central to Foucault's understanding of *askēsis*.[46] Pierre Bourdieu brings the listening posture specifically to bear on the field interview. In a way similar to Foucault, Bourdieu invokes the language of 'spiritual exercise' and 'conversion' in his account of what goes into interviewing well:

> In effect, it combines total availability to the person being questioned, submission to the singularity of a particular life history . . . I would say that the interview can be considered a sort of spiritual exercise that through forgetfulness of self aims at a true conversion of the way we look at other people in the ordinary circumstances of life.[47]

The Songhay elder told Paul Stoller, 'You must learn to sit with people, Monsieur Paul. You must learn to sit and listen.' Such sitting and listening implies the practice of *leisure*. In Roman Catholic Christianity, leisure is a basic human good (and therefore also a right). It is, as Josef Pieper claims, 'the basis of culture'.[48] I once complained to an anthropologist friend about theologians who claimed to be doing 'ethnography' when they gave no indication of any knowledge of the highly developed tradition of theoretical reflection *on* ethnography – for instance, its epistemological pre-suppositions, its limits as a method – in anthropology. I opined, 'Ethnography is more than just hanging out,' to which he replied, 'Yes, it is deep hanging out.' As discussed earlier, such practice of the leisure of deep hanging out is often in tension with institutional requirements for results to be produced within a specific timeframe.

Time hanging out with your research subjects might tempt you to think that you have managed to achieve, without remainder, Malinowski's desideratum of seeing things from a 'native' point of view. He wanted to 'wake up every morning to a day present-ing itself to me more or less as it does to a native'. This would enable the researcher 'to grasp the native's point of view, his rela-tion to life, to realize his vision of his world'.[49] However, as when I misinterpreted Ojara's act of hospitality, often enough we not only miss aspects of the lives of our research subjects but also, in large part because of the presuppositions we bring to the field, having noticed them we interpret them dramatically incorrectly. Fieldwork, therefore, requires the practice of *epistemic humility*. Post-'interpretive turn' ethnographers ground their humility in the practice of reflexivity, which means, in short, turning their theories back on themselves, and in making their social location, their 'positionality', clear both in their fieldwork and in their pub-lic representations of their research subjects. The aim of these practices is to keep in check any epistemic hubris.

Living between two worlds, opening up the senses and the affect, and sometimes the sheer physical grind of fieldwork are all taxing on the researcher. You will find yourself exhausted in ways untouched by library research. *Care and love of the self* are necessary; Foucault interprets *askēsis* primarily in relation to such care of the self.[50] Fieldwork can be a lonely activity. That it is also often emotionally charged compounds the diffi-culty. Doctoral programmes only sometimes address through their curricula the issues of physical and psychological stress in the field, and the researcher is often without adequate interper-sonal support. Geraldine Lee-Treweek writes of such 'emotional danger' that the 'answer would seem to be planning, forethought and peer and/or collegial support when necessary. These strategies seem straightforward but in reality one has to work at creating a support network and asking for extra support is often not easy.'[51] Lee-Treweek sought out a therapist; I added an acupuncturist and more. Religious communities have traditions of spiritual direction and sometimes have in-house spiritual directors. Use them; use them all. In the best way, take advantage of them.

And what about our obligations toward others, our research subjects in particular? What do we owe them beyond informed consent and confidentiality? Experimental science often just pays them a few dollars and that is the end of it. Ethnographers with any conscience are not let off so easily. Though such engagement is sometimes hotly debated in anthropology, it is important for any ethnographer to think through – and attempt to follow through on – the practice of *solidarity with and love of the other*. Once again, Olum of Pabbo's 'J'accuse!': You come and steal our knowledge. You steal our culture. You come and talk to us about our knowledge and our culture and then take it all back with you. And we have nothing left. He is telling us that unless it is converted into something that they themselves can use, academic research on the poor is simply another instance of colonial extraction, no less so than mining for minerals, as culture is collected and borne away. Without a deeper and more steadfastly manifested love of and solidarity with the subjects of research, scholarship conducted in such settings is mere plunder, another Scramble for Africa.

Writing and publishing, which by themselves fall short of what you owe to your research subjects, provide one means of repaying part of the debt of hospitality to your research subjects, but only if you practise what ancient Greeks, and Foucault after them, called *parrhēsia*, or frankness of speech, and what the New Testament and early Christianity called 'witness' (*martyria*/μαρτυρία). Fieldwork offers you access to the unnoticed and unspoken parts of society. There will always be persons who want those parts to remain hidden. That 'you always have the poor with you' (Mark 14.7; John 12.8) is in large part a function of the fact that we always have the rich and powerful with us as well. Solidarity with and love of the poor and marginalized in writing with the kind of particularity that ethnography requires will bring resistance from the rich and powerful – you can count on it, especially if that writing is published beyond the closed circle of the academy. Foucault stresses that *parrhēsia* highlights *probation*; that is, that life is a test. And it is for this reason, among others, that we need an *askēsis* of fieldwork.

## Notes

1 Many commenters date the start of the 'interpretive turn' in anthropology later, but Dennison Nash and Ronald Wintraub make the case that elements of it began as early as the 1950s. See Dennison Nash and Ronald Wintraub, 'The Emergence of Self-Consciousness in Ethnography', *Current Anthropology* 13, 5 (1972), 527–42. A key text for this shift is James Clifford and George E. Marcus, eds, *Writing Culture: The Poetics and Politics of Ethnography* (Berkeley, Los Angeles, CA and London: University of California Press, 1986).

2 See, for instance, Anthony Kwame Harrison, 'Ethnography', in *The Oxford Handbook of Qualitative Research*, ed. Patricia Levy (Oxford and New York: Oxford University Press, 2015), 224, 228–30, 243.

3 Michel Foucault, *The Hermeneutics of the Subject: Lectures at the Collège De France, 1981–1982*, trans. Graham Burchell (New York: Picador, 2005), 321–22.

4 Foucault, *Hermeneutics*, 326.

5 Foucault, *Hermeneutics*, 322, citing Marcus Aurelius, *Meditations* VII.61.

6 Foucault, *Hermeneutics*, 16.

7 Foucault, *Hermeneutics*, 15–16, 207–17, 252–54. 'There can be no truth without a conversion or a transformation of the subject' (15).

8 Foucault, *Hermeneutics*, 372–73.

9 Foucault, *Hermeneutics*, 321.

10 On the Christian foundations see Christopher Herbert, *Culture and Anomie: Ethnographic Imagination in the Nineteenth Century* (Chicago, IL: University of Chicago Press, 1991). On its secular character see Charles Stewart, 'Secularism as an Impediment to Anthropological Research', *Social Anthropology* 9, 3 (2001), 323–28; Henri Gooren, 'Anthropology of Religious Conversion', in *The Oxford Handbook of Religious Conversion*, ed. Lewis R. Rambo and Charles E. Farhadian (Oxford and New York: Oxford University Press, 2014), 111, n. 144; Claude E. Stipe, 'Anthropologists versus Missionaries: The Influence of Presuppositions', *Current Anthropology* 21, 2 (1980), 165–79.

11 Henrietta L. Moore, 'Global Anxieties: Concept Metaphors and Pre-Theoretical Commitments in Anthropology', in Henrietta L. Moore and Todd Sanders, *Anthropology in Theory: Issues in Epistemology* (Malden, MA, and Oxford: Wiley Blackwell, 2014), 363–76.

12 See, for instance, Michael Lambek, *The Ethical Condition: Essays on Action, Person, & Value* (Chicago, IL and London: University of Chicago Press, 2015).

13 For instance *Current Anthropology*, one of the leading journals in the field, recently published, as a featured article with multiple respondents, an essay making a substantively Christian religious case for theological modes of reasoning in the discipline of anthropology. See Eloise Meneses, Lindy Backues, David Bronkema, Eric Flett, and Benjamin L. Hartley, 'Engaging the Religiously Committed Other: Anthropologists and Theologians in Dialogue', *Current Anthropology* 55, 1 (2014), 82–104. Even more broadly, the proceedings of a panel presentation given at the International Union of Anthropological and Ethnological Sciences relating anthropology to multiple theological traditions – Hare Krishnan, Islamic, and Pagan as well as Christian – appeared as a special section in the *Australian Journal of Anthropology* 24 (2013).

14 Nancy Scheper-Hughes, 'The Slow Death of the Roman Catholic Church' (titled 'What's a Catholic to Do When Her Church is Corrupt and Moribund' in the print version), *CounterPunch* (18 Nov. 2011), at http://www.counterpunch.org/2011/11/18/exclusively-in-the-new-print-issue-of-counterpunch/. Scheper-Hughes also points to the disanalogy between secular anthropological and religious ways of being in the world when she adds, 'I am grieved and not relieved by my loss of a faith that once gave beauty, richness and fullness to my life.' Yes, she says, secular anthropology offers an alternative discipleship, 'but it is cold comfort for the former believer, when the mystery is gone and with it the light has gone out of one's soul'.

15 See, for instance, Harrison, 'Ethnography', 225; Carole McGranahan, 'What is Ethnography? Teaching Ethnographic Sensibilities without Fieldwork', *Teaching Anthropology* 4 (2014), 23–36.

16 McGranahan, 'What is Ethnography?' 23–24.

17 See, for instance, Hayley Henderson, 'Toward an Ethnographic Sensibility in Urban Research', *Australian Planner* 53, 1 (2016), 28–36; Deborah Keisch Polin and Arthur S. Keane, 'Bringing an Ethnographic Sensibility to Service-Learning Assessment', *Michigan Journal of Community Service Learning* (Spring 2010), 22–37; and Barbara Prainsack and Ayo Wahlberg, 'Ethnographic Sensibility at the Interface of STS, Policy Studies, and the Social Study of Medicine', *BioSocieties* 8, 3 (2013), 336–59. Daniel Neyland, who is a business professor, organizes his book *Organizational Ethnography* into ten 'sensibilities'; see Daniel Neyland, *Organizational Ethnography* (London: Sage, 2008).

18 Christopher Gill, 'Introduction', in Epictetus, *Discourses, Fragments, Handbook*, trans. Robin Hard (Oxford: Oxford University Press, 2014), xxiv–xxv; Pierre Hadot, *Philosophy as a Way of Life*, ed. Arnold I. Davidson (Malden, MA/Oxford: Blackwell Publishing, 1995). For the integral relationship between theory and practice in Epictetus, see John M. Cooper, 'The Relevance of Moral Theory to Moral Improvement in Epictetus', in *The Philosophy of Epictetus*, ed. Theodore Scaltsas and Andrew S. Mason (Oxford and New York: Oxford University Press, 2007), 9–19.

19 'Hospital', in Lesley Brown, ed., *The New Shorter Oxford English Dictionary*, vol. 1 (Oxford: Clarendon Press, 1993), 1266.

20 Michael H. Agar, *The Professional Stranger* (2nd edn; San Diego, CA: Academic Press, 1980).

21 See, for instance, Kirin Narayan, 'How Native is a "Native" Anthropologist?' *American Anthropology* 95, 3 (1993), 671–86; and B. M. Brayboy and D. Deyhle, 'Insider–Outsider: Researchers in American Indian Communities, *Theory into Practice* 39, 3 (2000), 163–68.

22 See Akhil Gupta and James Ferguson, eds, *Anthropological Locations: Boundaries and Grounds of a Field Science* (Berkeley, CA: University of California Press, 1997).

23 Lucius Annaeus Seneca, *On Benefits*, trans. Miriam Griffin and Brad Inwood (Chicago, IL: University of Chicago Press, 2014); Jacques Derrida, *Given Time: 1: Counterfeit Money*, trans. Peggy Kamuf (Chicago, IL: Chicago University Press, 1992); Jacques Derrida, 'Hospitality', in Derrida, *Acts of Religion*, ed. Gil Anidjar (New York and London: Routledge, 2002), 356–420; John Taylor, *Classics and the Bible: Hospitality and Recognition* (London: Duckworth, 2007); John Koenig, *New Testament Hospitality: Partnership with Strangers as Promise and Mission* (Eugene, OR: Wipf & Stock, 2001); John Milbank, 'Can a Gift Be Given? Prolegomena to a Future Trinitarian Metaphysic', *Modern Theology* 11, 1 (1995), 119–61; and Milbank, 'The Transcendality of Gift: A Summary in Answer to 12 Questions', *Revista Portuguesa de Filosofia* 65 (2009), 887–97.

24 Bronislaw Malinowski, *Argonauts of the Western Pacific* (1922) (London: Routledge & Kegan Paul, 1966); and Marcel Mauss, 'Essai sur le don. Forme et raison de l'échange dans les sociétés archaïques', *L'Année Sociologique* (1925), translated as *The Gift: Forms and Functions of Exchange in Archaic Societies* (Glencoe, IL: The Free Press, 1954).

25 The name is a pseudonym.

26 Paul Stoller and Cheryl Olkes, *In Sorcery's Shadow* (Chicago, IL and London: University of Chicago Press, 1987), 11.

27 Lao Tzu, *Tao Te Ching*, chap. 11, lines 1–6, trans. Victor H. Mair (New York: Bantam Books, 1990), 16. Mair, following the Ma-wang-tui manuscripts discovered in 1973, orders the chapters of the *Daodejing* differently than most translations of the text. In most translations, the

relevant paragraph here is numbered 48. Unless otherwise indicated, I follow the numbering and arrangement predominant among the various translations.

I use the more recently preferred Hanyu Pinyin rendering of the Chinese into English even where my source texts use the older Wade-Giles romanization of the language. For instance, I use *Daodejing* rather than *Tao Te Ching*, and Laozii rather than Lao Tzu. For consistency's sake, in the text I make these changes even in quotes from sources that use the Wade-Giles. However, in the text citations in the notes I use the sources' own renderings so that the reader will have no problem looking them up.

28 Lao Tzu, *Tao Te Ching*, chap. 37, lines 1–2, trans. Red Pine (Port Townsend, WA: Copper Canyon Press, 2009), 74. I use Red Pine's translation here. My practice is to use the version and translation that seems clearest relative to the point in question.

29 Lao Tzu, *Tao Te Ching*, trans. Red Pine, para. 63, lines 1–3. Mair translates, 'Act through nonaction, / Handle affairs through noninterference.'

30 Lao Tzu, *Tao Te Ching*, trans. Red Pine, para. 81, lines 14–15.

31 Lao Tzu, *The Way of Lao Tzu (Tao-te ching)*, trans. Wing-Tsit Chan (Upper Saddle River, NJ: Prentice Hall, 1963), 240; Thomas Cleary, trans. and ed., *The Taoist Classics*, vol. 1 (Boston, MA: Shambhala, 2003), 47.

32 The most extensive treatment of the concept of *wu-wei* in Chinese thought is in Edward Slingerland, *Effortless Action: Wu-Wei as Conceptual Metaphor and Spiritual Ideal in Early China* (Oxford and New York: Oxford University Press, 2007).

33 Stephan Schuhmacher and Gert Woerner, eds, *The Encyclopedia of Eastern Philosophy and Religion* (Boston, MA: Shambhala, 1994), 421; Lao Tzu, *Tao Te Ching*, trans. Mair, 138; and Eva Wong, *Taosim: An Essential Guide* (Boston, MA and London: Shambhala, 2011), 25.

34 Kenneth S. Cohen, *The Way of Qigong: The Art and Science of Chinese Energy Healing* (New York: Ballantine Books, 1997), 93.

35 *Qi* can also be rendered 'spirit', 'life energy', or 'vapour'; *gong* can also be translated 'practice' or 'exercise'.

36 Lao Tzu, *Tao Te Ching*, trans. Red Pine, chap. 15, lines 7–12.

37 Lao Tzu, *Tao Te Ching*, trans. Red Pine, chap. 64, lines 10–15.

38 Lao Tzu, *Tao Te Ching*, trans. Red Pine, chap. 73, lines 1–5. Lines 8–12 continue, 'the Way of Heaven/is to win without a fight/to answer without a word/to come without a summons/and to plan without a thought.'

39 Lao Tzu, *Tao Te Ching*, trans. Red Pine, chap. 76, lines 1–13.

40 Jean Roche, *La religion et la magie Songhay* (1960) (2nd edn; Brussels: Université de Bruxelles, 1989), 17; quoted in Paul Stoller, *The Cinematic Griot* (Chicago, IL and London: University of Chicago Press, 1992), 84.

41 Hortense Powdermaker, *Stranger and Friend: The Way of an Anthropologist* (New York and London: W.W. Norton, 1966).

42 Paul Stoller, *The Taste of Ethnographic Things* (Philadelphia, PA: University of Pennsylvania Press, 1989), 6–7, 10–11, 56–57; Stoller, *The Cinematic Griot*, 18, 19, 21, 23, 213, 219, 220; Paul Stoller, *Sensuous Scholarship* (Philadelphia, PA: University of Pennsylvania Press, 1997), 26.

43 Mair emphasizes the similarities and even claims a strong historical link between Daoism and the beliefs and practices of Indian Yoga. See Mair, 140–48 and 155–61.

44 For helpful treatments of the affect in fieldwork, see Sherryl Kleinman and Martha A. Copp, *Emotions and Fieldwork* (Newbury Park, CA, London, and New Delhi: Sage, 1993).

45 Here I am in agreement with David B. Wong, 'The Meaning of Detachment in Daoism, Buddhism, and Stoicism', *Dao: A Journal of Comparative Philosophy* 5, 2 (2006), 207–19. With regard to Ignatian detachment or 'indifference', George Ganss explains in a note, '"Indifferent": undetermined in one thing or option rather than another; impartial; unbiased; with decision suspended until reason for a wise choice are learned; still undecided. In no way does it mean unconcerned or unimportant. It implies interior freedom from disordered inclinations.' Saint Ignatius, *The Spiritual Exercises of St Ignatius*, trans. George E. Ganns, S.J. (Chicago, IL: Loyola Press, 1992), 151, n. 20.

46 Foucault, *Hermeneutics*, 333–52.

47 See Pierre Bourdieu, et al., *The Weight of the World: Social Suffering in Contemporary Society* (Stanford, CA: Stanford University Press, 1999), 609, 614.

48 Josef Pieper, *Leisure: The Basis of Culture* (San Francisco, CA: Ignatius Press, 2009).

49 Malinowski, *Argonauts*, 7. Anthony Kwame Harrison makes a helpful distinction regarding Malinowski: 'He had no desire to become a Trobriander but rather an intense desire to take on a native standpoint', Harrison, 'Ethnography', 235.

50 'This is a work of the self on the self, an elaboration of the self by the self, a progressive transformation of the self by the self for which one takes responsibility in a long labor of ascesis (*askēsis*)', Foucault, *Hermeneutics*, 16. See also Michel Foucault, *The Care of the Self: The History of Sexuality*, vol. 3, trans. Robert Hurley (New York: Vintage Books, 1986).

51 Geraldine Lee-Treweek, 'The Insight of Emotional Danger: Research Experiences in a Home for Older People', in Geraldine Lee-Treweek and Stephanie Linkogle, eds, *Dangers in the Field: Ethics and Risk in Social Research* (London and New York: Routledge, 2000), 130.

# 6

# Just Don't Call It 'Ethnography': A Critical Ethnographic Pedagogy for Transformative Theological Education

## NATALIE WIGG-STEVENSON

The complaint I hear most often from students is that they don't know how they will *apply* what they have studied in theological school in their ministry once they graduate. Over-exposure to this metaphor nearly causes hives to erupt on my skin each time I hear it. 'What if we imagined something more interesting to do with your theological education than *apply* it?' I repeatedly ask them. The blank stares this vague question inspires on their faces, however, serve each time to indict my own pedagogical inadequacy. My question should be described as vague rather than, say, open-ended because I too have been fumbling for a better metaphor than application to describe what I think the practical dimension of theological education involves.

I have been assigning various versions of ethnographic research and writing to my students over the past few years in the hopes that such ad hoc experiments might produce a better metaphor and, more importantly, a better pedagogy for that metaphor's implementation. As I've done so I have realized how much my vocation as a theological educator is shaped by a desire to partner with my students – as we all partner with God – in the practices of justice I believe the Gospel of Jesus Christ heralds. But this is a vision with a level of idealism matched only by its level of abstraction. And neither of these is a descriptor we ethnographic theologians particularly value. So why on earth do I think that teaching ethnographic practices to my theology students could even begin to help us in this ridiculously lofty pursuit? What role can ethnography play as we shift from metaphors of *application* to metaphors of *transformation* for describing the practical import of theological education?

My hunch going into the conversations out of which this book has emerged was that using ethnography in traditional practices of theological education created as many pedagogical problems as it did pedagogical possibilities. And those conversations revealed I was not alone in my struggle. In this essay I thus demonstrate how ethnography situated within transformative (rather than traditional) pedagogies for theological education cannot be taught as another siloed, coherent scholarly discipline. Instead, what we might call ethnographic impulses, habits, dispositions, modes of engagement, and analysis can all be taught under the aegis of contextual theology for the purpose of cultivating in students a critical theological habitus. Of course, teachers who are scholars of ethnography and theology will teach in ways that draw on their scholarly embodiment of both disciplines. But we can do so in ways that are oriented to conscientizing our students to the socio-theological transformation for which their contexts yearn.

In order to make this argument, I first outline what problems might occur when ethnography is used in traditional approaches to theological education (i.e. approaches shaped by what Paulo Freire has famously called a *banking* model of education). Next, I articulate what it might look like to reimagine or, better, to re-perform aspects of Freire's transformative pedagogical scripts in my privileged North American context. This reframing of transformative pedagogy for the oppressors creates a foundation for reflecting on the use of ethnography in theological education. I close with some practical insights into the somewhat counter-intuitive claim this essay makes: if you want to teach ethnography for transformative rather than traditional theological education, then my advice to you would be, *just don't call it ethnography.*

## Diagnosing the Problem: Ethnography as One More Account from which to Withdraw

Most theological educators, whether we received our doctorates five years ago or 35, were almost certainly trained in a model that required we mastered the Christian traditions before we were allowed to do anything creative with them: I had to write my comprehensive exams before I could write my dissertation before I could write my first academic book, and so on. No matter how far we stray, or even flee, from our scholarly origin stories, it is likely that our attempts to be 'good teachers' still perform aspects of those novice/master scripts. It is normal in a Western model of education to expect that students understand a text before they construct something creative out of it. Indeed, if we had to choose, we would probably rather that our students understand without creativity than be creative without understanding. In as much as these master/novice scripts shape our *teaching* instincts, then, they also shape our students' *learning* instincts, whether those students arrive to their programmes fresh from university or having taken a long break from higher education. Despite their desire to play creatively with texts, students typically find that doing so distracts from rather than reinforces their understanding.

As a result of this dynamic, and despite the fact that most educators and even many students now know at least the gist of Freire's banking model theory (if only by osmosis), our dominant theological education practices still prioritize a system in which 'expert' teachers fill up 'receptacle' students with supposedly vital information about the theological traditions. The gap between where we were and where we want to be as teachers and learners is difficult to bridge, precisely because of the ways in which we carry *where we were* in our bones. We might want to raise students' critical consciousness to facilitate their capacity to transform those same traditions, but our pedagogies can often struggle to reflect that desire. Teaching liberation is really difficult, as is learning liberation. And in a culture that increasingly instrumentalizes education toward capitalist ends, not to mention the rapidly dwindling resources for supporting theological education, it often feels like we lack the time and space to get beyond the basics, in other words, beyond the content. Liberation, particularly in the minority world, feels paradoxically like a luxury.

The problem, as Freire describes it, is that education as banking divorces knowledge from the conditions of its creation, leaving students unable to recognize, let alone interpret, those conditions for themselves.[1] Receiving information abstracted from reality, students furthermore do not learn how to produce knowledge for themselves. Like trust-fund kids, students whose education begins with banking learn only to bank, because the process of banking forms them as too passive to do otherwise. To further unpack the metaphor, then, education is not even reduced to the status of a *commodity*, which would be bad enough. Rather, education is reduced to some abstract valuation (money) that is merely collected, stored, and then spent. When exchange rates fluctuate (the humanities, and theological education in particular, are down right now), there may be moments of panic that lead people to question the goods of the whole system. But rarely does anyone suggest we dismantle it all together. Rather, we merely tinker with it, trying to boost its efficiency enough such that when we make our withdrawals they can be worth just enough to be able to afford whatever we want to spend them on. But the spending is key.

Within such a model it becomes difficult to imagine the practical dimensions of education, particularly theological education, as anything more than application: education gives us information, and information is a resource we hand over in appropriate moments to get out of them what we need. We know this intuitively from the requests our students make of us. For example, a common refrain from the classroom when students read the works of historical figures like Anselm or Luther is, 'But how can we make this preach?' Or they ask, 'What good is understanding Calvin's view of God's sovereignty to me when I'm comforting a grieving congregant?' Let alone, what good might a complex critical retrieval of that same theological concept offer? And they're right: if the Divine becoming flesh, sinners justified by faith, and the revelation of God's glory are all pieces of theological information to be plucked up whole and traded for pastoral success via the transactions of preaching and pastoral care, then, no, they don't have too much value.

When fragmented areas of study become bank accounts from which students are expected to withdraw, then the addition of any new topic to a curriculum or particular course takes on the character of simply one more account. I know I have fallen prey to this pedagogical dilemma when trying to incorporate ethnography into my own teaching. Excited by the ways it has enlivened the contextual and practical dimensions of my own scholarship, I find myself inadvertently seeking to impart ethnography to my students as a coherent discipline for them to master and use in (i.e. apply to) their faith contexts. The students, overwhelmed by yet another new siloed discipline to master, get bogged down in details: how to create an acceptable IRB/REB proposal, the difference between emic and etic or qualitative and quantitative, ontological epistemological what?! They struggle to observe the forest holding together all the participating trees.

As a result, instead of letting ethnographic impulses serve theological or pastoral ends, students stall out at trying to *do a good ethnography*. Their struggle in turn exacerbates my pedagogical desire to help them achieve their (now misguided) goal, making it difficult for me to remember that a student discovering ethnography for the first time and using it in such a limited way likely cannot accomplish anything approaching a *good ethnography*. Once they have got the good ethnography, I find myself thinking, against my better teaching self, then they can *move on* to using it/ applying it pastorally.

In other words, I might teach them the basic terms, basic methods, and basic questions, as well as how to get through an IRB/ REB proposal. But I don't manage to get to the goods of cultivating curiosity, losing oneself in a theoretical text that helps illuminate a confusing human activity, frittering away an afternoon in unstructured conversation with a research partner, or letting data sit for long enough to see what bubbles up from forgotten memories in the field. All the magic of ethnographic practice, the stuff that I believe gives it value for theological and pastoral practice, gets lost. And my students find they have one more set of half-learned knowledge to try – and likely fail – to apply to their work upon graduation.

The wild and often desperate ride of theological education provides rare opportunities for us as teachers to step back, take a breath, and reflect deeply enough on what we are doing (i.e. the mistakes that we are making) to be able to create more than Band-Aids for what we know are broken approaches. The gift of the symposium out of which this collection of essays was born was, for me, one of those rare moments. The wisdom and, more importantly, the vulnerable grappling of our colleagues around the table pressed me to think more radically into my pedagogical decisions than I had previously managed to do. They helped me see that I had been introducing ethnography into my teaching because I wanted my students to better contextualize their theological labour in concrete practices of social awareness and analysis. I wanted our theological work together both to bubble up from everyday practice and return to that practice in transformative, justice-seeking ways. In other words, I wanted our shared practices of teaching and learning to enact some kind of material, spiritual liberation. No small goal! But I was inadvertently continuing to use a banking pedagogy to try to get there. As Freire has cautioned again and again, nothing short of pedagogical revolution that completely dismantles our explicit and implicit uses of the banking model can achieve social (and, relatedly, theological) revolution. If I want to use ethnography to enact a more liberative theological contextualization, then the ethnography I teach needs to be contextualized within a more liberative theological pedagogy. It is to this topic that we now turn.

## Transformative Education for the Oppressors (of Whom I Am One)

I must begin by coming clean about my use of these pedagogies. As Peter Elbow avers in his article 'The Pedagogy of the Bamboozled', too many teachers imply that they follow Freire's principles without realizing they do not, thereby *bamboozling* both their students and themselves. There are two possible reforms for this dilemma, Elbow argues: 'start really doing what Freire describes; or stop implying that you do'.[2] I want to forge a third way, however, based in Freire's own suggestion: 'In sum, my educational experiments in the Third World should not be transplanted to the First World, they should be *created anew*.'[3] Instead of trying to use, apply or follow Freire's principles or methods in my context, I'm seeking to open his pedagogy up, reimagine it, and perform it not only with awareness of the moments when my performance entails slippage and change, but also with acknowledgement that it will slip without my even knowing. Perhaps the best metaphor for what I am doing as I improvise around Freire's script in my classrooms is that of a sitcom actor trying to perform Shakespeare in the food court at the mall.

Freire's pedagogy was not created in or for a classroom like the one in which I teach: a middle-class, Canadian, privileged university classroom filled predominantly with bodies racialized as white. And yet his pedagogy is still relevant (vital, in fact) for that classroom so long as in it I am seeking to disrupt and dismantle its insidious colonial constitution. As Henry Giroux has rightly demonstrated, when academics who 'inhabit the ideology of the West' appropriate Freire's work, we 'reduce it to a pedagogical technique or method', thereby stripping away the 'profound and radical nature of its theory and practice as an anti-colonial and postcolonial discourse'. Our ability to use the right terms – *problem-posing, conscientization, education for critical consciousness,* and so on – therefore 'speaks less to a political project constructed amidst concrete struggles than to the insipid and dreary demands for pedagogical recipes dressed up in the jargon of abstracted progressive labels'.[4] First and foremost, improvising around Freire's pedagogical scripts in my context requires recognition that the land on which I teach was stolen from its First Peoples to my gain as one of its Settlers.[5] Even the most inadequate version of an ethical response I can have to that original sin must then reorient our classroom's telos away from a pedagogical agenda that trains producers for the globalized marketplace (that realm of so-called *neo*-colonization) toward one that engages decolonial practices instead. Any use of ethnography in theological education oriented thus will likewise need to take account of the ways in which not only anthropological and sociological but also theological discourses and practices have been complicit in and drivers of the colonial project. And it needs to take account of how that colonial project has shaped and continues to shape our daily lives.

This leads to my second point, that for Freire the students' lives or, rather, as Elbow puts it, 'the students' perceptions of their own lives – always reflected back to [them] as a problem or source of contradictions', must be the subject of study.[6] In Freire's teaching context, the process of action/reflection brings students to critical consciousness of the social forces that form the injustice of their situations. As they gain this critical consciousness, students become equipped to act upon that injustice in order to transform it. In the privileged, progressive, anti-hierarchical Canadian context where I teach, a pedagogical process that lifts questions out of the contexts of students' lives sounds enough like adult-learner approaches to teaching/learning that it is worth explicitly distinguishing the two. Freire's critical interrogation of the problems posed, as well as the significance placed on their cultural constitution, belies a mistaken assumption at the heart of the adult-learner model: that 'individuals should do and be what they desire and that their desires are basically good'.[7] But as Monette points out regarding student-centred learning approaches: 'needs assessment actually promotes oppression when the paradigm or set of norms is uncritically assumed, whether the paradigm originates from society, an institution, or an educator'.[8] Improvising around Freire's pedagogical scripts in my particular context therefore entails interrogating the power and privilege that give rise to the very questions my students and I ask about the injustices that make possible our life together.

Among the many motivations I have for introducing ethnography into the theology courses I teach, a desire to bolster students' independence and capacity to articulate their own research questions is one. So I have mistakenly introduced ethnography as a coherent discipline or practice, tried to put it in conversation with theology as a coherent discipline or practice, and tried to orient both together toward generative questions about context and social transformation. When I did this, I found myself so short on time and space for doing any one of the pieces well that I tried to simplify things by letting each student's personalized question serve as the foundation for our work together. The time we spent critically interrogating that question's ever-shifting foundations was little to nil. Besides, I told myself, these questions were already rich and insightful, rich and insightful *enough*, anyway. Moreover, the students understood themselves to know their own 'learning needs' adequately, such that they tended to experience any interrogation of them as an affront to their own educational agency, an affront that required negotiation that also used up valuable time. In a true Freirian model, we would have spent that ample time unpacking their understanding of agency and how that understanding contributed to the questions they brought, as well as whose needs their articulated learning needs eclipsed and erased, as well as why they experienced such conversations as offensive. But with all the other needs pressing on a twelve-week syllabus, who has time for that?

Part of my teaching involves directing a programme in contextual education that has courses at all three levels of the MDiv curriculum. At the beginning of each of these courses, students write a series of brief analytic vignettes that share biographical details oriented to articulating their sense of pastoral vocation. This biographical writing then serves as the foundation for their student-centred learning in each course. Over the years, as I have endeavoured to shift the assignment from an exercise in personal storytelling to an exercise that raises critical consciousness about context, exploring the differences between biography and critical autoethnography has proved helpful. As I understand it, the key difference between these two genres that focus on personal narrative is that the former tells a story of the self, while the latter intentionally uses the self as a critical lens on the wider culture.[9] It is only autoethnography, then, that accounts for and analyses the various cultural dynamics that contribute to the self and to which the self's constituted agency also contributes, in the modes of maintaining and/or dismantling.

In many ways this 'biography' assignment has stayed the same over the years: students still tell me their story as it pertains to their vocation. But now they are asked to tell it with specific reference to the systems of power, privilege, and oppression that shape and are shaped by their experience. So a story about how a gap year spent at an ashram in India (biographical narrative) informs a particular student's understanding of personal prayer as embodied (vocational narrative) must now include at least a brief engagement with how that student's status in terms of economics, class, ethnicity, and citizenship made such a trip possible (analytics of privilege). In this way the student comes to awareness – is conscientized – to the ways in which their vocation, as well as their strategies of vocational preparation, are shaped by privilege and are dependent upon while also sustaining systems of oppression. Such reflection should also, in this model, stimulate continued reflection for the student on how their personal piety might now be shaped by an experience of exoticizing religious practice perceived as *other*. Infused with the principles of autoethnography (without the student ever explicitly studying autoethnography), a straightforward biographical assignment facilitates an arrival at our shared work that both values *and* critically deconstructs the particular nature of that arrival. In other words, ethnography oriented toward transformative pedagogical ends ignites the student's critical awareness of how their learning-self is formed by and oriented to the wider context in which they live and its inherent power dynamics.

And this leads to my final point. In Freire's pedagogy, the goal of education is not just transformation for the student, or even for the student and teacher together; the goal, rather, is for the student and teacher to become allies in a shared labour of transforming the world – or at least the small part of the world they inhabit. Elbow points out a number of impediments to pursuing these principles in North American education contexts. Not least among these is the fact that Freire was teaching in something more like a voluntary consciousness-raising group; he was not teaching in an institutionalized university setting, and he was not teaching for credit.[10] His work therefore was not beholden to bodies who assessed educational outcomes for the purpose of accrediting degrees. '[Western] institutional education', Elbow points out, 'grew up through society's need to bring its young into its own culture.'[11] In other words, Western pedagogy is designed largely to conform to and reproduce Western culture, not to decolonize (i.e. dismantle) that culture. As a result, most people teaching in Western institutions do not define the 'goal of their course [as] a particular set of partisan activities designed actually to change some social, personal or political situation'. Likewise, despite the lip-service given to free and radical thought, most educational institutions (even among the humanities) 'are not comfortable accepting partisan action as the goal [of education]; especially not if the action starts to be effective'.[12]

I have to believe that it is still possible for the university classroom – though increasingly beholden to neoliberal, capitalist ends – to be a site where teachers and students together ignite their desire and orient their activity toward acts of cultural revolution, no matter how small those acts might be. The theological classroom in a post-Christendom culture perhaps especially bears the responsibility as well as the possibility for fostering this type of counter-cultural insurgency. Part of the work of theology entails imagining the alternate reality in which the last shall be first, the first shall be last, every valley shall be filled in and every mountain and hill made low (Matt. 19, 20; Mark 10; Luke 13; Isa. 40; Luke 3). Such a vision is not the happy inclusivity of liberalism; it is the radical dismantling and redistribution of power and privilege:

But woe to you who are rich,
    for you have received your consolation.
Woe to you who are full now,
    for you will be hungry.
Woe to you who are laughing now,
    for you will mourn and weep.

(Luke 6.24–25, NRSV)

This means that in the largely privileged context in which I teach, my students and I need to partner in self-sabotaging acts of justice-making; we need to work together to pursue our own woe.

Improvising around Freire's pedagogical scripts in my classroom context therefore entails something more than simply learning from and with my students, difficult though that task may be, given my broken desire to hang on to my own privilege as their teacher. I make this pedagogical commitment because I believe that my students can hold me accountable for pursuing acts of justice that alone my life cannot bear and alone my will cannot desire. I have already unpacked how attempts to improvise around Freire's pedagogical scripts must recognize that my humanity is intertwined with my students' humanity, which is intertwined with the humanity of people whose oppression produces our privilege. For Freire, education should take us deeper into our vocations to become more human. Recognizing the intersectional nature of our human constitution should therefore also commit us to a project of shared humanization, both for those who are present in the classroom and for those who are absent from it.

What makes our project so flawed and perhaps even impossible is that *absence*; for the most part, the shared labour of our classroom has to function in the key of hope. It must gesture toward the possibility of forging unlikely friendships beyond the borders of our classroom's space and time. Such hopeful gestures would be facile and empty, however, if when those typically missing students broke through the barriers of their exclusion, we ignored the potential gift of their presence to disrupt and reconfigure the status quo of our practice. Justice cannot be pursued outside relationships; indeed, imagining I can pursue justice alone entails a false grasping toward constituting my own justice expertise. While I grieve at the moments when students have borne the burden of the growing edges of my ignorance, I also have been grateful for their willingness to engage, lead, and teach me, as well as to partner with me to disrupt my teaching for its permanent reconfiguration. In recent years, this has happened for me when my first Indigenous student courageously called out my colonial privilege, when my first transgender student courageously called out my cisgender privilege, and when my first Muslim and Buddhist students courageously called out my Christian privilege.[13] These courageous callings out led to partnerships that increasingly constitute the core of who I am as a teacher in ways that have challenged, surprised, and humbled me. Those who called me out constitute the expanding circle of friendships toward which I am now responsible when I teach.

In the unfortunately more common experience I have of these crucial students being missing from the classrooms where I teach, however, ethnography offers insight, albeit fragmented insight, into the forms of oppression that constitute my and my students' privilege. In fact, engaging ethnographic texts and practice in this way necessitates that we do so for the purposes of dismantling that privilege and, by extension, the systems that hold it together. This means that at the most basic level, any ethnography introduced into theological teachings must inherently critique objectifying research relationships. People and their practices cannot be treated as data for interpretation. There can be no research *informants* or *subjects*, only research *partners*. Too often students of theological ethnography imagine they have met the ethical obligations of their research relationships if they have shared their final paper with their research community to receive their rubber-stamped approval. What I am suggesting here, however, digs deeper than the final ethnographic product; indeed, it makes that product somewhat irrelevant. Rather, I am suggesting a way of imagining one's relationship with one's research partners and I am suggesting a particular understanding for one's own attitudinal role in the field. We theological teachers and students who draw on ethnographic impulses to orient ourselves to revolutionary acts of justice must submit ourselves to the authority of the people whose oppression creates our privilege. We must participate, observe, and ask questions not to create our own agendas for justice, but rather as co-conspirators in the revolution our partners seek. And as the teacher, I must make space for the possibility that as a teaching tool, a *good ethnography* might be little more than a reflection on why such a thing is impossible.

## Just Don't Call It Ethnography

Theology and ethnography are both cultural practices that produce distinct forms of academic knowledge. Each has the power to intervene in, critique and reconstruct the other. Indeed, in ethnographic approaches to academic theology these distinct disciplines overlap and interfere and become intermingled such that they are difficult to tease apart. Nevertheless, theology's tendency toward idealized visions of practice can benefit from ethnography's critical rigour at interpreting contexts, while ethnography's commitment to relativism can bolster the status quo in ways that theological activism can disrupt. It should be clear by now that in my own teaching (as in my scholarship) it is this interpermeation of disciplines that I seek, rather than some vision in which two coherent, distinct disciplines are added together. Given this intentionally murky image, then, I want to close with a couple of themes that have run across these reflections that culminate in the advice that when using ethnography for transformative theological education, *just don't call it ethnography*.

First, by not calling it ethnography, we open the possibility of teaching *ethnographically* rather than teaching ethnography. By this I mean that we liberate ourselves from the need to teach one more coherent discipline in the midst of competing coherent disciplines. So, for example, I incorporate ethnographic values like reflexivity, curiosity, and participation into assignments that ask students to surface, analyse, and begin to deconstruct their social privilege in relation to a thick description of a field trip we have taken or of their contextual education site placement. Furthermore, when students are tasked with writing social and theological analyses of concrete contexts in their pastoral work, guidelines informed by ethnographic values also press them to practise patience, empathic listening, and attentiveness in ways that open them up to the people they encounter rather than allow them to instrumentalize those people toward their assignments' ends.[14] By extension, then, without ever assigning ethnographic readings on 'the crisis in representation',[15] or anything so technical, I nevertheless use ethical questions arising from that crisis to help students reflect on how various people appear in their thick descriptions and social analysis assignments.

As is clear, then, when I teach students reflexivity, representation, description, and attention, for example, I do so with my own awareness of how those values are situated within a wider, ethnographic disciplinary framework. But in teaching these values as consciously arising from that situatedness, I don't spend time unpacking that whole scholarly, disciplinary world for my students. For many of us, teaching in this way would require a shift from *teaching* our scholarly disciplines (i.e. as a canon of content) to *teaching from* our scholarly disciplines (i.e. as transposed into a set of pedagogical strategies and values). If such a prospect sounds difficult to those of us whose doctoral training taught us how to be scholars, but not how to be teachers, I would offer – yep, it sounds so simple, but I certainly struggle with it myself! Nevertheless, it is crucial that we figure out how to do it, because it is precisely that challenge that could open up a host of vital pedagogical questions about the nature of the connection between research and teaching. And it could do so in ways that would enliven both.

Second, by teaching ethnographically without calling it ethnography, we open up the space to teach more radical, justice-oriented approaches to ethnography. Teaching ethnography as a coherent discipline requires giving students the basics before we can teach them the outliers; in other words, we never find the space to teach more radical approaches to research or, at least, we never teach them well. Yet as anthropologist Norman Denzin has pointed out, whereas traditional ethnography seeks to represent culture for the purpose of increasing our knowledge about it (an approach which may or may not inspire greater social awareness about dynamics of power, privilege, and oppression), critical, more radical approaches to ethnography alternatively 'work to expose the ways in which power and ideology shape self, desire and human consciousness in concrete institutional and interactional sites'. Critical approaches to ethnography do the important work of interrogating the ways in which everyday culture is 'embedded in the naturalized commonsense realities of capitalism, the media and the neoliberal corporatist state'.[16] Critical ethnography entails a form of reflexive, critical consciousness in relation to context, whereby its practitioner learns how to produce knowledge in that context and even how to transform that knowledge, thereby transforming the context around it. When traditional approaches to ethnography are taught within traditional approaches to theological education, the result unsurprisingly is a theological approach that serves primarily to preserve a theological status quo. More transformative ethnographic approaches are required for a more transformative theological pedagogy and for an approach to theological construction that has the power to transform the context around it.

It is important to note, however, that teaching critical approaches divorced from their traditional lineage is not the same thing as teaching ahistorically. More radical, critical approaches to ethnography are grounded in a historical framework that takes seriously the colonial context of anthropology's birth. They intentionally critique the ahistorical approach of traditional ethnography that ignores these implications and thereby inadvertently reproduces colonial forms of knowledge production. Once again, then, by teaching ethnographically from within the context of our own scholarly ethnographic expertise – without teaching the content of that expertise – we become liberated as teachers to situate our teaching within a decidedly decolonial framework.

Finally, I hope that it is clear that while my examples in this essay have focused on teaching basic degree level students (i.e. students working on pastorally oriented theological degrees such as the MDiv and MPS, or Master in Pastoral Studies), everything I have outlined here also has import for transformative education of theological doctoral students as well. A knot of trends, concerns, and possibilities in doctoral theological education connects in the issues I have raised here: doctoral dissertations in the theological disciplines seem to be engaging ethnography faster than we are producing scholars who can supervise such projects; doctoral students are increasingly attempting to connect their scholarly work with the contexts of everyday life; many doctoral students are trying to bridge their scholarly work with their activism; doctoral students are endeavouring to connect their scholarly work with their (activist) teaching; we are increasingly recognizing and responding to the need to educate doctoral students not only as scholars but as teachers too. The work so many of us are trying to do at the intersection of ethnographic theology, transformative pedagogy, and theological education has the potential to produce fresh insight not only for a shifting ecclesial terrain, therefore, but also – I hope – for a shifting academic one too. At least, my hope is that the work I am engaging at these intersections can contribute to both. And I remain ever hopeful that my students will continue to show me the way as they achieve things I so often fail to achieve myself.

## Notes

1 Paulo Freire, *Pedagogy of the Oppressed*, trans. Myra Bergman Ramos (2nd edn; New York: Bloomsbury, 2000), 72–73.

2 Peter Elbow, 'The Pedagogy of the Bamboozled', *Soundings: An Interdisciplinary Journal* 56, 2 (1973), 247.

3 Paulo Freire, *The Politics of Education: Culture, Power and Liberation* (South Hadley, MA: Bergin & Garvey, 1985), 190; italics original.

4 Henry A. Giroux, 'Paulo Freire and the Politics of Postcolonialism', *Journal of Advanced Composition* 12, 1 (1992), 15.

5 Emma Battell Lowman and Adam J. Barker, *Settler: Identity and Colonialism in 21st Century Canada* (Halifax, NS: Fernwood Books, 2015).

6 Elbow, 'Pedagogy', 248.

7 Maurice Monette, 'Paulo Freire and Other Unheard Voices', *Religious Education* 74, 2 (1979), 550.

8 Monette, 'Paulo Freire', 554.

9 Tony E. Adams, Stacy Holman Jones, and Carolyn Ellis, *Autoethnography: Understanding Qualitative Research* (New York: Oxford University Press, 2015); Natalie Wigg-Stevenson, 'You Don't Look Like a Baptist Minister: An Autoethnographic Retrieval of "Women's Experience" as an Analytic Category for Feminist Theology', *Feminist Theology* 25, 2 (2017), 182–97.

10 Elbow, 'Pedagogy', 248.

11 Elbow, 'Pedagogy', 253.

12 Elbow, 'Pedagogy', 250.

13 I teach in a historically Christian theological school that in recent years has begun pastoral programmes in Muslim and Buddhist studies.

14 Mary Clark Moschella, *Ethnography as Pastoral Practice: An Introduction* (Cleveland: Pilgrim, 2008).

15 For foundational texts related to the crisis in representation, see James Clifford and George E. Marcus, eds, *Writing Culture: The Poetics and Politics of Ethnography* (Berkeley, CA: University of California Press, 1986); and George E. Marcus and Michael M. J. Fischer, *Anthropology as Cultural Critique: An Experimental Moment in the Human Sciences* (Chicago, IL: University of Chicago Press, 1986).

16 Norman Denzin, *Performance Ethnography: Critical Pedagogy and the Politics of Culture* (Thousand Islands, CA: Sage, 2003), 33.

# 7

# Teaching and Researching Practical Theology: A Liberative Participative Approach to Pedagogy and Qualitative Research

## ANTHONY G. REDDIE

My participative approach to undertaking practical theology seeks to use models of experiential learning such as exercises and games, role-play and drama as an interactive means of engaging with adult learners. The goal is that they be impacted by, learn from, and contribute to the development of new knowledge concerning the theory and practice of Black theology.[1]

A related part of that ongoing effort has been concerned with working with predominantly white lay people in terms of conscientizing them to live out their Christian faith as anti-racist ambassadors for a liberative model of Christianity. This work often sees me leading workshops on Christian discipleship for lay people across the United Kingdom. The underlying epistemological framework for this particular approach to Christian faith formation draws from the radical tradition bequeathed to educators by the great Paulo Freire. Using Freire's scholarship as a pedagogical resource I have developed a participative approach to practical theology that combines teaching and qualitative research. This work begins with creating participative exercises that operate as a form of engaged pedagogy and are undertaken for the added purpose of creating qualitative research that seeks to generate new practical theological knowledge for the field.

This essay outlines the intersection of participative pedagogy and qualitative research methods.

## Participative Engaged Pedagogy as Practical Theology

Paulo Freire's ground-breaking work in devising appropriate pedagogies for teaching marginalized and oppressed peoples is legendary.[2] Freire developed a philosophy of education that challenged poor and oppressed people to reflect upon their individual and corporate experiences and to begin to ask critical questions about the nature of their existence. The radical nature of this critical approach to the task of teaching and learning brought Freire to the attention of the military government in Brazil in 1964. He was subsequently imprisoned and then exiled. In exile he began to refine his educational philosophy and method.

Freire's concern for the radical and revolutionary intent of education as the basis for socio-political change forms the epistemological framework for my pedagogical approach to teaching and engaging in practical theology. While Freire thus provides the underlying philosophical approach to the pedagogical intentionality of my work, the more specific practical theological dimensions have been influenced by British scholars as such as Paul Ballard, John Pritchard, Duncan Forrester, and Elaine Graham, who have theorized around the development of practical theology as a model of reflective activity in which the theologian interrogates the connections between the theory and practice of Christianity in a diverse range of contexts and settings.[3]

Practical theology is an overall framework for the Christian faith that uses differing models of thinking, from psychology, counselling, education, and sociology, for example, as ways of looking at God's action in the world. One of the central tasks of practical theology is to consider the relationship between, on the one hand, how the Church and individual Christians have *considered* faith and, on the other hand, what individuals and the

Church actually *do* in their lived attempts to give expression to what they believe.

My work as a participative educator underpins the pedagogical approach to practical theology that is concerned with transforming the critical consciousness of predominantly lay learners within a workshop context. In using participative education as a means for exploring anti-racist discipleship, I am concerned with providing an accessible basis for the radical re-interpretation of the Christian faith for the transformation of ordinary people. This pedagogical approach to practical theology is undertaken, as we shall see, by means of participative exercises that also serve as models of qualitative research.

In undertaking the bulk of this work in relatively informal workshops, I have developed a creative and participative pedagogy for teaching practical theology and also for engaging in qualitative research. I have identified this form of theological education work and qualitative research as a form of performative action. Performative action requires that we creatively engage with the Other in a socio-constructed space – often a workshop setting – in which all participants promise to engage with the Other in a fashion that affirms mutuality, cooperation, and a shared commitment to the production of new knowledge.[4] The production of new knowledge is not simply for the purposes of passing exams or writing term papers; rather, the desire is to create new forms of knowing for the express purpose of changing behaviour and developing better praxis in terms of Christian discipleship.

This process of performative action operates within often informal workshop settings, in which I seek to create a safe space that affords predominantly ordinary lay people the opportunity to reflect critically on self and on their engagement with others as Christian disciples within contexts and cultures that inform their experience as human beings.

In this participative pedagogical approach to practical theology I have used a variety of exercises and activities for enabling participants to explore their feelings and emotions in that safe space. The exercises allow them to adopt imaginary roles and to 'park' their sometimes extreme feelings within a comparatively safe 'rest area', where they can notionally ascribe responsibility for their anger, frustration, or sense of tension to the fictional persona of the character they have adopted in the exercise. In the various exercises, participants, by means of conversation and interaction, have the opportunity to reflect on their action within the context of a central activity. They can assess their agency and their responses for their truthfulness to God's gracious activity in Jesus Christ, juxtaposed with the historical and contemporary experience of racism and oppression.[5]

The participative element of the work challenges learners to decide how they will inhabit particular spaces and places in order to assess in what ways they are playing out learned pathologies that are often informed by the specious binaries of *them* and *us*.[6] What would happen if participants were enabled to take on the persona of the Other in order to live out their realities and experiences within a participative exercise? To what extent would these experiences change their subjective self and their concomitant consciousness?

The modus operandi of this approach to practical theology is intended to offer participants new models of being Christian in a context where white nationalism and racism are on the rise.

## Participative Liberationist Methodologies in Practical Theology

It has always been my desire that people, especially marginalized and oppressed individuals and communities, should be enabled to play an active part in shaping and reworking the participative, theologically reflective processes of the workshop. For this to happen, an interactive, participative philosophy of education needed to be developed. Working within the broader framework of an action-research methodology, I wanted to find an educational philosophy that would equip ordinary people to be agents in the practical theological research and teaching work I was undertaking.[7]

In the context of this work, the scholarship of Augusto Boal has proved invaluable.[8] Boal's ideas on drama/theatre as a means of consciousness-raising and problem-solving owe much to the pioneering work of Paulo Freire. Like Freire, Boal was born in Brazil. He was raised in Rio de Janeiro. He was trained in chemical engineering and attended Columbia University in New York in the late 1940s. Despite his formal interest in chemical engineering, Boal's vocation was the theatre, and in his early teens, he had displayed an aptitude for performance that marked him out for the remainder of his life.

Like Freire's thought, Boal's work has proved highly influential for liberationist theorists and practitioners across the world. Whereas Freire focused on pedagogy and critical consciousness, Boal efforts were directed at theatre-based educational philosophy. Like Freire's scholarship, Boal's approach had a political dimension, which drew the attention of the military authorities in Brazil. In 1971 he was arrested and tortured; he eventually went into exile, first in Argentina and then in Europe.[9]

Boal's approach to drama/theatre was to collapse the emotional and conceptual distance between the performer on stage and the observer in the audience. In one famous incident, Boal stopped a performance in order that a disgruntled spectator could mount the stage and offer an alternative version to the untruth she was witnessing in the stage performance. This incident proved pivotal for his development and career, for from it emerged Boal's notion of a 'Theatre of the Oppressed'.

His 1971 book of that name created a self-conscious and deliberate re-conceptualization of theatre to the end of assisting oppressed poor peoples to name and construct alternative realities to the subjugating and inhibiting versions that confronted them daily, by means of participatory theatre.[10] The link between theatre and politics, Boal argued, is not a new phenomenon. He traced the roots of theatre as a response to and a mirror of contextual realities that date back to the Greeks and the writings of Aristotle and Plato.[11] The concept of theatre of the oppressed gained international prominence when Boal organized the first international festival of theatre of the oppressed, in Paris in 1981.

I have utilized Boal's notion of theatre of the oppressed to enrich my participative approach to practical theological work, in engaging people in critical, performative workshop-based scholarship.

Boal's classic text (republished in 2000) remains the most detailed explication of the conceptual ideas that underpin theatre of the oppressed. An important dimension of Boal's concept is formed by identification with characters in the play and awareness of the extent to which they are free, able to exercise self-determination, as subjects, and are not purely objects onto which external factors are grafted.[12] In *Theater of the Oppressed*, but also in later works, Boal not only refined the conceptual basis of his ideas around participatory theatre, but also added a number of practical training elements to the panoply of techniques and workshops that have grown out of his original theory.[13]

Boal's work is concerned with helping participants in the theatre, whether performers or spectators (he collapses the two into the 'spect-actor'),[14] to interrogate truth by inhabiting a character and exploring potential new concepts within the confines and structure of the play.[15] This blurring of the line between actor and spectator finds concrete expression in the observer's ability to interrupt the performance and mount the stage to offer an alternative or a corrective mode of action.[16] The improvisatory action that ensues carries within it the potential to create a cathartic and therapeutic space in which the pain and restricted selfhood of the oppressed can be rehearsed and examined.[17]

In order that this concept of participative, liberative theatre might come alive and deliver fresh insights into the lives of the oppressed, the underlying themes or subtexts for any performance must be concrete and contextually relevant to the participants. In Boal's words, 'The chosen subject must be an issue of burning importance, something known to be a matter of profound and genuine concern for the future spect-actors.'[18]

The importance of locating key themes that speak to the experience of people in the workshops resonates with a central idea in the work of Thomas Groome, a highly influential liberationist practical theologian.[19] Groome describes 'generative themes' as 'some historical issue, question, value, belief, concept, event, situation . . . that is likely to draw participants into engagement'.[20] The use of generative themes is an attempt to locate substantive subtexts on which an overarching approach to critically shared theological inquiry can be developed. In the context of my participative approach to practical theology, I have used Boal's work, augmented by Groome's creative understanding of generative themes, to provide the methodology and content for this workshop-based approach to shared, practice-based theological reflection and research.

The model of practical theology I have developed is predicated on a participative critical pedagogy that seeks to enable ordinary lay people to engage in performative action and specifically in critical reflection on the nature of anti-racist models of Christian discipleship. The significance of Freire's and Boal's work does not lie only in the methodological insights it has provided for my participative approach to practical theology, for Freire and Boal also both provide an important nexus of radical educational approaches to conscientization and expressed theological paradigms found in liberation theology. The combination of liberation theology as the content for theological reflection with the critical pedagogical methodologies of liberative education gives rise to the participative model of practical theology I outline in this essay.

## Participative Engaged Pedagogy as Qualitative Research

The pro-Brexit vote in the United Kingdom (23 June 2016) clearly demonstrated a barely concealed exceptionalism and sense of entitlement upheld by predominantly white English people. The xenophobia underpinning the Leave campaign reminded many of us that 'true Britishness' equals whiteness, and that those deemed Other, be they 'migrants' living in the United Kingdom or 'foreigners' in Europe, are distinctly less deserving in the eyes of many white British people. A romantic nostalgia for the past and a time when Britain had the biggest empire the world has ever seen is predicated on an intrinsic estimation of Britain as superior, a value often seen in alliances such as Britain First or other groups on the political Right who want to 'make Britain great again'. Black British social commentator Gary Younge has noted, 'Not everyone, or even most, of the people who voted leave were driven by racism. But the leave campaign imbued racists with a confidence they have not enjoyed for many decades and poured arsenic into the water supply of our national conversation.'[21]

I have sought to interrogate the construct of whiteness within the body politic of the United Kingdom through qualitative research. This research challenges white learners to reflect critically on what it means to be white and whether this socially constructed phenomenon can be deconstructed and remade so that it becomes something more than simply a site for unreflective privilege and entitlement.

The use of participative exercises creates a scholarly connectivity between, on the one hand, teaching and learning that conscientizes students in the classroom and, on the other hand, the creation of new knowledge within the wider purview of practical theological research. This model of qualitative research is predicated on a participative teaching and learning process. Its natural corollary is a model of liberative theological reflection that is undertaken by means of participative exercises through which new theories and concepts for Christian praxis are enacted. This form of scholarship thus develops new knowledge by means of a participative pedagogical engagement.

In these participative workshops I have often used a particular experiential exercise as a way of enabling white students to reflect on the powerful but hidden normative strength of whiteness.[22] The exercise is a form of qualitative research in that it explores theological anthropology among people engaged in various forms of Christian ministry with a view to creating new knowledge in the field.

The exercise begins with each participant receiving a piece of paper on which is printed a series of four concentric circles. The participants look at the innermost circle and are asked to put down one term, or at most two, that define them. This term is central to how they see themselves at that moment. It may be factual (male, female, man, woman) or it may be a characteristic (kind or loving), or a relational term (mother, uncle, child of God) or generic (human being), or something else. I try not to say too much, for fear of suggesting what the participants might name. The term is located in the innermost circle as it is most central or most important to how that individual understands themselves as a human being.

The exercise continues with successive movements out from the central circle, with the participants invited to put down further terms that define them. When different terms have been placed in all the circles, I ask participants to share what they have listed. Is there anything immediate to note about where particular terms have been placed? The exercise is a practical, experiential-participative qualitative research method for exploring the theological positionality of Christian disciples. The exercise combines participative pedagogy and qualitative research to challenge participants to reflect critically on what it means to claim that we are created in the image of God. African American theologian Dwight Hopkins has shown that being a black human being is a concept both complex and often illusory.[23] Black and womanist theologians have repeatedly argued that one cannot take as axiomatic any sense of what it means to be a black human being that has not in itself been both a bold, critical act of self-assertion and a determined act of will.[24]

When asking participants to reflect on the terms they have used in the exercise, I have often found it illuminating to ask what is *not* stated by those terms. I have used this exercise on myself on many occasions, most usually when carrying it out with others in a workshop setting. I have a golden rule of never asking anyone to do something I am not prepared to do myself, and I therefore ensure that I also complete the exercise.

The exercise generates new knowledge drawn from qualitative research methodology in challenging participants to notice what they have not recorded. In one case, I failed to write down 'male'. Yet women in the various groups with which I have worked very often, if not always, make reference to their gender – perhaps in terms of a role (wife, daughter) or directly as 'woman' – in one of their inner circles. For those for whom it applied, often the terms 'black' and 'woman' appeared together, for example in the form 'black woman'. Much later, when reflecting on my different circles I also realized that nowhere in my circles had I written the term 'heterosexual'.

Over the many years I have been using this exercise as a form of engaged pedagogy and a qualitative research method, I have come to realize that those who define themselves in marginal terms will often seek to name aspects of their identities that speak to their sense of marginalization. Thus, women will more readily record 'female' or 'woman' than men record 'male' or 'man'. Similarly, disabled people will often name their disability when those termed 'able-bodied' will make no reference to what is perceived as their normality. The same applies with the distinction between 'heterosexual', on the one hand, and 'gay', 'lesbian', 'bisexual' or 'transgendered', on the other. In all the years I have been using this exercise, I have only witnessed one able-bodied person put down that term or an equivalent in one of their circles. Such epistemological insight constitutes the exercise's use as a qualitative research method.

I complete this exercise, along with others, in order to see how my own responses change over time and context. When using this exercise with participants in workshop settings and classrooms, I have begun to add 'heterosexual' to my own circles precisely because it is one of the things I take for granted. One of the research outcomes is recognition of the way in which our tacit 'normality' shapes notions of power and privilege in human anthropology, for issues such as masculinity, sexuality, and ability confer not only this supposed normality but often also power on those who can claim and use such terms. Thus, the normality of maleness and masculinity is assumed within our Christian traditions and in the Bible, which is replete with such a notion.[25]

I have used this exercise predominantly with white students, as a means of helping them recognize their whiteness and its possible impact on their sense of solidarity with black people in the urban context.[26] I ask simply, 'For those for whom it applies, how many of you have placed the term "white" anywhere in your circles?'

The responses from the different groups with members for whom this question applies have been fascinating. For the most part, white people training for ordained ministry fail to put down the term 'white' anywhere in their circles. When black people have been in the workshops, they *always* place the term 'black' somewhere within the first two circles.

In reflecting on the exercise, I ask the white participants to consider the ways in which they have been able to ignore the materiality of their whiteness. Why did it not occur to many of them that being white might be significant for how they construe their identities? And what impact might the symbolic power of their whiteness have on their ability to engage with the Other?

In my final reflections in the debriefing session I assert that I am not suggesting that white participants must put the term 'white' in one of their circles. And if they do choose to acknowledge it, I insist that I am not telling them where the term should be placed. But I am challenging them to reflect on what privileges and opportunities are accrued by the simple fact that one is white. These reflections are undertaken within a multi-disciplinary, intersectional framework that is similar to the forms of analysis advocated by womanist theologians, in that issues of gender (how many put down the terms 'man' or 'male' or 'able-bodied' or 'heterosexual'?), class, sexuality, and disability are also discussed and reflected upon.[27]

The exercise enables me to undertake practical theological research that engages issues of race, identity, power, and context in Christian ministry and discipleship. This method, however, not only is a form of participative work that enables exploration of theological anthropology as a social inquiry, but also operates as template for students to undertake their own enquiries under the guidance of the placement supervisors.

This and other exercises not only have been used to enable students to reflect critically on their experience in learning about and being immersed into practical theology, but also seek to provide them with opportunities to undertake their own research projects.[28] So, for example, I have encouraged students to use this participative piece of work to undertake their own forms of qualitative research, particularly into contextual theological anthropology in practical theology.

An important aspect of students' learning in practical theology is undertaken in assessed supervised ministry placements, where they are encouraged to reflect on their experience and gain the confidence to enact classroom learning in ministerial practice. Students are often encouraged to undertake a small-scale piece of qualitative research that challenges them to juxtapose inherited learning from the classroom and critical epistemological insights gleaned from their research inquiries. Utilizing the work of John Swinton and Harriet Mowat, students are encouraged to see this exercise, along with other forms of participative research, as an opportunity to engage in qualitative research that throws light on current practical theological issues in anthropology, pastoral care, Christian education, and homiletics.[29] The exercise discussed in this article, for example, has given rise to qualitative research that poses critical questions related to the theological anthropology of whiteness and the ways in which issues of entitlement and superiority can be dispelled or reinforced through the research process.[30]

As a practical theologian, I am eager that all participants in the workshops become anti-racist Christians committed to living out a radical and liberative faith that means standing alongside others in solidarity against injustice. In particular, I want white participants to become Christian activists who will resist the toxic tentacles of racism. The use of this exercise as a form of qualitative research has allowed students to discover for themselves the limits of transformative change from this form of practical theological engagement.

For example, on occasion the research projects undertaken by students have challenged the findings of my own research, on which much of my teaching has been based. In the case of the participative exercise I have described, some students have recorded that none of the participants reported any of the liberative insights I have attained in my research activities. Such inquiries in practical theology therefore appear heavily dependent on context and the reflexivity of the researcher and seem often to eschew the kind of replicability one often sees as axiomatic in more positivistic, quantitative forms of research.[31]

This participative, liberative model of practical theology contains the radical and profound challenge that new knowledge and truth can emerge from Christian practice. Truth and the discernment that gives rise to epistemological insight are not solely expressed in and through ordained authority figures or formally educated, often-male leaders at the apex of their respective societies or communities. This model of practical theology is a form of bottom up, transgressive critical pedagogy in which epistemology is shaped by ordinary people, often individuals who possess no power or authority within their respective churches or wider society. The exploration that I model and encourage provides critical reminders of the unique significance of context and the mercurial and rich learning that emerges from the thick descriptions of human participants.[32]

## Conclusion

In the final analysis this overarching approach to practical theology asserts the importance of personal, subjective, and affective learning as a conduit for a transformative, anti-racist practice of Christian discipleship. It utilizes a critical nexus of liberative pedagogy and practical theological reflection via performative forms of embodied learning to raise the critical consciousness of learners and bring about new theological knowledge.

The learning that emerges from these creative and critical encounters enables participants to reflect on their own embodied subjectivity in order to be cognisant of self and thus engage in a more informed manner with the Other. It is my contention that the subjective and experiential basis of this approach to anti-racist Christian discipleship lies at the heart of the God who makes Godself known in personal encounters with all people, through the humanity of Jesus, in the power of the Holy Spirit.

It is my hope that this form of practical theology pedagogy and qualitative research will allow all people to embrace a Christian discipleship built on a process of conscientization that enables learners to see themselves as potential agents of change whose lives embody the liberative spirit of God that is revealed in the person and the work of Jesus.

## Notes

1 See Anthony G. Reddie, *Acting in Solidarity: Reflections in Critical Christianity* (London: DLT, 2005); *Dramatizing Theologies: A Participative Approach to Black God-Talk* (London: Equinox, 2006); *Black Theology in Transatlantic Dialogue* (Basingstoke and New York: Palgrave Macmillan, 2006); *Working against the Grain: Re-imaging Black Theology in the 21st Century* (London: Equinox, 2008).

2 For essential works by Paulo Freire see *Pedagogy of the Oppressed* (1970) (New York: Herder & Herder, 1999); *Education for Critical Consciousness* (1973) (New York: Continuum, 1990); and *A Pedagogy of Hope: Relieving Pedagogy of the Oppressed* (New York: Continuum, 1999).

3 Paul Ballard and John Pritchard, *Practical Theology in Action* (London: SPCK, 1996); Duncan B. Forrester, *Truthful Action: Explorations in Practical Theology* (Edinburgh: T&T Clark, 2000); Elaine L. Graham, *Transforming Practice: Pastoral Theology in Age of Uncertainty* (Eugene, OR: Wipf & Stock, 2002).

4 Jose Irizarry, 'The Religious Educator as Cultural Spec-Actor: Researching Self in Intercultural Pedagogy', *Religious Education* 98, 3 (2003), 365–81, and Clark C. Abt, *Serious Games* (New York: Viking, 1970).

5 Dale P. Andrews, 'African American Practical Theology', in *Opening the Field of Practical Theology: An Introduction*, ed. Kathleen A. Cahalan and Gordon S. Mikoski (New York: Rowman & Littlefield, 2014), 11–29.

6 Kelly Brown Douglas, *What's Faith Got to Do with It? Black Bodies/Christian Souls* (Maryknoll, NY: Orbis, 2005).

7 On action research see John Swinton and Harriet Mowat, *Practical Theology and Qualitative Research* (London: SCM Press, 2016); Helen Cameron, *Talking about God in Practice: Theological Action Research and Practical Theology* (London: SCM Press, 2010).

8 Augusto Boal, *Theatre of the Oppressed* (London: Pluto, 2000).

9 Boal, *Theatre of the Oppressed*.

10 Boal, *Theatre of the Oppressed*.

11 Boal, *Theatre of the Oppressed*, 1–50.

12 Boal, *Theatre of the Oppressed*, 83–95.

13 For later works see Augusto Boal, *Games for Actors and Non-Actors* (London: Routledge, 1992), *Rainbow of Desire* (London and New York:

Routledge, 1995); and *Legislative Theatre* (London and New York: Routledge, 1998).

14 Boal, *Theatre of the Oppressed*, 126–30.

15 Boal, *Games.*

16 Boal, *Games*, 210–23.

17 Boal, *Rainbow*, 18–27.

18 Boal, *Rainbow*, 6.

19 Thomas Groome, *Christian Religious Education* (San Francisco, CA: Jossey-Bass, 1999).

20 Thomas Groome, *Sharing Faith* (San Francisco, CA: Harper, 1991), 156.

21 Gary Younge, 'After this Vote the UK Is Diminished, our Politics Poisoned', Guardian, 24 June 2016, https://www.theguardian.com/comment isfree/2016/jun/24/eu-vote-uk-diminished-politics-poisoned-racism.

22 Anthony G. Reddie, *Is God Colour Blind? Reflections on Black Theology for Christian Ministry* (London: SPCK, 2009), 37–52.

23 Dwight N. Hopkins, *Being Human: Race, Culture and Religion* (Minneapolis, MN: Fortress, 2005), 1–52.

24 Emile M. Townes, *Womanist Ethics and the Cultural Production of Evil* (New York: Palgrave Macmillan, 2006).

25 Mary Daly, *Beyond God the Father* (London: Women's Press, 1986); Daphne Hampson, *After Christianity* (London: SCM Press, 1996).

26 Anthony G. Reddie, 'Exploring the Workings of Black Theology in Britain: Issues of Theological Method and Epistemological Construction', *Black Theology: An International Journal* 7, 1 (2009), 64–85.

27 Reddie, 'Exploring the Workings'.

28 See by Reddie, *Dramatizing Theologies*; *Working against the Grain*, and *Is God Colour Blind?*

29 Swinton and Mowat, *Practical Theology.*

30 See Reddie, *Is God Colour Blind?*

31 Swinton and Mowat, *Practical Theology.*

32 On thick description, see Clifford Geertz, *The Interpretation of Cultures* (New York: Basic Books, 1973).

# 8

# I Am Not a Sociologist: Reflections on Sociological Research in Theology

## BRETT C. HOOVER

When I present my research on parish life, I often begin by stating, 'I am not a sociologist.' Occasionally, if the audience looks old enough, I add, 'But I play one while doing research.' The echo is of an oft-mocked series of 1980s television commercials, where soap-opera actors who played doctors promoted Vick's Formula 44 cough syrup saying, 'I am not a doctor but I play one on television.' One might expect that I do this, as a pastoral theologian, to dampen the expectations of methodological rigour expected of social scientists. Yet I have committed myself to doing responsible qualitative research that meets the standards of the discipline of sociology. I have presented some of my work at sociological conferences, and some of it has been reviewed in journals of sociology. I try to make sense of my conclusions in serious theoretical dialogue with the sociology of religion, and I am happy to contribute to that discipline in some small way if I can. Instead, by saying that I am not a sociologist, I wish to make my ultimate aim clear. I research the social processes that make up the everyday life of Christians, both within their faith communities (*ad intra*) and in the larger society (*ad extra*), so that I might offer responsible theological analysis of the questions and dilemmas that arise in that everyday life in the interest of reforming Christian practice.

## Practical or Pastoral Theology

In the Reformation traditions of Christian theology, engaging in social scientific work in the service of theological analysis and reformed practice is considered part of the work of practical theology. Many Catholic theologians like me speak of this work as practical theology largely to distinguish it from the study of ministerial skills (homiletics, pastoral care, spiritual direction, liturgical leadership) more common at seminaries or pastoral institutes that is generally described as pastoral theology. Some of the desire to make this distinction comes from university theologians who worry that pastoral theology in Catholic seminaries has lost theoretical and methodological rigour.[1] The dynamic should come as no surprise since the university liberal arts system largely values critical analysis and publication in peer-reviewed venues while Catholic seminaries during the last two pontificates have struggled with pressures toward ideological conformity. Another force driving the distinction is a worry that therapeutic psychology exercised too much influence over pastoral theology from the late 1970s to the 1990s, resulting in a surfeit of individualistic perspectives and a substitution of psychological for theological vocabulary in areas like spirituality.[2]

I would argue, however, that it is unwise for Catholic theologians to reject the moniker of pastoral theology too hastily. In Hispanic ministry and theology, for example, Catholic pastoral theology retains a self-conscious connection to the robust methodological trajectory that began with Catholic Action in the early twentieth century. The Young Christian Workers (the *Jeunesse Ouvrière Chrétienne* or JOCists) in France and Belgium, under the guidance of the priest (and later cardinal archbishop) Joseph Leo Cardijn, developed a practical approach to ministry among factory workers who no longer affiliated themselves with the Catholic faith. They engaged in correlative study of the problems inherent in industrial contexts and Catholic social teaching. This 'see–judge–act' approach spread around the world through Catholic Action organizations like the Young Christian Students, the Christian Family Movement, and other groups for students, workers, and professionals. In the latter half of the twentieth century, see–judge–act found a home in Latin American base communities, and through those communities it had an impact on the development of the hermeneutical methodologies of Latin American liberation theology. The *Encuentro* theological reflection and planning process that characterized Hispanic ministry in the 1970s and 1980s took up see–judge–act, and Hispanic ministry organizations like *Instituto Fe y Vida* elaborated the methodology while using it in the context of pastoral ministry.[3] Finally, Catholic Action methodology was joined to Ignatian discernment modalities to form the pastoral circle of Jesuit tradition.

This rich methodological trajectory has frequently made space for social scientific research and theory in the service of theological analysis and practical reform. During the Catholic Action era in the United States, labour priests and Catholic sociologists used sociological theory and methodologies not only to help make sense of Catholic social teaching but also to enact social reform.[4] A generation of liberation theologians in Latin America, wanting both to understand the poverty and oppression of their context and to work for change, took to the study and use of a 'humanistic' (i.e. non-materialist) Marxist social theory and analysis. According to Enrique Dussel, the critical development of *liberation* as a soteriological lens depended on the Latin American 'sociology of dependency' that critiqued capitalist approaches to economic development.[5] Also in recent decades, many of those engaged in mission and social justice work have relied on social scientific tools and theoretical perspectives to engage in rigorous but practical social analysis as part of their practice of the pastoral circle.[6]

I envision my use of rigorous qualitative research and theoretical perspectives from sociology as a way of taking seriously the call of the Salvadoran liberation theologian (and martyr) Ignacio Ellacuría for theology to grasp 'historical reality'. For Ellacuría the primary place to encounter God was amidst human struggles for transformation in the concrete world. He and other liberation theologians reacted to a European theological tradition they saw as insufficiently attentive to the social, political, and economic struggles of the poor. Ellacuría believed that theologians must not only understand these struggles but also take responsibility for them. He wanted to create a theology that took up the concerns of the poor and marginalized, part of a larger project to transform the University of Central America into an institution devoted to the transformation of society in the service of the poor.[7]

In my own rather different context I envision sociological theory and methods as tools that that enable more precise understanding of the social processes in which Christians' struggles for transformation are embedded in the concrete world. This more precise understanding of the 'historical reality' of the contexts I study and in which I live as a Christian minimizes my own biases in interpreting the dilemmas of the present moment. By doing so, I hope not only to create responsible contemporary interpretations of the Christian tradition but also to co-operate with faith communities in the renewal of Christian practice against the horizon of the Reign of God. In this way, theological reflection can become more responsive to everyday pastoral needs as well as to the systemic injustices that dog our faith communities' attempts to do good in our particular world. This is my limited attempt to grasp and to take responsibility for the historical reality of my own context.

## Ministerial Challenges

Like many pastoral and practical theologians, I came to grasp the reality of that context and feel responsibility for it not from studying theology but within the work of ministry. Trained in a pastorally oriented graduate school of theology, I was prepared for ministry by a deep engagement with the North Atlantic Catholic theology that emerged in the wake of the Second Vatican Council (1962–5), including, for example, the systematic theology of the German Jesuit Karl Rahner, the moral theology of the American ethicist Charles Curran, and the North American approach to liturgical studies at institutions like the University of Notre Dame and Saint John's University in Collegeville, Minnesota. Then I walked into a ministerial world dominated by a diverse group of young urban professionals working in finance or entertainment, an aging working-class white community, and a multicultural Hispanic immigrant community living in nearby tenements or city housing projects. I found that the preparation I had received was only half of what I needed to understand these communities and to accompany the people of the parish constructively. Most of my studies had emerged from a particular cultural consensus, a very optimistic American interpretation of Vatican II rooted in the experience of the post-war boom for Euro-American Catholics. I grew up within the context of this consensus, in which we worked to unlearn a nineteenth-century pessimism about the modern world and participate in a rational renewal of liturgy and ministry that we believed could move the Church forward. Ironically, there was more than a hint of nineteenth-century faith in progress in this consensus.

After Master's level theological study, however, I found myself immersed in ministry in an urban, multicultural context increasingly remote from that cultural consensus. Most of the dilemmas we faced in ministry – mutually unintelligible cultural realities in the same parish, the brutal demands of work in different sectors of the economy, spirituality for people facing their limits, young people bewildered by the foreign language of religion, and a rising awareness of social anxiety and uncertainty symbolized by the 9/11 attacks – did not figure prominently in the formation I had received. In fact, some of the theologians and pastoral leaders I had known seemed determined to avoid addressing such dilemmas, particularly those associated with the sheer size and breadth of the demographic changes facing Catholicism.

After nearly a decade in ministry, I moved into academia with the hope that I might participate in a renewal of pastoral ministry formation with these new social facts in mind. I found my way into a multicultural community of scholars quite aware of the changes upon us and the new world of ministry. I studied critical and postcolonial theory with Protestant scholars, US Hispanic theology with a Mexican-American Jesuit, and recent trends in practical theological methodology with a Filipino Catholic practical theologian who had pioneered community-based research in religious education. I went to the University of California, Berkeley to be trained in qualitative research by cultural anthropologists. Ultimately I moved away from cultural anthropology, with the discipline going through an anti-theoretical phase in its efforts to come to terms with its colonial past. Instead I found my way to the theory-rich traditions of sociology, especially the sociology of religion with its 'new paradigm' focus on the structures and dynamics of religious organizations and the overall place of personal agency amidst cultures and communities.

Even in the midst of this serious immersion in the theoretical and methodological traditions of the social sciences, I remained a theologian. Like other constructive (and liberation) theologians, I came to the social sciences hoping to avoid constructing complex interpretations of Christian tradition that rested too much upon one person's take on a particular philosophical school and not enough on the reality of Christian life in the concrete world. I worried about rooting theology in naïve interpretations of the social realities around us. The sociology of religion gave me a theoretical framework and methodological rigour to better interpret the social realities of ecclesial and societal life. Unlike some other branches of sociology, it places a high value on qualitative research and not just on quantitative work. I found new paradigm research on congregational life particularly helpful, especially with its emerging focus on immigrant communities. At the same time, there was a relative lack of sociological research on Catholic faith communities, despite their size and reach, and despite a brief mid-twentieth-century burst of Catholic sociological study of parishes.[8] I turned toward qualitative investigation of Catholic parishes for a decade of fruitful research, specializing in what I called the 'shared parish', where multiple ethnic or racial communities preserve worship and ministry according to their own languages and traditions but share parish leadership and facilities.

## Qualitative Research in the Sociological Tradition

In the plainest language, qualitative research is a disciplined use of our senses, in large part a form of disciplined watching and listening. Both watching and listening are practices, basic repeated actions we learn as children and refine as young adults. Cultural rules school us in the proper procedures of each practice – who is allowed to watch whom and when, and who should or even must listen to whom under what conditions. Our cultural formation and the power asymmetries with which we live introduce implicit biases in the way we watch and listen. Thus many men presume they have the right to stare at beautiful women but do not have to listen to them. Many people (including some non-white people) feel less of a responsibility to attend to the activities of the non-white people around them (making them effectively 'invisible') and less of a responsibility to register the opinions of those of races or ethnicities other than the dominant group. Qualitative research, like much educational and professional formation today, aims to introduce correctives where implicit biases shape practices like watching or listening. Those of us trained in helping professions like psychotherapy, social work, and ministry learned how to listen in a particular way – with clearly expressed emotional empathy for all who come before us yet retaining enough detachment to see what the person speaking may not see in order to help them. Some of us were also trained to attend *more* carefully to the activities of people at a power disadvantage in society, to offset the biases we learned in cultural formation. This practice is one way of embodying what theologians refer to as the preferential option for the poor.

Training for qualitative research in the sociology of religion disciplines its practitioners to watch and listen more carefully than they might in daily life, but usually in contained spaces and times and with a particular research question in mind. It invites us to bracket our own assumptions about what is going on, to delay interpretation until we have as much information as possible. To do that, we have to become as aware as possible of our own biases, preferences, and privileges – what researchers call reflex-ivity. In the past, ethnographers and other qualitative researchers were trained for objectivity. At its best, this training promoted enough detachment to see what insiders cannot see, but at its worst it freed the researcher from having to be more critical of his or her own assumptions. In sociology, all researchers attend in particular to social processes – how people function in groups and as groups. Quantitative sociology mainly uses surveys and statistics to determine correlations and possible trains of causality in social processes. But since social processes are often complex and difficult to untangle, sociologists also use qualitative research to try to surface new explanations of how social processes work, and then they submit their conclusions to further testing by repli-cation across social fields or quantitative study.

## Researching Shared Parishes

I brought this particular tradition of qualitative study to research of shared parishes. I found that shared parishes arose organically in US Catholicism to accommodate demographic change due mostly to post-1965 immigration. Yet one might say that most of the history of Catholicism in the United States is a study of the impact of immigration. Though US history began with few Catholics and very little Catholic infrastructure, nineteenth-century immigration changed all that. For decades, Catholic parishes were formed primarily to accommodate one immigrant group or another. Many were called national or ethnic parishes and focused on one ethnic or language group. As immigration increased from Catholic regions in Ireland, Germany, Poland, Italy, and other places, the Church grew so fast – especially in urban areas – that any infrastructure created was generally insufficient. Then in the early twentieth century a new wave of anti-immigrant, anti-Catholic, and anti-Jewish sentiment brought the great machine of immigration to a relative halt. The Great Depression and the Second World War ensued, and for five decades Catholic parishes participated in the grand national experiment in 'Americanization', what we now call assimilation. National and ethnic parishes gradually disappeared.

After the Second World War, renewed waves of Catholic immigration swept over the nation, beginning with the migration of *braceros*, labourers from Mexico. After the Hart-Celler Act of 1965, global economic and political forces drew ever larger numbers of immigrants from Latin America, East and South Asia, and to a lesser extent the Middle East, Africa, and Oceania. Catholic immigrants came from Latin America, the Philippines, Vietnam, Korea, and even nations with tiny Catholic populations such as China and India. The phenomenon began in the gateway cities and regions – California, New York City, Chicago, Florida, and Texas – but spread by the 1990s to most parts of the country. But this time, US Catholicism already had an infrastructure of churches, priests, and other pastoral workers. Thus, though some of these migrants have found their way into ethnically (or linguistically) unique parishes, research suggests that most worship at shared parishes.[9] The twentieth-century history of assimilation among white Catholics has made the sharing somewhat unexpected. Furthermore, the authority structures of Roman Catholicism do not place the decision to share a parish in the hands of lay leaders, as would occur within a congregational or semi-congregational polity in many Reformation traditions. The groups that share a parish are yoked together, happily or unhappily, and often with considerable asymmetrical power relationships between them, shaped by those relationships in the larger society.

In order to understand the ecclesiological implications of that yoking and discover possibilities for renewed practice in Catholic communities, I spent a decade doing qualitative research in such parishes, first in a year-long project (2007–08) studying a parish in the Midwest I call All Saints, and later in a two-year study (2012–14) of three shared parishes in Southern California.[10] I turned to sociological research in part because ecclesiology is notoriously idealistic. Theologian Nicholas Healy has argued that very often the images of Church discussed in theological articles and church documents bear at best only a partial resemblance to the actual faith communities that make up that Church. Healy sees them as near Platonic types of Church, and he wants us to develop a 'prophetic-practical ecclesiology' that both describes the 'concrete' Church and calls it to eschatological fullness.[11] In a friendly challenge to postliberal theology, Christian Scharen argues that we need more 'judicious narratives' of ecclesial life to temper our Christian narratives about the Church.[12] With my qualitative research at Catholic parishes, I hoped to get at some of those judicious narratives.

## Uncovering Power Dynamics

My decade studying shared parishes yielded, as I had presumed it would, many stories about the way in which the language barrier (and related culture clash) complicated the negotiations involved in sharing a parish. A dearth of bilingual adults could cleave a parish into mutually incomprehensible worlds, often seen oppositionally. At All Saints, the parish I studied in the Midwest, that mutual incomprehension was everywhere:

> Interviews revealed people in both communities who had little contact with and no information about people from the other community . . . One thirty-something mother from the Latino community, when asked about the presence of two cultures in the parish, said in a distracted voice, 'No me afecta.' 'It doesn't affect me.' Henry McKellar, a longtime Euro-American parishioner in his eighties, summed it up: 'We've got two parishes now, one Mexican and one English, and we pray that they can be more combined than they are today.[13]

During that time of research, I found myself frequently called into service to explain these worlds back and forth. I answered queries about the financing of parishes in Mexico (as in the United States, by donations) and about the possible participation of English-speaking Catholics in the Ku Klux Klan (unthinkable, fortunately). At one of the Southern California parishes I studied, Holy Nativity, African American leaders vociferously complained at the Hispanic community's apparent unwillingness to participate in liturgy planning, but that unwillingness took on a different tone to me when I discovered that the only translator for those meetings was the pastor, whose efforts in Spanish were sincere but spotty.

Language and culture clashes I expected, but the more vexing problem in shared parishes turned out to be power asymmetries. At All Saints many in the recently arrived Mexican immigrant community felt besieged in being required to meticulously account to Anglo leaders at the parish and school for the condition of parish rooms they regularly used. Some of the same people expressed their gratitude for being 'allowed' to use the church and facilities. After a decade at the parish, they still felt like (and were sometimes treated as) guests rather than members of the family. At Saint Martin de Porres, an old Mexican mission parish now located in an affluent town on the Southern California coast, the small remaining Spanish-speaking community did not meaningfully participate in church renovations, and pastoral council members could not say why. At Queen of Heaven, in an overwhelmingly Latino suburb of Los Angles, a relatively affluent Filipino community nevertheless felt like second-class citizens until a new (Mexican-American) pastor solicited their concerns. At Holy Nativity, a historically African American parish in urban Los Angeles, a debate over the wording of the parish mission statement – whether it should contain the word 'Hispanic' – exposed complex asymmetries in the parish. On the one hand, it showed how reluctant some African American parishioners were to afford Latino/a parishioners equal status in the parish. On the other hand, many of those same people seemed motivated by struggles by African American Catholics to preserve their cultural traditions over and against unsympathetic white Catholic leadership, both within the parish itself and across the archdiocese.[14]

These power asymmetries brought to light the way local faith communities often reproduce unjust conditions in the larger society. Ironically, church teaching and a biblical witness so clearly in favour of the poor and marginalized and asserting the equal dignity of all the baptized may serve to hide these conditions in our parishes and congregations. It may seem difficult to reconcile the things we say about the Church – that it is the Body of Christ, a Trinitarian communion, a sacrament of divine unity – with the reality of societal injustice as embedded in the local faith community. A sacramental view of ecclesial unity, the kind we Catholics cling to along with our Orthodox and Anglican brothers and sisters, can half-consciously divert our attention away from the actual relationships between different groups of believers. Religious individualism may make it difficult to come to terms with a communal sinfulness that few persons consciously (or publicly) claim as their own. Pastoral leaders may even feel that those who draw attention to these manifestations of societal inequity mean to insult their leadership or express a lack of confidence. Yet an honest ecclesiology requires that we come to terms with this manifestation of the sin of the Church and attend to the *ecclesia semper reformanda*.

## Interdisciplinary Challenges

Qualitative research in dialogue with sociological theory helped me surface the racial and ethnic power asymmetries in shared parish life and understand how they are shaped by larger societal dynamics. The strength of sociology as a discipline is its willingness to train empirical tools on social processes no matter how disruptive the results may prove. This commitment emerges from a modern empirical epistemology that presumes human beings can study the world they inhabit in a disciplined way and discover how it works. Contemporary sociology nuances this epistemology by acknowledging that the world is not simply 'out there' but also socially constructed by human beings.[15] Such an epistemology encouraged – in reality demanded – that I see what was there and how it worked. It required that I examined the power relationships in shared parishes in some detail, not only as they were manifested in the structures of the parish (such as unequal representation on parish staffs) but also in the ordinary ways people understood and interacted with one another. This gave me a fuller and more precise picture of power dynamics among unequal groups in shared parish life, a vexing problem that traditional theological reflection might well have overlooked or even purposefully ignored.

That possibility also has epistemological roots. Christian theologians and pastoral leaders have traditionally operated under an epistemology that values divine revelation and our continuing interpretations of that revelation. When empirical data conflicts with highly prized interpretations of revelation, we have not always reacted well. The most famous examples have emerged from historical conflicts between church authorities and scientists, such as the censure of Galileo Galilei during the Catholic Reformation or twentieth-century Fundamentalist and Evangelical resistance to the theory of evolution. But similar conflicts have also erupted around empirical data on social processes within churches. In the late 1940s, the Jesuit sociologist Joseph Fichter completed a comprehensive study of a Southern parish and found that parishioner habits did not necessarily correspond to Catholic teaching regarding the necessity of weekly Mass attendance. He also noted that parishioner attitudes about racial segregation were more in line with Southern cultural norms than with Catholic social teaching.[16] After the publication of the volume reporting these findings, church leaders managed to block any further publication of Fichter's study.[17] Of course, such resistance by authority does not change facts – physical or social – uncovered by empirical research. After being forced to recant his observations about the earth's movement around the sun, Galileo allegedly quipped, 'And yet it moves.'

At the same time, the empirical epistemology of sociology has limitations for theologians. Sociologists of religion study the phenomena of religion, but they bracket questions of the transcendent truth or the moral significance of such phenomena. Kevin Christiano, William Swatos, and Peter Kivisto propose such an approach in their textbook on the sociology of religion:

For the sociological study of religion what matters is not whether God exists or whether the soul is immortal or how evil comes to be defined, but the fact that people act on beliefs that God does or does not exist, that there is or there is not life after death, that evil is or is not a real power operating in the world.[18]

An empirical epistemology may demand that I accept the reality of social facts like the power asymmetries at shared parishes, but it does not necessarily make judgements about the meaning or moral significance of those social facts. Without sociological training, I might have missed the racially or ethnically charged power asymmetries in shared parishes, but it was theological reflection that suggested the unacceptable distance between those asymmetries and a Christian vision of the *ekklesia*.

The 'racial formation' most people receive in US society has the effect of normalizing racial and ethnic inequalities.[19] But an ecclesiology of communion, for example, presumes that baptism must stand as the foundational identity that orders the community, not race or ethnicity. Nor should we think of this struggle over power asymmetries due to identity markers as a contemporary development in theology. In the earliest Church, Saint Paul remonstrated with Galatian Christians for claiming superior status for those asserting Jewish identity through circumcision and observance of dietary law (Gal. 1–3). In the Acts of the Apostles, Luke exposes the neglect of Greek-speaking widows by Aramaic-speaking leaders in the daily distribution of food, a matter that forced the apostles to select a new class of Greek-speaking leaders (Acts 6.1–7). Thus, it is continuing reflection on a theological vision of the Church rooted in the revelation of God in Jesus Christ that makes parish power inequities rooted in race or ethnicity untenable. This recognition presents clear ethical demands for the reform of Christian practice. Not only must pastors and parish leaders take practical steps to rebalance the scales of power in favour of deprived communities, but they must also reshape the organizational culture of the local faith community so that all members become conscious of the threat of these asymmetries and take responsibility for addressing them as they arise.[20]

What I hope has become clear is that the kind of pastoral theology I do is no matter of simple 'borrowing' of sociological data to draw theological conclusions.[21] More in-depth interdisciplinary scholarship requires that the researcher retain a certainly clarity about the methodologies of the different disciplines, their epistemological roots, and how they can or should interact. The interaction between those methodologies and epistemologies may produce fruit greater than the sum of the disciplinary parts, as I hope I have shown here. But it may also lead to conflict, either over the data itself or over its meaning and implications. To avoid or at least understand such interactions and potential conflicts, pastoral and practical theologians who engage in social scientific research (including qualitative researchers of many stripes) cannot simply hold themselves accountable to the standards of their own discipline. We need to have one eye on social science and the expectations it bestows on us with the gift of qualitative research. This is not to say that we should become social scientists. As I noted in the beginning, I have always tried to retain clarity about my own location and aims as a scholar. I am not a sociologist, even if I play one when I do qualitative research.

## Notes

1 Kathleen A. Cahalan, 'Roman Catholic Pastoral Theology', in *Opening the Field of Practical Theology*, ed. Kathleen A. Cahalan and Gordon S. Mikoski (Lanham, MD: Rowman & Littlefield, 2014), 229–32.

2 See D. J. Tidball, 'Practical and Pastoral Theology', in *New Dictionary of Christian Ethics and Pastoral Theology*, ed. David J. Atkinson and David F. Field (Downers Grove, IL: Intervarsity Press, 1995), 46–47.

3 See Edward Arnouil and Carmen Cervantes, *The Prophets of Hope Model* (Winona, MN: St Mary's Press, 1997), 46–51.

4 See, for example, the works of the priest-sociologist John A. Ryan. For a consideration of Ryan's work, see Francis L. Broderick, *Right Reverend New Dealer, John A. Ryan* (New York: Macmillan, 1963).

5 Enrique D. Dussel, 'Theology of Liberation and Marxism', in *Mysterium Liberationis: Fundamental Concepts of Liberation Theology*, ed. Ignacio Ellacuría and Jon Sobrino (Maryknoll, NY: Orbis, 1993), 85–102.

6 See, for example, Frans Wijsen, Peter Henriot, and Rodrigo Mejía, eds, *The Pastoral Circle Revisited: A Critical Quest for Truth and Transformation*

(Maryknoll, NY: Orbis, 2005), and Maria Cimperman, *Social Analysis for the 21st Century* (Maryknoll, NY: Orbis, 2015).

7 Robert LaSalle-Klein, *Blood and Ink: Ignacio Ellacuría, Jon Sobrino, and the Jesuit Martyrs of the University of Central America* (Maryknoll, NY: Orbis, 2014), 198–227.

8 Tricia Bruce, 'A Brief History of Sociology and Parishes in the United States', in *American Parishes: Remaking Local Catholicism*, eds. Gary Adler, Tricia Bruce, and Brian Starks (New York: Fordham University, forthcoming).

9 Hosffman Ospino, *Hispanic Ministry in Catholic Parishes* (Boston, MA: Boston College, 2014), 14.

10 As the reader will expect, all parish names here are pseudonyms.

11 Nicholas H. Healy, *Church, World, and the Christian Life: Practical-Prophetic Ecclesiology* (New York: Cambridge University Press, 2000), 1–51, 154–85.

12 Christian Scharen, '"Judicious Narratives", or Ethnography as Ecclesiology', *Scottish Journal of Theology* 58, 2 (2005), 125–42.

13 Brett C. Hoover, *The Shared Parish: Latinos, Anglos, and the Future of US Catholicism* (New York: NYU Press, 2014), 61.

14 Brett C. Hoover, 'Power in the Parish', in *American Parishes*, ed. Adler, Bruce, and Starks.

15 See Thomas Luckmann and Peter Berger, *The Social Construction of Reality: A Treatise in the Sociology of Knowledge* (New York: Anchor, 1966).

16 See Joseph Fichter, *Dynamics of a City Parish*, vol. 1 of *The Southern Parish* (Chicago, IL: University of Chicago Press, 1951).

17 See Joseph Fichter, *One-Man Research: Reminiscences of a Catholic Sociologist* (New York: Wiley, 1973).

18 Kevin Christiano, William H. Swatos, Jr., and Peter Kivisto, *Sociology of Religion: Contemporary Developments* (3rd edn; Lanham, MD: Rowman & Littlefield, 2016), 27.

19 Michael Omi and Howard Winant, *Racial Formation in the United States* (2nd edn; New York: Routledge, 1994), 53–76; see also Stephen Conrell and Douglass Hartmann, *Ethnicity and Race: Making Identities in a Changing World* (2nd edn; Thousand Oaks, CA: Pine Forge Press, 2007), 75–106.

20 On shaping the organizational culture of a faith community, see Jackson Carroll, *God's Potters: Pastoral Leadership and the Shaping of Congregations* (Grand Rapids, MI: Eerdmans, 2006).

21 On borrowing see Julie Thompson Klein, 'A Conceptual Vocabulary of Interdisciplinary Science', in *Practicing Interdisciplinarity*, eds. Peter Weingart and Nico Stehr (Toronto: University of Toronto Press, 2000), 3–24.

# 9

# Teaching Spirituality with Qualitative Research Methods

## BOYUNG LEE

How might social justice leaders not only generate hope for others, but also sustain hope for themselves despite the many hopeless situations they face? How can they stay in anti-oppression work while being discriminated against because of race, religion, gender identity, or some similar defining feature? These are the questions and challenges that many of my students and I wrestled with in my Spiritual Formation for Leadership class, a required class for entry students in Master of Divinity, Certificate in Spiritual and Social Change, and Master in Social Transformation programmes at Pacific School of Religion in Berkeley, California, where I taught for 15 years. Attempting to answer these questions, I designed my class in different ways using various pedagogical modes, but I found qualitative research methods most helpful in working with students at Pacific School of Religion who had particular needs.

In the Spiritual Formation for Leadership class I typically had about 45 students from over twenty religious backgrounds, which included various Christian denominations, Judaism, Islam, Buddhism, diverse Native/Indigenous spiritual traditions, as well as students without any religious affiliations. About 60 per cent of the class that I taught identified themselves as members of LGBTQ communities, and about 40 per cent of the enrolled students came from racial/ethnic minority contexts. The ratio of Master of Divinity students to other degree students was almost equal. Approximately 50 per cent of the enrolled students came from non-governmental organizations, healthcare services, legal communities, higher education, hi-tech industries, or similar, and the majority planned to return to the same workplaces, hopefully with deepened theological and spiritual foundations. Despite their widely different religious and work backgrounds, all of these students expressed a deep commitment to social justice, which they wanted to pursue from a spiritual/theological perspective in their various contexts. Most of them openly shared their wounds and burn-out from working at the frontlines of social justice movements and were seeking spiritual renewal.

Such needs and challenges, along with the grim statistic that about 35 to 40 per cent of pastors leave ministry for good within the first five years because of burn-out and a sense of hopelessness,[1] have prompted theological educators, myself included, to pay particular attention to the formation dimension of our teaching. The situation also calls for a pedagogy that helps our students increase their spiritual depth in order to generate hope in a world where many feel hopeless. In this chapter I present a pedagogical model for spiritual formation that is an intersection of 'engaged spirituality' and qualitative research, focusing on the participatory observation methods of Paulo Freire. Specifically, using my own teaching context as a case study, I demonstrate why and how qualitative research methods can function as critical pedagogical frameworks for teaching spirituality and spiritual formation in theological classes.

## Engaged Spirituality: Spirituality that Leads to Action for Social Justice

Engaged spirituality, a concept borrowed from Thich Nhat Hanh's 'Engaged Buddhism', is spirituality that nurtures people in their deepest being so that they can engage in social justice activities that move the world toward peace, justice, compassion, and wholeness.[2] Engaged spirituality sees spirituality and liberation not as either/or options but as both/and, because spirituality is viewed as a life committed to 'living a dual engagement: engaging with those resources that provide spiritual nurture *and* engaging with the world through acts of compassion and justice'.[3] While the concept of engaged spirituality was popularized by Thich Nhat Hanh, its actual practice has a long history in Christian spirituality.

Through years of teaching the spiritual formation class, I found the notion of engaged spirituality extremely helpful in addressing my students' need to deepen their own spirituality for social justice leadership as well as in challenging their assumptions about spiritual formation. In spite of their commitment to different social justice causes, some of my students understood spirituality as paying attention to inner well-being through soul-quieting spiritual practices, such as silent meditation. For these students, spiritual nurture often presupposed taking time off from daily busyness and retreating to nature or places where they would not be disturbed, and thus it was something they could not afford to do frequently.

The assumption that silence and solitude are necessary conditions for spiritual nurture has a long history in Western Christianity and its practices. For example, Cynthia Bourgeault, a popular leader of centring prayer, defines contemplative prayer as 'a wordless, trusting opening of self to the divine presence', and declares that 'silence is the normal context in which contemplative prayer takes place'.[4] Standing in the long line of the Western Christian contemplation tradition, Bourgeault suggests that contemplation is akin to silence and quiet meditation, and along with other contemplative prayer leaders she maintains that by extinguishing external noises through a retreat from the requirements of mundane living we can return to life and work with a renewed body and spirit. This silence-based approach is a pre-condition of most Western Christian spiritual practices, such as the Prayer of Examen, *Lectio Divina*, the Four-Stranded Garland Prayer, Contemplative Listening, and Christian Guided Meditation. Many practical guidebooks to such prayer practices suggest practitioners should prepare themselves with silence, to quiet their minds before they move on to the particular practice.

Practitioners are asked to calm themselves before engaging in contemplative spiritual practices through which they hope to encounter the Divine. They are to do so by finding a physically quiet place, closing their eyes, engaging in a breathing exercise, and/or imagining themselves in a serene natural environment.[5]

Barbara Holmes, a womanist theologian, observes that viewing silence as the prerequisite for contemplation and spiritual practices is a very Eurocentric understanding of Christian spirituality. She argues that in African American Churches contemplation includes but does not require silence, noting, 'Instead contemplative practices can be identified in public prayers, meditative dance movements, and musical cues that move the entire congregation toward a communal listening and entry into communion with a living God.'[6] Yet in the European and American context, contemplation and silence are believed to be synonymous. Holmes argues that contemplation as silence is a much narrower view than the original early Church understanding of Christian contemplation, particularly that of desert spirituality. Defining contemplation as 'an attentiveness of spirit that shifts the seeker from an ordinary reality to the *basileia* of God', Holmes broadens the scope of contemplation beyond silent meditative practices, which often require that practitioners carve out time from life's multiple demands.[7]

Encountered by God's spirit through interactive spiritual practices, the community is then called to engage in God's reign building work on earth through contemplative witness: standing for justice, creating a beloved community,[8] performing acts of mercy, fighting against unjust power, and engaging in prophetic proclamation and action, for example. Holmes suggests that what Martin Luther King Jr., Rosa Parks, Gandhi, Nelson Mandela, and many other justice movement activists practised are examples of contemplative witness.[9] In other words, contemplation charges people to be in the world creating God's reign, where justice and peace flourish for all people. In this regard, James Noel, a scholar of African American Christianity, says that in African American spirituality there is no contradiction between contemplation and social action.[10]

Contemplation as a companion to social justice in and for the world is in line with the definition of spirituality provided by liberation theologians Dorothee Sölle, Robert McAfee Brown, and Gustavo Gutiérrez.[11] Brown asserts that spirituality and liberation are 'two ways of talking about the same thing, so that there is no necessity, or even a possibility, of making a choice between them'.[12] Janet Parachin and Joseph Nangle respectfully apply Eastern understandings to say that spirituality coupled with liberation is engaged spirituality.[13] This form of spirituality commands those who engage in spiritual practices to look 'at reality, especially the great – and small – struggles for human liberation, from God's perspective, seeing possibilities where others might not' and then engage in action to remedy the reality.[14]

The notion of engaged spirituality also resonates with the original meaning of contemplation attributed to the desert elders of North Africa.[15] The desert elders retreated to the wilderness to live ascetically, fighting against the devil that was believed to rule over the dead buried there. It did not take long for them to perceive, however, that communal living would be required if they were to maintain their psychological and spiritual sanity, and thus they formed monasteries and spiritual communities. Pilgrims from the city came to these communities for prayers and spiritual advice and then returned to their lives in the city. This rhythm of retreat and return was a critical aspect of desert spirituality and anti-imperialist – against the Roman Empire – and not necessarily silent in nature, it was expressed through diverse communal contemplative practices.[16] The desert elders' contemplative prayers happened in all areas of their lives where God also acts – that is, the intrapersonal, interpersonal, natural/cosmic/environmental, and systematic/structural arenas of human living – and took various forms.[17]

Holmes observes that the communal spirituality of the desert elders started changing in the twelfth century with the assumption that 'the contemplative life was reserved for professional clerics or solitary individuals gifted by God in intensely mystical ways'.[18] As Western European Christianity became the dominant power along with colonialism, the view of contemplation as silent meditation became the norm. Eurocentric Christianity's equation of contemplation with silence, Holmes further asserts, is the reason many African American Christians have refused to embrace silent forms of contemplative practices. As a survival mechanism from colonialism, racism, and other forms of systematic oppression, the oppressed intentionally disengage from meditative and reflective practices that might evoke the traumatic memories and consciousness they have stowed away.[19] Instead, they find coping mechanisms in interactive and outspoken contemplative practices that give them a voice and an outlet, such as shouting, singing, clapping, or dancing.

All these factors suggest two pedagogical points for teaching spirituality. First, separating spirituality from social justice actions is problematic. Supporting my students' needs, namely healing after burn-out and renewal for continuous social justice ministries and activism, requires a curriculum that is well-balanced between the personal and structural pursuits of compassion and justice. Second, nurturing one's spiritual well-being can include solitude and silence but does not have to. Pedagogically this means offering diverse contemplative spiritual practices – both quiet and not quiet – for students with different needs and styles of spiritual engagement.

## Teaching Engaged Spirituality through Qualitative Research

What pedagogical methods exist to help my students nurture and deepen their personal spirituality, through which their vision and commitment to social justice, their communal connections, and their compassion for human beings and the world might be generated and sustained? Or more fundamentally, how can spirituality, which helps people connect with their deepest selves and God, be taught so that these individuals become leaders for social justice? I have found qualitative research reframed through critical pedagogy extremely helpful in addressing these tasks. Specifically, the Freirean participatory observation approach provides great insight for teaching engaged spirituality to a diverse group such as that which comprised my former students.

Brazilian educator Paulo Freire was influential not only in the field of critical pedagogy but also in critical social research. As described below, Freire involved the people he studied as partners in the research process.[20] They would join researchers in investigation, examination, criticism, and reinvestigation, as subjects learning about their own reality more critically and systematically. This process enabled them to take the necessary actions to build more just and equitable life conditions for themselves and others. Unlike traditional research methods, where researchers are expected to take a neutral position and bracket their personal views of certain social issues, Freirean research begins from the conviction that there is no value-free research and researchers can never be separated from the ideological assumptions of their societies.[21] Because Freirean researchers view confronting the social injustices that are rooted in unequal power relationships and structures as central to their research, theirs is an intentional and critical departure from traditional research methods. Freirean researchers regard research as a transformative endeavour and believe that researchers should be 'unafraid to consummate a relationship with emancipatory consciousness'.[22] Freirean researchers therefore aim to expose and change the causes of human suffering by raising the critical consciousness of participants, who in turn engage in communal transformative actions.

Raising the critical consciousness of participants, which Paulo Freire called conscientization, is fundamental to Freirean research and education.[23] Freire defined conscientization as 'the process in which men, not as recipients, but as knowing subjects, achieve a deepening awareness both of the socio-cultural reality which shapes their lives, and of their capacity to transform that reality through action upon it'.[24]

To this end he advocated problem-posing research that interrogates challenging issues in participants' lives, especially oppressive social phenomena, through dialogical inquiry between the researcher and participants and among participants, who systematically analyse identified problems and make constructive action plans for change as part of a learning community.[25] In other words, critical consciousness is raised through a continuous dialectical and praxis-oriented process in a communal context: unlearning, learning, and relearning. This dialectical process aims to disrupt the unequal and oppressive power dynamics of class, race, sexuality, gender and identity and other hegemonic agenda hidden in scholarship, both in schools and in the greater society beyond the classroom and studied communities.[26] Since my class was not about teaching qualitative research methods per se, but about helping students cultivate and deepen their own engaged spirituality, I considered the Freirean research method compatible with my requirements.

Freire's participant observation method, which he developed for literacy training, shows what Freirean qualitative research looks like in a given context. In his book *Pedagogy of the Oppressed*, Freire documented the origins of his critical research and teaching method: he moved from teaching Portuguese using traditional teaching methods to employing methods relevant to his learners' desire to improve their lives; he moved from telling them what to memorize to helping small groups struggle together for mastery; and he moved from teaching in a culture of unquestioning assumptions to one of empowering the peasants to generate hope and action for their own lives.[27]

More concretely, Freire's participant observation literacy training method had four phases.[28] The first phase was study of the learners' context, gained by spending an extended period in their communities, participating in informal conversations with residents, observing their culture, listening to their life stories, and identifying the community's key and recurring words and themes, which were then to be used in teaching. In the second phase, the teaching team chose 'generative words' from their collected vocabulary lists that were later used to help students develop elementary skills in decoding and encoding print. Freire believed that generative words should have emotional attachments for the learners that evoked their unjust social, cultural, and political living conditions. In the third phase, generative words with emotional provocation were presented in the form of drawings of familiar scenes from the life of the community. Each scene depicted conflicts found within the community for students to recognize, analyse, and attempt to resolve as a group. In the course of solving the problem depicted in the picture, learners 'named' the embedded generative words, giving teachers the raw material for developing reading and writing exercises. In the fourth and final phase, learners worked with a discovery card containing a generative word separated into its component syllables, giving them the opportunity to recombine syllables to form other words in their vocabulary.

This four-phase method clearly shows a process of conscientization. It starts with getting to know the participants' life circumstances, and the learning process and materials are closely related to their reality. The method is also communal. Through a communal research and learning process, participants are encouraged to be co-researchers and learners for one another, and to find a solution for their communities while implicitly learning how to read. This learning process is also very political because it challenges participants to ask the *why* questions about their reality, and to imagine and find ways to build a more just world.

I was drawn to using Freirean participant observation for teaching engaged spirituality for the following reasons. First, as the process emphasizes participants' own experiences and current context as the starting point of education, this method, in conversation with the rigorous studies and healing practices of engaged spirituality, could help my students bring forth their spiritual needs and also find ways to nurture their spiritual leadership for social change. Second, Freirean participant observation highlights that the purpose of research and learning is to help participants critically assess the world they live in, pay attention to power dynamics and dominant ideological assumptions, and find their role in creating an alternative world. Because many of my students came from backgrounds of social justice activism and ministry, often with experiences of being wounded and burned out, they tended to be suspicious of anything with the appearance of a mainstream ideology. Starting with their own experiences helped ease them into the course, which in turn led them to critically analyse their own assumptions as well as their experiences with the dominant society. The Freirean research and pedagogy process was also helpful for those who were relatively new to critical thinking, as the starting point of the method is their own life world.

Third, Freirean research and pedagogy is highly communal. Participants are challenged to identify and solve problems together. A new and emancipatory knowledge is generated through a communal process. This communality was a critical element for my students to learn. Despite their lived experiences of discrimination, those students who came from dominant cultural contexts tended to be very individualistic in their pursuit of spiritual nurture. Their major focus was on their own wounds and on seeking healing for these alone, without paying attention to the fact that their unacknowledged privileges could harm others. Other students who had worked at small non-profits as the sole programme officer and executor at times either implicitly or explicitly bypassed the communal problem-solving process.

For these and other compelling reasons, I designed a class on spiritual formation for leadership using the Freirean participant observation framework, and a description of that class follows below.

## Combining Engaged Spirituality and Freirean Qualitative Research

The Spiritual Formation for Leadership class was aimed at helping students sustain themselves as people and as social justice leaders through rigorous academic studies accompanied by spiritual nurture and witness. There were students from a variety of backgrounds and with needs of many kinds, as described earlier in the chapter. These diverse backgrounds made the class very exciting and generative, as they opened new and constructive ways for each student to think about their spiritual leadership for social change. At the same time, the diversity of the class created tensions and conflicts that resembled many of the students' ministry and social justice work contexts. It was therefore important both for me and for the students to develop an operating definition of engaged spirituality that everybody could agree to as the starting point for our study together. For this purpose, I started the first day of the class with an invitation to students to briefly share their response to the question 'What nurtures your spirit?' as a part of their self-introduction. Building on what they shared, I then introduced a broad definition of engaged spirituality, one that I integrated from the work of Sandra Schneiders, Joseph Driskill, and Barbara Holmes: the study of spirituality is concerned with the lived experience of faith, the communities that nurture it, the practices that sustain it, and the moral life which embodies it. In other words, spirituality is concerned with all of life as it is lived and experienced by believers – their beliefs, ethical stands, actions, motivations, historical context, social location and all other salient influences on the lived experience of their faith in a community.[29] This operating definition helped me then introduce the reasons for studying spirituality for social change through a layered participant observation method, which the class engaged with throughout the semester. The following explanations were given to my students in the first two class sessions: (1) to understand the tradition(s) that have shaped us, (2) to explore the spirituality of others in a way that is fair and just to them, (3) to understand issues of our world more deeply, as most of the injustices in our world intersect with oppressive theologies and spiritualities of dominant groups, (4) to provide leadership for spiritual communities for social justice, and (5) to nurture/deepen our own spirituality.

In addition to lectures, reading discussions (first hour of the class), learning/practising a Christian contemplative practice (second hour of the class), and being in a covenant group with a leader (third hour of the class), the students undertook assignments that encouraged them to study and practise engaged spirituality using the Freirean critical research method. Those assignments are discussed in the next section.

## Learning Engaged Spirituality

### *Step One*

Before they wrote their first paper, 'Reflection on the Spirituality of One's Own Community', I introduced the students to the Description–Analysis–Evaluation–Response method of participatory observation as a means of framing their paper (see Table 1). This paper had a dual purpose: to provide an opportunity for students to make a critical assessment of how their own faith community had shaped their view of spirituality, so that they might see their own theological/spiritual assumptions and biases, and to help them learn and practise ethical observation methods. In their first assignments in seminary, most students tend to write very passionate, evaluative and judgemental papers on their own communities, and thus I found myself spending a substantial time commenting on their papers, offering further explanations of the four-step paper guidelines, and repeating the guidelines in the class.

The guidelines presented a condensed version of the participatory observation method, but they were intended to help students learn the importance of paying attention/listening and of thick descriptions, starting with their own communities, which they thought they knew well. This exercise surprised some students as they noticed things of which they had previously been unaware but that positively and negatively shaped their own spirituality.

| Description | Analysis | Evaluation | Response |
|---|---|---|---|
| The student provides *a thick description* of what s/he/they observed: you clearly and respectfully describe what you observe without making judgemental statements, and let the observed community speak for itself. During your visit, try to take field notes describing what you see, hear, feel, notice including physical environments, and feel free to quote your notes in the paper. | The student provides careful analysis of the observed community's distinctive spirituality *in its own context* to understand why and how that community does what it does: you support your analysis with the community's available resources such as the webpage, historical documents, etc. | The student provides thoughtful and thorough theological-socio-cultural evaluations (theology, race, ethnicity, gender, class, etc.) of the observed community's distinctive spirituality with supportive literature. Here you bring your previous training from different disciplines and experiences to make some evaluations of what you have observed. | The student offers an emerging characteristic, distinction, or pattern of the observed community's spirituality, and makes constructive suggestions and comments to the observed community, whether/how the community is observing engaged spirituality or not. The student also makes critical reflections on her/his/their learning from this observation for her/his/their own current and future ministry contexts and spiritual leadership for social change. |

*Table 1. Four-step guidelines for first assignment (observation method), from syllabus for Spiritual Formation for Leadership course.*

## Step Two

This introduction to participatory observation was expanded in two ways. First, a social justice ministry/activism site was assigned to each covenant group, which comprised about eight students. The students were first to research the site through available literature and online material as a group, and later in the semester they visited the site, again as a group, to conduct observations and interviews in order to understand how spirituality for social transformation was at work there. For the fall 2016 class, five sites were chosen by the instructor and the Director of the Contextual Learning Office (DCLO) of Pacific School of Religion after they had reviewed each student's application prior to the semester:

- The Health Reform Forum of the Allen Temple Baptist Church in Oakland, in partnership with Alameda County Health Department
- Urban Adamah, a Berkeley-based educational farm and community centre that integrates Jewish tradition, sustainable agriculture, mindfulness, and social action
- CultureStrike, an arts-based social justice strategy hub, particularly for migrant artists, women artists, and artists of colour to create alternative narratives and culture change
- Berkeley or Oakland City Council, the legislative body that governs the city, which has a reputation for being the most progressive legislative body in the country
- First Congregational Church of Berkeley, a typical mainline congregation, the majority of which is white, with a progressive theology

In each instance, Pacific School of Religion either had an existing long-term relationship with the site or was cultivating a new partnership with it. Within each covenant group, the students, along with their group leader, were expected to help one another gain as much information about their site as possible, including its mission, history, work, and spirituality.

While they were learning about the site independently as a group, the students were introduced through their readings to some of the markers of engaged spirituality embodied in the life of social justice leaders. For example, in *Engaged Spirituality: Ten Lives of Contemplation and Action* by Janet Parachin they studied the life and activism of Howard Thurman, Elie Wiesel, Marian Wright Edelman, Thich Nhat Hanh, Rigoberta Menchú, and others. The class also included sessions on African American spirituality, focusing on race, and diverse communal and liberation spiritual practices from the Global South, such as Korean communal prayer practices. Kingian nonviolence principles, Courageous Conversations about race as a spiritual practice, and various Protestant spiritual practices were also introduced. These topics, which were designed to invite students to reflect on what it means to be a spiritually and theologically rooted leader for social change, provided opportunities to generate markers and characteristics of engaged spirituality, communally and individually, that the students could use in the interpretation of their observations on their sites.

For their mid-term project each student was required to write a research paper about a social justice leader in the field of their ministry interests – a public figure or an individual they knew. In this paper, students were to explore how their chosen leader's spirituality was forming and informing their leadership and then identify the characteristics of that leader's engaged spirituality as well as the learning they had taken away for their own leadership. Students' definitions of engaged spirituality would later serve as another lens for analysis and interpretation during their site observations. As with the first reflection paper, students were asked to follow the Description-Analysis-Evaluation-Response framework, but this time their description and analysis were to have more depth. As preparation for this paper and the coming site visit, I gave more explicit instructions on the four-step framework, differentiating in particular between observation and interpretation. I also lectured on interview methods, how to generate open-ended interview questions from observations, and ways to conduct focus groups (students seldom reach this last-named stage in this introductory class). These methods were introduced not only as approaches to be deployed on the site visit, but also as ways of conducting needs assessments for the final course project, on teaching, and in their ministry and social justice work contexts, where many of the students will develop curricula for diverse groups and for leadership training from theological/spiritual perspectives.

## Step Three

Later in the semester, regular class sessions were no longer held. Instead, each covenant group spent an initial minimum of three hours on its assigned site, with each student required then to spend six additional hours after the visit on further observations, interviews, and other activities before they turned in their observation paper near the end of the semester. After initial contact with each site had been made by the instructor and the Director of Contextual Learning Office, all the logistics for the group's visit, including the timing and the activities they were invited to participate in, were handled by the group via their group leader. Before their visit, each group was required to create an ethical behaviour covenant for while on the site and to review the methods for participatory observation provided in my lecture and handouts. When the students were at their site, a host or hosts would usually introduce them and invite them to participate in certain routine activities (negotiated with myself and the DCLO in advance). They were then allowed unstructured observation time and interacted with regular participants of the site programmes and/or staff at the site. The site visit typically ended with a community gathering at which my students could ask the host and/or regular participants questions. After the site visit, each group was required to meet to debrief, to compare field notes, and to generate follow-up questions and action plans, including whether they wanted to organize group or individual visits for further observations and interviews.

After completing a total nine hours of site visits, students submitted their observation papers, which were expected to fully utilize their pre-visit research, initial and follow-up visits/interviews, and their field notes. Again they were required to frame their papers using the Description–Analysis–Evaluation–Response format. In terms of content, the students were first to describe what they had observed in detail and then analyse how engaged spirituality was at work at the site by interpreting its characteristics, patterns, and embodiment in light of what they had learned about engaged spirituality in class. Students were also expected to provide in-depth reflection on what it means to create a community of engaged spirituality that was based on their participant observations and on the insights they had gained for their own spirituality and leadership.

## Step Four

As a final project in which the students were to bring together everything they had learned in the class, they created a teaching project for a group of people of their choice (non-class members) to help increase awareness of social justice grounded in spirituality. They were to incorporate a spiritual practice they had experienced either in the class or in their covenant group. This exercise encouraged students to think about how to bring both participant observation and engaged spirituality to their ministry and activism, because the assignment required them to outline the needs of their participants, assessed through listening, research, observation, and other methods. In other words, students had to show why the chosen topic (the *what*) and process of teaching (the *how*) of their project would meet the needs of their participants, beyond what they think helpful for their participants. The critical importance of listening and of particular contexts in pastoral and social justice ministries was reiterated in this final project.

In general, the students responded to the Freirean qualitative research methods very positively. In their course evaluations, most of them listed the site visit as the most important component of the class. Even though a fully developed version of qualitative research methods was not taught, students expressed their appreciation of a new critical tool they could use when listening and for understanding the contexts of their various ministries. These responses, they felt, would help them create ministries that emerged from the people.

Concretely, I learned that qualitative research methods could help my students and me in a number of ways. First, we learned to listen deeply to the needs of the people and the various contexts of our ministries in a rapidly changing world. Faith community leaders, who are expected to provide pastoral and prophetic leadership, should be able to read the patterns of change and the needs of people in this changing world. Second, we learned to integrate theory and practice, and also personal and communal spirituality. The pastoral and prophetic leadership based on engaged spirituality that my students are expected to provide can be exercised only when they are equipped with deep theological thinking and pastoral praxis and can see the systematic causes of injustice that lie beyond individual human sufferings. Theories isolated from the reality of living in the world and practices without critical analyses are neither healthy nor generative. Third, qualitative research methods helped my students develop a deep appreciation of the hermeneutics of both generosity and suspicion. They quickly learned how to deconstruct texts and contexts through critical analysis. Although sometimes they did so without fully understanding the reasons behind certain past actions and the role of the object of their critique in the life of the people, I witnessed how by engaging in qualitative research my students learned to appreciate what they observed before making critical evaluations. Such attitudes sometimes helped them discover realities and possibilities that they did not expect to find. Fourth, with skills learned through qualitative research engagements, my students grew together to form a healthy learning community where collaboration and different opinions were respected, even though the process of learning required more patience and harder work than a typical class. This benefit of the Freirean participant observation method was especially important when the class was exploring difficult topics such as anti-racism as a spiritual practice.

## Conclusion

The Spiritual Formation for Leadership class described in this chapter is unique in terms of the diverse make-up and needs of the students, and thus some readers may think that such a class is not feasible in their own teaching contexts. It is not my expectation that readers will transfer my class as it stands to their own context. I wanted to demonstrate in this chapter that qualitative research methods can form an important and helpful pedagogical framework for theological classes. Depending on the context and needs of the theological institution and its students, different methods of qualitative research may be required. Spiritual formation that heals a hurting world requires varied forms of teaching and learning. I found my own pedagogical niche in qualitative research, and I invite others also to explore this old and yet new teaching partner.

## Notes

1 Jason Helopoulos, *The New Pastor's Handbook: Help and Encouragement for the First Years of Ministry* (Ada, MI: Baker Books. 2015), 201.

2 Janet W. Parachin, *Engaged Spirituality: Ten Lives of Contemplation and Action* (St Louis, MO: Chalice Press, 1999), 2.

3 Parachin, *Engaged Spirituality*, 2.

4 Cynthia Bourgeault, *Centering Prayers and Inner Awakening* (Lanham, MD: Rowman & Littlefield, 2004), 5 and 7.

5 For examples see works such as Adele Ahlberg Calhoun's extensive handbook on spiritual practices, *Spiritual Disciplines Handbook: Practices that Transform Us* (Downers Grove, IL: IVP, 2015), especially parts 2 and 7.

6 Barbara A. Holmes, *Joy Unspeakable: Contemplative Practices of the Black Church* (Minneapolis, MN: Fortress Press, 2004), 42.

7 Holmes, *Joy Unspeakable*, 32–38, with quotation on p. 43.

8 The beloved community is a concept of community of justice and compassion popularized by Martin Luther King, Jr. See further 'The King Philosophy' page of The King Library and Archives in Atlanta, http://www.thekingcenter.org/king-philosophy#sub4.

9 Holmes, *Joy Unspeakable*, 138.

10 James Noel, 'Contemplation and Social Action in Afro-American Spirituality', *Pacific Theological Review* 22 (1988), 25.

11 Dorothee Sölle, *The Silent Cry: Mysticism and Resistance* (Minneapolis, MN: Augsburg Fortress Press, 2001), Robert McAfee Brown, *Spirituality and Liberation: Overcoming the Great Fallacy* (Louisville, KY: Westminster Press, 1988), and Gustavo Gutierrez, *Spiritual Writings*, selected by Daniel G. Groody (Maryknoll, NY: Orbis, 2011).

12 Brown, *Spirituality and Liberation*, 18.

13 Parachin, *Engaged Spirituality*, and Joseph Nangle, *Engaged Spirituality: Faith Life in the Heart of the Empire* (Maryknoll, NY: Orbis, 2008).

14 For the quotation see Nangle, *Engaged Spirituality*, 47.

15 Holmes, *Joy Unspeakable*, 27; Michael Battle, 'Liberation', in *The Blackwell Companion to Christian Spirituality*, ed. Arthur Holder (Malden, MA: Wiley-Blackwell, 2011), 523.

16 Holmes, *Joy Unspeakable*, 34; Battle, 'Liberation', 522–26; Columba Stewart, 'Christian Spirituality during the Roman Empire (100–600)', in *The Blackwell Companion to Christian Spirituality*, ed. Holder, 86–87.

17 See Joseph D. Driskill, 'Spirituality and the Formation of Pastoral Counselors', *American Journal of Pastoral Counseling* 8, 3/4 (2006), 82–83, and Elizabeth Liebert, 'Supervision as Widening the Horizons', in *Supervision of Spiritual Directors: Engaging the Holy Mystery*, ed. Mary Rose Bumpus and Rebecca Bradburn Langer (Harrisburg, PA: Morehouse, 2005), 125–46.

18 Holmes, *Joy Unspeakable*, 36.

19 Holmes, *Joy Unspeakable*, 30.

20 Joe L. Kincheloe, Peter McLaren, and Shirley Steinburg, 'Critical Pedagogy and Qualitative Research', in *The Sage Handbook of Qualitative Research*, ed. Norman K. Denzin and Yvonna S. Lincoln (Thousand Oaks, CA: Sage, 2011), 164.

21 Joe L. Kincheloe, 'Describing the Bricolage: Conceptualizing a New Rigor in Qualitative Research', *Qualitative Inquiry* 7, 6 (2001), 679–92.

22 Kincheloe, McLaren, and Steinburg, 'Critical Pedagogy', 164.

23 Ana Maria Freire and Donaldo Macedo, eds, *The Paulo Freire Reader* (New York: Continuum, 2000).

24 Paulo Freire, *Cultural Action for Freedom* (Cambridge, MA: Harvard Educational Review and Centre for the Study of Development and Social Change, 1970), 27.

25 Paulo Freire, *Pedagogy of the Oppressed* (New York: Continuum, 1970), 71–86.

26 Zeus Leonardo, *Race, Whiteness, and Education* (New York: Routledge, 2009), 19; Michael Apple, *Ideology and Curriculum* (New York: Routledge Falmer, 2004), 77–98.

27 Freire, *Pedagogy of the Oppressed*.

28 Paulo Freire, *Education for Critical Consciousness* (New York: Bloomsbury Academic, 1974).

29 See Sandra M. Schneiders, 'The Study of Christian Spirituality: Contours and Dynamics of a Discipline', *Christian Spirituality Bulletin* 6, 1 (1998), 3–21; Joseph D. Driskill, *Protestant Spiritual Exercises: Theology, History, and Practice* (Harrisburg, PA: Morehouse, 1999), and Holmes, *Joy Unspeakable*.

# The Researcher as Gamemaker: Teaching Normative Dimensions in Various Phases of Empirical Practical Theological Research

## TONE STANGELAND KAUFMAN

In books and articles based on qualitative studies, the findings are usually neatly presented and discussed, and the reader easily gets the impression that the process has been rather nice and tidy. However, this is seldom the case. As an inexperienced PhD student, I came across a Norwegian book entitled *Historien om et kvalitativt forskningsprosjekt* [The story of a qualitative research project].[1] This book was different from most publications on methodology as it simply told the story of a research project, thereby making the messiness of such a process explicit. As a reader I was allowed backstage, so to speak, an experience that was formative for my understanding of the research process. It was somehow encouraging to realize that a seasoned professor also experienced difficulties in gaining access to her field, the frustrations of cancelled appointments, a wilderness of data, and the confusion of various theoretical perspectives, not to speak of the personal challenges that are also part of qualitative research processes.

Most PhD dissertations and Master's theses have (or at least should have) a chapter on 'method', a term whose Greek roots mean 'after the way' (*meta odos*). When I supervise graduate students, I usually tell them that the methodology chapter, like the book I referred to above, should aim to make the decision trail

for the study transparent in a way that allows the reader to follow the path taken by the research, including its messy detours.
As questions of normativity in many (often implicit) ways influence the entire research process, it is particularly significant to
reflect on and make explicit the understanding and use of normativity in qualitative research and dissertation work. This topic is
the subject of this chapter, where emphasis is given to the supervision of graduate students in theological education in the field
of practical theology. As a point of departure we can adopt my
earlier definition: 'the terms "normative" and "descriptive" are
used as opposite positions on a continuum where "normative"
denotes an explicitly evaluative position making value claims,
whereas the "descriptive" end of the continuum entails a minimum of explicit value claims'.[2] It should be noted that 'normative' does not equal 'prescriptive', as I understand the latter to be
a narrower term.

My teaching and research have led me to reflect on and write
on normativity, and I begin by giving a few examples of how I
have encountered questions of normativity in my own work. I
also account for how these experiences have shaped my understanding of normativity in my writing and teaching. In the main
part of the essay, I seek to show how issues to do with normativity come to the fore during the phases of a PhD research project.
The structure of the body of the essay is therefore inspired by the
process of writing a doctoral or Master's thesis or of conducting
a qualitative research project more generally.

## Commonplaces

One day in 2007, while working on the analysis of my empirical
material for my PhD research, I had an epiphany. I was sitting
in my office looking at the works on Christian spirituality on
my bookshelf and thinking, what am I missing? Something didn't
quite make sense. And then it struck me: What did St John of
the Cross, Teresa of Avila, and Dietrich Bonhoeffer have in common? Yes, precisely! None of them had the daily responsibility

of children.[3] I had sensed a discrepancy between what I had read in the history of Christian spirituality literature and my own empirical data material established by in-depth interviews with Norwegian pastors serving in local parishes. What the latter had told me about their spirituality seemed far more everyday-like, and parenting was a significant part of their account, also in terms of how their spirituality related to their pastoral ministry. Moreover, I realized that a majority of the authors from the Christian spirituality literature had written from within a contemplative atmosphere, often living in monastic communities where spiritual practices were built in. In addition, many of them had lived under extreme conditions or wrote about extraordinary spiritual experiences, such as the visions of Julian of Norwich or St John of the Cross's 'dark night of the soul'.

Largely by coincidence I then picked up Bonnie Miller-McLemore's book *In the Midst of Chaos*, in the American Academy of Religion exhibition hall that same year.[4] And partly because I did so, I ended up exchanging the theological voices I had planned to engage in my dissertation: Dietrich Bonhoeffer, Henri Nouwen, and Kenneth Leech were replaced by Bonnie Miller-McLemore, Elizabeth Dreyer, and Gordon Lathrop. My exchange of theological conversation partners was implicitly a *normative* move as it influenced in a profound way the results of my research and thus my normative understanding of clergy spirituality (and spirituality more generally). Yet, I did not use Miller-McLemore's book or the other theological resources as a theological norm or measuring rod by which I evaluated the spirituality of the interviewees in my study. Rather, these theological writings and voices served as analytical lenses and conversation partners in the research process.

## Engaging Normativity in Practical Theology

In the following discussion I offer a few examples of how questions of normativity have been crucial in my own research. First, I have come to consider reflexivity a significant interpretive key in turning naïve and implicit normative notions and values (normativity as pitfall) into explicit normative claims that might contribute to a more nuanced understanding of the phenomenon under investigation (normativity as ally).[5] While the former form of normativity tends to confirm assumptions held by the researcher at the outset of the study, the latter might surprise the researcher and contribute to novel knowledge production. I therefore explicitly challenge students to pay attention to normative dimensions and assumptions both in their own work and when they read and comment on the work of fellow PhD students and other scholars. A crucial part of this process is to make what is implicit explicit so that such normative assumptions do not form blind spots. Hence, I aim to complexify the concept of normativity by distinguishing between different aspects or dimensions of normativity.[6]

In a previous book chapter on conundrums in practical theology I chose to write about *normativity* in what is often termed descriptive work.[7] As a non-native English speaker, I fell in love with the word *conundrum*, a term that captures that which cannot be resolved easily, or perhaps cannot be resolved at all, in the dilemmas we explored in the book. Over and over again I experience students and seasoned scholars alike struggling with the conundrum of normativity in qualitative practical theological research. As I wrote in that earlier chapter on conundrums in practical theology:

> I hardly ever sit through a session where a paper presenting empirical research framed in practical theology is discussed without anyone mentioning the relationship between the descriptive and the normative. Frequently, the author is accused of being too normative, which often means their normativity is implicit, tacit, off the page, or at least between the lines. However, the critique might also go the other way around: The text is considered to be 'insufficiently theological' or 'insufficiently normative,' although the two are not identical. The former critique is often posed by one of the social scientists in the room, whereas the latter is usually voiced by one of the scholars inclined to systematic theology. The researcher is at

one and the same time faulted if they do include normative assumptions *and* faulted if they do not.[8]

How, then, can students and scholars approach and deal with the conundrum of normativity in 'descriptive work'?

## The Researcher as Gamemaker

Natalie Wigg-Stevenson foregrounds *the research question* as key in making normative theological claims based on an ethnographic study in theology.[9] Although sympathetic to and inspired by Wigg-Stevenson's approach, I believe it is even more accurate to say that it is the overall research design *and* entire research process that contribute to producing normative theological claims.

When looking back at my own research as well as the work of other scholars, I have been struck by how many small and large decisions the researcher makes, and how these decisions influence the analysis and (normative) argument of the study. Examples of such research decisions include the sampling of research participants, the establishment of the material and relationships that emerge in the field, the research question, the theoretical perspectives selected, the epistemological paradigm in which the work is situated, the analytical strategies used, the argument made, and how all of these elements are put together in a research design. Such decisions are not normatively neutral. Quite the opposite. A normativity is embedded in the research design and research process, and the researcher has the normative power to orchestrate the research process and make decisions that influence what emerges as normative spirituality, ecclesiology, or theology as the result of a qualitative study in practical theology. Thus, in this essay I suggest that in describing the researcher we can draw on the character Seneca Crane from Suzanne Collins's *Hunger Games* and apply the metaphor of the Gamemaker, for 'the researcher, as Gamemaker, is to a certain extent in the position to control the "game board" of the research'.[10]

There are usually no explicit and fixed criteria according to which the researcher makes such normative decisions in the research process. This kind of implicit normativity therefore tends to pass under the radar. Although the researcher (student and scholar alike) cannot step out of the role of Gamemaker, they can be a *responsible* Gamemaker. To do so entails being transparent about their assumptions, location, and pre-understanding, as well as giving warrants for the choices made. A responsible Gamemaker, then, practises *self-reflexivity*. How can self-reflexivity and an awareness of various normative dimensions be fostered when working with graduate students and their qualitative research projects? In the following I address this question as I walk the reader through the process of writing a qualitative PhD thesis in practical theology. When doing so, I seek to distinguish between different kinds of normativity. I also present a heuristic model that helps identify theological voices in the research.

## Supervision and the Methodology Chapter

Students who approach me because they want to do qualitative research framed within practical theology for their Master's or PhD thesis are often motivated by a passion for the Church. Not infrequently they want to change current Church practice in their field of study. Yet their normative notions and values regarding the phenomenon they would like to research are often partly hidden from the students themselves, or they are implicit or intuitive rather than explicit. Therefore, at the outset of the research process I have my students write a paper on (1) why they want to undertake the research, (2) what their preliminary assumptions and hunches are, and, not least, (3) how they position themselves in relation to the topic of investigation and field of research. The purpose of this paper is to help them uncover some of these underlying and often highly normative theological notions and values. Moreover, some of these initially normative values might be interpretive keys for their research process.[11]

In my experience, the fostering of self-reflexivity related to a given research project is an ongoing process. It might begin with an assignment of the type described above, with students required to write reflection notes about their implicit and explicit assumptions. Throughout the process, too, I keep asking my students to distinguish between their normative stances and positions prior to or in an early phase of the research and those that emerge during the research process itself as a result of their analysis and interpretation of the data.

Issues of normativity should be attended to not only in the methodology chapter but also throughout the entire thesis. Hence, when examining a PhD thesis, I often look at how the methodology chapter is reflected in the rest of the dissertation. It is not uncommon for me to recognize a discrepancy between the intentions spelled out in this chapter and what is written out in the rest of the text. One practical piece of advice I recommend students be given is that they constantly write and revise the methodology chapter to keep it close to the actual research process and the normative considerations made throughout the journey. This practice includes reading the entire thesis in light of the methodology chapter toward the end of the study in order to make sure the decision trail is apparent.

One simple pedagogical tool that I have found helpful also in terms of fostering self-reflexivity has been to have students write a short memo or reflection note soon after each of our meetings. Here they briefly reflect on our conversation and how they will follow it up. Moreover, in various phases of their research, I might ask my students to write what some authors call 'morning pages', a 15- to 30-minute writing exercise in which students uncritically write what they think and feel about their research and also where they stand on their current choices, experiences, observations, analyses, and what they read by other scholars. Reflecting on these notes, as well as on the students' general observations, experiences, and findings, often fosters awareness of varied understandings of normativity. This contemplation also covers choices that the researcher will have made prior to and during the phase that involves establishing the empirical material for the project. The student might reflect on why a certain sampling approach has been chosen over other possible approaches, the kind of data collected, or, eventually, the kind of (normative) theological knowledge that this approach might produce in relation to the research question. In the field site the researcher establishes relationships with the research subjects or interviewees, and in my own research I have found it helpful to reflect on such interactions in terms of their possible role in the production of the empirical data and in my analysis and interpretation of the material.

My aim in this regard, then, is to train students to be able to distinguish between various forms of normativity and to note how normativity is inherent in the entire research process. Forms of normativity include *evaluative normativity* (often in the shape of theological norms), *prescriptive normativity* (often the outcome of a practical theological research process in the form of advice for a revised practice), *rescriptive normativity* (a hermeneutical normativity, see below), as well as the overall reflexive normativity exercised by the researcher as Gamemaker. In the doctoral programme at my institution, MF Norwegian School of Theology, Religion and Society it has become more common for research and the supervision of doctoral students to be carried out collaboratively. Some PhD students write their dissertations as part of a larger research project and thus become part of a research team. They benefit from taking part in ongoing research and membership of a research community in terms of conversations, feedback, responding to others, and networking. They have a research community that understands their work and in a certain way provides a safe space for them. The students are also encouraged and invited to present their current work at an early stage, receiving feedback from colleagues whose understanding of normativity in qualitative practical theological research might differ quite significantly from their own. This latter experience is an important part of fostering self-reflexivity, as they may find their intuitive and implicit normative notions and values challenged. Moreover, when the students work collaboratively, they may have colleagues who will play devil's advocate in relation to their preferred positions and findings. Have they simply found what they were looking for or are they willing to be surprised by the unexpected? I have experienced for myself the temptation of rejoicing in my initial and favoured findings. I therefore keep challenging my students to pay particular attention to the part of the material that questions, problematizes, or nuances their preferred findings and to observations that do not quite fit into the overall pattern of their initial argument.

As normativity concerns not only the methodology chapter but also the entire dissertation thesis, I have found supervising students in groups helpful and also responding to ongoing graduate work thematically across several dissertation texts rather than looking simply at one paper at a time. The first respondent (usually a faculty member as the principal respondent, with a student as an additional respondent) might read all the introductions, another the analyses, a third the discussions, and a fourth the methodology chapters. This procedure can be implemented with a special emphasis on normativity when normativity is the thematic focus of the seminar. This approach enables a respondent to see things that might have otherwise gone unnoticed, as it enables them, for example, to compare introductory or methodology chapters and thus to go into depth with one theme instead of responding to a larger text written in its entirety by one student. Reading through four drafts of methodology chapters, I encounter various ways of going about this task and can also see how ideas from one thesis could enrich and enhance another.

## Theological Voices

As we saw in the discussion of my spirituality study, I first exercised normative power as Gamemaker by choosing three theological conversation partners and then, as the research process went along, exchanged them for three other theological resources with different normative perspectives on spirituality. As this example illustrates, the choice of theoretical perspectives also entails normative dimensions, and therefore calls for self-reflexivity on the part of the researcher that will make such choices explicit. Graduate students in practical theology face the challenge of sorting between theological and theoretical voices, frameworks, and resources in their dissertation work. I usually ask the students I supervise to specify how they understand and use the term 'theory' and what role 'theory' is given in their work. In particular, students are encouraged to be clear how extant theory relates to the data they assemble and their analysis of that data. This issue is also relevant for the role theology plays in their research. What are considered normative theological sources and why? Is tradition or, more specifically, a given theological tradition ready-made or in the making? What normative status does tradition have for a particular scholar?

One heuristic tool useful in this regard is the *Four Voices of Theology* model developed by the British research group Action Research – Church and Society (ARCS).[12] This framework distinguishes between four 'theological voices':

- the *espoused* voice – what is expressed verbally in the empirical field site
- the *operant* voice – what is enacted in the empirical field site
- the *normative* voice – Scripture and ecclesial traditions at work in the empirical field site as well as normative theological voices that can be drawn in by the researcher at various stages of the research process
- the *formal* voice – theological reflections and studies from the academy, which are usually brought into the research process by the academic scholar, either in the empirical field site or at a later stage of the research process[13]

Although I am positively inclined toward this model, the work of the ARCS team raises questions. Highly relevant for our topic of normativity is the tension between claiming the 'mutual engagement' of these four voices and granting the normative voice of the ecclesial tradition a privileged position, an attitude that acknowledges an asymmetrical relationship between the four voices.[14] Still, students and scholars have found this heuristic model useful because it enables them to see different theological voices in their work. For example, the distinction between the espoused and operant voices often helps them spot discrepancies between what is enacted and what is verbally expressed in the field site.

Moreover, less evident in the work of ARCS is the role the researcher or research team plays in weighing these theological voices when making normative theological claims based on fieldwork.[15] This essay seeks to draw attention to precisely this normative dimension. Hence, I deploy the metaphor of the Gamemaker to acknowledge and make explicit the power and responsibility of the researcher in negotiating these various theological voices from Church (*normative theology*) and academy (*formal theology*) as well as these various *operant* and *espoused* theologies identified in the field site. The significance of the researcher's role as Gamemaker should not be underestimated. Being a responsible Gamemaker means being particularly aware of two crucial questions related to a qualitative research process: Which voices are included and drawn into the conversation? and What roles are these voices allowed to play? Both of these questions are also relevant for issues of normativity, and I remind students to attend to them throughout the research process.

In the research referred to above, I did not use the works of Miller-McLemore, Dreyer, Lathrop or other academic and ecclesial authorities such as Scripture, the Creed, or Luther as the normative standard for, or means of measuring, the spirituality of my research participants. As I have noted elsewhere, this kind of 'evaluative normativity is what we often automatically associate with the term "normativity," and in certain Lutheran contexts, Luther can always be drawn as a non-negotiable trump card!'[16]

## Analysis, Argument, and Discussion: Rescriptive Normativity

Although I would argue that some kind of analysis is constantly taking place during the entire research project, there is also a particular phase where the researcher attends more specifically to analysis of the empirical data. And this phase entails normative dimensions, not least a more hermeneutically oriented normativity closely related to the analysis. The foregrounding of everyday spirituality in my own PhD work was a *normative* move that grew out of my account and analysis of the empirical data, as described in the story above. I have in previous works called this a *rescriptive normativity*, acknowledging that an account of a research process 'is not simply "a mere description" of the practice field, but a re-description, a re-making, and thus a *rescription*'.[17] The study and the research process contributed to widening and challenging my normative understanding of clergy spirituality, as it opened my eyes to the significance of an everyday spirituality, not only for lay people (as had been claimed before) but also for clergy. Hence, as I have previously argued, 'this rescription also includes normative theological dimensions, and is consequently a contribution to the production of theological knowledge', even if it is different from the evaluative normativity described above.[18] Still, this rescriptive normative move was influenced by the specific theological conversation partners found in the literature that I as researcher and Gamemaker brought into dialogue with the data.

In the following I give an example of a rescriptive normativity that happened primarily in the field site, in establishing the empirical data. In her ethnographic study Wigg-Stevenson brought in traditionally normative theological doctrines (such as God as the Trinity or models of atonement) for members of her adult Sunday School class to argue about and wrestle with. However, these doctrines were *not* treated as normative standards against which the theological reflections and positions of the Sunday School participants were measured and evaluated. Rather, indeed on the contrary, they were consciously engaged, rejected, and reaffirmed.[19] This practice, then, contributed to the development of the research participants' normative theology and, consequently, to the production of theological knowledge. However, the reflections of the research participants were not allowed to automatically trump the theological doctrines either. Yet, because of the acknowledgement that the normativity embedded in ecclesial practices should also be considered a significant theological voice, there seems to be a real *mutuality* among the various theological conversation partners in her work. Wigg-Stevenson makes the case that it is possible to make normative theological claims based on ethnographic work but these claims must be discerned, articulated, and argued in a transparent way.[20] The researcher as Gamemaker is in a position to grant these different voices various roles and priorities. Yet the Gamemaker cannot fully control either the outcome of the conversation or the normativity that emerges from it.

Sometimes normative approaches are mixed in a way that blurs not only the understanding of the phenomenon under investigation but also the overall argument of the thesis. Thus, throughout the research process and also when I comment on drafts, I keep asking students to distinguish between approaches to normativity and how normative and theological voices are used in their work. Why is one particular theological voice or resource granted priority over alternative or competing voices? What are the normative criterion or criteria used for the dissertation's argument? – a question to which students must pay particular attention as they seek to make an overall argument for the dissertation toward the end of the research process.

## A Prescriptive Outlook?

Master's degree students in particular but also PhD students tend to want to end their theses with a prescriptive outlook. I try to make the students aware of the kind of normative stance this is, and I also challenge them to consider whether this prescriptive normativity is actually built on the analysis of the material, or if it is rather what they would have argued prior to doing the research or independent of its findings. Not infrequently the student's preferred positions show up in this last chapter despite the analyses of the material. What I here call *prescriptive* normativity is similar to the kind of normativity that Don Browning termed 'strategic' and that John Swinton and Harriet Mowat referred to as 'revised' theology, that is, the last stage or the outcome of a practice–theory–practice cycle in practical theology.[21] As I noted in an earlier publication, 'Prescriptive normativity thus often takes the shape of prescribing a good, helpful, or relevant way to conduct a certain practice. Prescriptive normativity is usually offered in the shape of concrete suggestions for concrete actions.'[22] Had my study been framed in terms of prescriptive normativity, it might have been framed as 'three ways to pursue a sustainable clergy spirituality'. While it is easy to equate normative with prescriptive, I find it more helpful to understand prescriptive normativity as only one dimension or only one kind of normativity.[23]


## Fostering Reflection

What kind of normativity is at stake in the various phases of PhD research? The three forms of normativity I offer in this chapter do not constitute an exhaustive list. My hope is, however, that researchers might be helped to distinguish between *evaluative*, *rescriptive*, and *prescriptive* normativity as well as the more overall *reflexive normativity* that the researcher as Gamemaker exercises. I can sum up this chapter by ending with some question on which a researcher might reflect when working on a qualitative research project in practical theology. (1) Whose voices are represented in the field site/in the empirical material and in the academic text? (2) Where is normativity, past and present, located? – In the theological tradition? If so, then in which tradition(s)? In academic texts written by theological scholars? If so, then in which ones? In the field site? If so, in which practices and which words? With the researcher who directs the research process, that is, with the Gamemaker? We can readily note that the normative voices are not in the singular but instead are plural, and that it is an ongoing task for students and scholars alike to justify which voices are brought in, why they are brought in, which roles they are given, and how they are used.

## Notes

1 Karin Widerberg, *Historien om et kvalitativt forskningsprosjekt: En alternativ lærebok* (The story of a qualitative research project: An alternative textbook), (Oslo: Universitetsforlaget, 2001).

2 Tone S. Kaufman, 'From the Outside, Within, or Inbetween? Normativity at Work in Empirical Practical Theological Research', in *Conundrums in Practical Theology*, ed. Joyce Ann Mercer and Bonnie J. Miller-McLemore (Leiden: Brill, 2016), 135.

3 See also Tone S. Kaufman, *A New Old Spirituality? A Qualitative Study of Clergy Spirituality in the Nordic Context* (Eugene, OR: Pickwick Publications, 2017), 4–6.

4 Bonnie J. Miller-McLemore, *In the Midst of Chaos: Caring for Children as a Spiritual Practice* (San Francisco, CA: Wiley Bass, 2007).

5 See Tone S. Kaufman, 'Normativity as Pitfall or Ally? Reflexivity as an Interpretive Resource in Ecclesiological and Ethnographic Research,' *Ecclesial Practices: Journal of Ecclesiology and Ethnography* 2 (2015), 91–107.

6 See Geir S. Afdal, *Researching Religious Education as Social Practice* (Munster: Waxmann, 2010); Jan-Olav Henriksen, ed., *Difficult Normativity: Normative Dimensions in Research on Religion and Theology* (Frankfurt am Main: Peter Lang, 2011).

7 Kaufman, 'From the Outside, Within, or Inbetween?'

8 Kaufman, 'From the Outside, Within, or Inbetween?' 134–35.

9 Natalie Wigg-Stevenson, 'From Proclamation to Conversation: Ethnographic Disruptions to Theological Normativity', *Palgrave Communications: Radical Theologies* (2015), 6, http://www.palgrave-journals.com/articles/palcomms201524.

10 I first used the concept of the researcher as Gamemaker in a presentation at the annual meeting of the American Academy of Religion in San Antonio in 2016. The concept is developed in Jonas Ideström and Tone S. Kaufman, 'The Researcher as Gamemaker: Response', in *What Really Matters? Scandinavian Perspectives on Ecclesiology and Ethnography*, ed. Jonas Ideström and Tone S. Kaufman (Eugene, OR: Pickwick Publications, 2018), from which this quotation is taken. For the original use of 'Gamemaker' see Suzanne Collins, *Hunger Games* (New York: Scholastic Press, 2008).

11 The main argument of this paragraph was previously published in Kaufman, 'Normativity as Pitfall or Ally?' 91–92.

12 Helen Cameron, Deborah Bhatti, Catherine Duce, James Sweeney and Clare Watkins, *Talking about God in Practice: Theological Action Research and Practical Theology*, London: SCM Press, 2010). I earlier

published a similar description of the Four Voices of Theology in Ideström and Kaufman, 'The Researcher as Gamemaker'.

13 Summarizing Clare Watkins, with Deborah Bhatti, Helen Cameron, Catherine Duce, and James Sweeney, 'Practical Ecclesiology: What Counts as Theology in Studying the Church?' in *Perspectives on Ecclesiology and Ethnography*, ed. Pete Ward (Grand Rapids, MI: Eerdmans, 2012), 177–78.

14 This is even more explicitly spelled out in the later works of Claire Watkins. See also Tone S. Kaufman, 'From the Outside, Within, or Inbetween? Normativity at Work in Empirical Practical Theological Research' in Mercer and Miller-McLemore, *Conundrums*, 141–42.

15 See also Elaine Graham's critique of a researcher who has left themselves largely off the page: Elaine Graham, 'Research Report: Is Practical Theology a Form of "Action Research"?,' *International Journal of Practical Theology* 17 (2013), 148–78.

16 Ideström and Kaufman, 'The Researcher as Gamemaker'.

17 Kaufman, 'From the Outside, Within, or Inbetween?' 147–49.

18 For cited text see Ideström and Kaufman, 'The Researcher as Gamemaker'.

19 Wigg-Stevenson, 'From Proclamation to Conversation', 5–6.

20 Wigg-Stevenson, 'From Proclamation to Conversation', 4.

21 Don S. Browning, *A Fundamental Practical Theology: Descriptive and Strategic Proposals* (Minneapolis, MN: Fortress Press, 1991); John Swinton and Harriet Mowat, *Practical Theology and Qualitative Research* (London: SCM Press, 2006).

22 Ideström and Kaufman, 'The Researcher as Gamemaker'.

23 Kaufman, 'From the Outside, Within, or Inbetween?'; see also Ideström and Kaufman, 'The Researcher as Gamemaker' and Afdal, *Researching Religious Education*.

# 11

# Qualitative Research at Emory: Ethnographic Insights and Notes from the Field

## NICHOLE RENÉE PHILLIPS

Candler School of Theology at Emory University, in Atlanta, Georgia, has developed a deep and rich tradition of using qualitative research in teaching theology students. Teaching has been by the likes of former professors and sociologists of religion Nancy Ammerman, Nancy Eiesland, and Steven Tipton and historian Thomas E. Frank, who incorporated congregational studies into his course curricula. We have continued that tradition into the present as professors from diverse disciplinary backgrounds, ranging from Christian social ethics to cultural studies to practical theology, either use the tools of or teach qualitative research, community, and congregational studies to educate students working for Master's degrees and for the Doctor of Ministry degree. As a sociologist of religion, I place myself within this tradition of forming theology students into ministers and other religious professionals and count myself as someone who earnestly engages practical theological concerns because the study of lived religion, community, and congregational life promises new understandings of how groups construct and reconstruct theological knowledge to offer novel and varied interpretations of social existence. In support of this view, I turn to a roundtable discussion and tribute to the late and renowned sociologist Robert N. Bellah that appeared in the December 2013 issue of the *Journal of the American Academy of Religion*, in which prominent sociologists debated the status of religion in American sociology.[1]

Interlocutors offered 23 theses to overcome the secularist (and at times parochial) nature of studying religion from a sociological perspective. Here I highlight one of the 23 theses about religion's status. Partnering with disciplines like theology enables a better conceptualization of religion (i.e. the turn to sociotheology) and doing more work in comparative, historical, and ethnographic methodologies would open up more penetrating sociological understandings of religion.[2] Participants in this roundtable discussion propose that basic literacy about religion accompanied by religious knowledge about beliefs, practices, language, narratives, rituals, identities, communities, and movements – the complexities of religion – will enhance the understanding of sociologists of religion of the human species and human social life.[3]

Like these scholars I believe a deeper understanding of theology is central to understanding social life. The study of Christian faith is not only about theological anthropology (i.e. human beings' relationship with God) and concomitant creeds and doctrinal confessions, but also about the study of 'theology as a social fact', which reveals how culture and community are construed by theology as a socializing force that shapes peoples' thoughts, actions, and meaning making.[4] Furthermore, a study of religious faith as the broad study of bodily practices in society, or, more specifically, a *sociology of the body* in the form of *the Church within society*. A focus on theology as a sociology of the body raises questions about *how* bodily practices in/of the Church influence society.

Additionally, the study of religious faith is an exploration of *embodied practices* – what sociologist, anthropologist, and philosopher Pierre Bourdieu termed *social habitus*.[5] Bourdieu developed the concept of *habitus* to display the unconscious and socially learned behaviours of groups and to explain the ways in which habitual actions, mindsets, and perceptions of persons and communities become a reflection of social order and structures.[6] According to practical theologian Christian Scharen, *social habitus* captures the diversity of communal and religious practices operating within congregations (and faith communities) as well as the specificity of church cultures.[7] Through observation of and participation in the habituated routines and daily activities of religious groups, a practical logic of (their) actions is produced. Scharen concludes that investigation of habitus cannot offer a portrait of the *ideal* Church (or faith community) but can frame interpretation of the religious and social identity of the people and additional understanding of a *concrete and real* Church – a 'flesh-and-blood' organizational body wrestling with ambiguities and particularities that include pain, pleasure, attendant suffering, and inquiries about communal and social life, as well as joys and tragedy.[8] And so, in this essay I offer reflections upon one method for teaching qualitative research – ethnography – to master's level theology students I encounter at Candler School of Theology whose desire is to conduct social, cultural, and religious analyses of groups through studies of communities and congregations.

## Ethnography: Merely a Journalistic Endeavour . . . or Not

My musings about ethnography as epistemology, method, and science were prompted by a question I received at my dissertation defence, in spring 2012. The professor and social ethicist who posed the question was not necessarily challenging my use of ethnography as one of the two major research methodologies for my work and project on the social scientific study of religious practices. Rather, he wanted clarification and a rationale for my use of this methodology, even though I had been educated and trained in the anthropology and sociology of religion by two distinguished dissertation committee members. Nevertheless, he asked, 'So why is ethnography not simply description?' Almost six years later, I don't quite remember how I answered his question. Yet, I do recall pointing out the value of ethnography as more than just description, as requiring analysis and the application of theories to interpret and understand social, cultural, and religious phenomena. That response seemed sufficient at that moment. Nevertheless, I have continued to ponder my now senior colleague's question, reframed to ask: Why is ethnography *not* merely a journalistic endeavour? Does ethnographic research produce data? If so, how? What kind of data? Journalists report on local and global events all the time and much of their writing *is* descriptive, so I wonder how I differ from them in what I do as a qualitative researcher. That initial question continues to drive my instruction of students about the nature and importance of qualitative research and ethnography for construing and elucidating the religious lives of local community members and the Christian faith of congregations.

At my institution I assign qualitative research methods to curricular projects and additionally teach research methods courses to Master of Divinity (MDiv), Master of Religious Leadership (MRL), and Master of Theological Studies (MTS) degree students. Teaching has helped me decode how I differ from a journalist in my reporting about religious, cultural, and social practices and phenomena as a qualitative researcher and ethnographer approaching the collection of data from a mixed-methods perspective (i.e. qualitative and quantitative). When I offer the basic research methods course in ethnography to our MDiv and MRL students, I entitle it 'Ethnographic Research for Ministry in Congregations and Communities', because the participants are being educated primarily for ministry and pastoral practice. However, when I teach the course to students pursuing a MTS degree, who are being educated for religious and academic professions, the course is offered in the Modern Religious Thought and Experience track as the methods course 'Ethnography in Church and Community'. I amend the course to meet the needs of each student sub-population.

In this essay I share a general overview for how I teach a basic ethnography course to these three degree streams. Ethnographic research methodology is an umbrella for research methods that can stand alone. For example, consider the following qualitative research methods that a researcher can employ to study lived religion without specifically doing ethnography: participation observation; direct and indirect observation; unstructured, semi-structured and focus group interviewing; grounded theory; life story and oral history.

When I teach basic ethnographic research methods, my aim is to showcase participation observation as cultural immersion into a community, which is what distinguishes ethnography from other qualitative research methods. I also seek to provide an in-depth treatment, a step-by-step study, on how to conduct 'good' ethnographic research and to explore why religious scholars and theologians are turning to this particular qualitative research methodology to interpret and comprehend human and religious experiences. I also aspire to critically engage the objections anthropologists and sociologists might have to the appropriation by religious scholars and theologians of an empirical research method commonly used by them to understand religious experience, the nature of God and the Church. All of these factors contribute to debates about social scientific and theological normativity.

In these courses what counts as data, as theologically and social scientifically normative, is the study of social systems, systems that include religious belief and practices. By applying the theories and methods of ethnography to research in communities, students produce a fuller portrait of community, congregations, and humanity. Ethnography becomes an organizing concept and principle for students' and my grapplings with the religion-science dyad in thinking about the ways in which religion and science can arrive at and represent 'truths' about human existence. Engaging the complexity of the religion-science dyad in pursuit of 'truth' is one of the premises of these basic research methods courses.

Related to this approach is the course goal of teaching students that contextuality or the 'situatedness' of socially constructed realities do not relativize such truths. Medical anthropologist Don Seeman makes this case in another way in his essay 'Divinity Inhabits the Social: Ethnography in a Phenomenological Key', where he argues that anthropology and theology must become conversation partners:

My point is not just that religions have social contexts (this much should be obvious), but that the basic phenomena of religious life manifest in social fields, and that despite any hand-wringing about disciplinary boundaries and objectives, this means that neither anthropology nor theology can afford to avoid the phenomenology of social life where divinity (for lack of better term) 'happens'.[9]

The second course objective is in accordance with Seeman's proposal, for the aim is to develop critical and comparative approaches to ethnography as social science and as theological construct. Seeman continues,

I should admit that my view of the potential collaboration between the two disciplines will require each of them to reconfigure to some degree around phenomenological concerns. The approach I want to advocate here insists, *inter-alia*, that confrontation with the plentitude of situated human experiences will bear more significant fruit for our purposes than any degree of abstract theorizing about cultural systems or theological constructs.[10]

That goal leads to a third course objective: to encourage intellectual rigour about participation observation, which distinguishes ethnography from other qualitative research methods. By way of participation observation, ethnographic research gives credence to and illumines a multiplicity of religious, social, and cultural narratives embedded in a particular setting. For students the multidimensionality of religious thought and cultural practices is captured via field study and course readings. In truth, these dimensions of human life might not be engaged were explorations not open to the complexity and phenomenology of *lived experiences*. Ethnography privileges the lived experiences of research subjects as the grounds for empirical research, for social scientific and theological normativity.

Over the last five years, in my process of teaching this basic ethnography course to three student populations and by applying qualitative research methods to parts of my other courses, students have attained more in-depth understanding of social questions and social phenomenon – a social world. They have accomplished this by analysing communities and congregations through the lenses of qualitative research methods and of ethnography as epistemology, method, and science. Undertaken with these lenses, ethnographic research has enabled these seminarians to decipher the social order, religious practices, cultural experiences, and beliefs of church members and local community constituencies.

## Ethnographic Epistemology

Anthropologist H. Russell Bernard writes:

> Phenomenologists try to produce convincing descriptions of what they experience rather than provide explanations and causes. Good ethnography – a narrative that describes a culture or a part of culture – is usually good phenomenology, and there is still no substitute for a good story, well told – especially, if you're trying to make people understand how the people you've studied think and feel about their lives.[11]

The starting point for ethnographic study in my qualitative research methods course is the study of culture. Informed by extensive educational literature on ethnographic research methods by sociologist Margaret D. LeCompte, medical anthropologist Jean J. Schensul, and community medicine and health anthropologist Stephen L. Schensul, I take students on a fifteen-week investigation of culture that leads them down a path to ultimately offering 'middle range' theories of culture as part of advancing a 'thick description'. That path is designed around LeCompte and Schensul's assertion that 'ethnographers begin and end their work with a focus on the mindset, patterns, and traits that constitute a people's culture'.[12]

Because ethnographic research captures the mundane and spectacular aspects of everyday life and the social relationships that anchor communal and cultural life at particular times and places, ethnography is an epistemological approach. The sources of *ethnographic epistemology* are the narratives, both social and cultural, that include the religious activities of peoples. These sources inform what we understand about the nature of knowledge, how we come to know what we know about communities; and what we name as the foundations for knowledge, while also attending to the presuppositions we hold about particular social phenomenon and groups. In sum, these suppositions and sources contribute to the *cultural production of knowledge.*

Here, epistemology is method.[13] Etymologically speaking, *method* in Greek is parsed into *meta* (after) and *hodos* (a travelling, way), which when put together can be translated to mean 'on the way'. Ethnography is the route researchers travel to garner insight into people's attitudes and behaviour; qualitative researchers who select this method of inquiry employ the close-up study of social collectives to determine how people construe meaning in their social worlds.

When ethnography is epistemology, a focus on local culture enables the investigator to make more global statements about social worlds, relying upon thick description to decode social behaviour and to generate new knowledge. Aldiabat and Le Navenec's findings support my contention.[14] Both researchers propose that ethnography is epistemologically anchored by and oriented toward *symbolic interactionism*, a sociological concept justifying the role of social relationships in human beings' ability to shape the world in which they live; symbolic interaction likewise asserts that human-to-human social interactions lay the foundation for people's understanding of their social realities. The concept is essential to describing psycho-social processes and to guiding researchers toward a pragmatic view, also a feature of ethnographic epistemology, that asserts that 'the empirical truth of reality can be emerged only by visiting the research field, observ[ing] the participants, and analyz[ing] their actual meanings in the real setting'.[15]

Sociologist of religion Justin J. Latterell offers a slightly different but consistent view of the type of social knowledge garnered from qualitative research:

My main course is an introductory survey of classical and contemporary sociological theories of religion, along with lots of case studies. It is not (primarily) a methods class. Thus, I use and rely upon sociological and (social) anthropological theories and case studies that exhibit diverse qualitative methods, and don't consciously teach qualitative research through a single philosophical lens. That said, my teaching and assigned readings do have a phenomenological and institutional bias: similar to anthropologist Don Seeman, I am very interested in observing and interpreting the 'lived experiences' of religious people(s). And similar to sociologist Steve Tipton, I am interested in understanding the ideas and practices that constitute social institutions, and catalyze or create social and institutional change.[16]

Latterell's comments are in line with my contention that ethnography is epistemology. As one qualitative research method, ethnography is educative about social institutions and processes of social change, yielding information about the social worlds of individuals and groups. It produces knowledge about their social arrangements, about how and why they think and act in the ways that they do. On that account, from mid-semester to the end of the course term, students are required to read ethnographies about churches and communities written primarily by scholars of religion, sociologists, and anthropologists who conduct ethnographic research and whose studies incorporate religion and religious belief in some form. Because I am intentional about forming theological ethnographers and theo-critical ethnographic researchers, I select ethnographies marked by the distinctions of gender, ethnicity, class, race, religion, and region, placing anthropology and sociology in conversation with theology even as I use social scientific theories and positivistic thinking to accomplish such goals.[17]

One of the ethnographies students read is Eric Ramírez-Ferrero's *Troubled Fields: Men, Emotions, and the Crisis of American Farming*, a study of the social, political, and economic complexities surrounding the collapse in the 1980s of the agricultural industry in parts of America and its effects on a rural north-western Oklahoma farming community, which witnessed an increased in the number of deaths of white male farmers by suicide.[18] Although the text targets a local culture, the author eventually makes a more general assessment of the positive and negative impact of technological innovation on family farms and by default on a more communal way of life. For the (white) men for whom farming was intergenerational, care of farm land shaped their masculinity by facilitating a special connection to God, allowing them to become conduits of the divine. Their cultivation of the farmland translated into acts of procreation that 'established an association between men as genitors and God as creator'.[19]

Seeman has proposed that

> theologies serve as important repositories of differentiated cultural knowledge that needs to be taken as seriously as any other data we [ethnographers] collect in fieldwork on societies in which they have played an influential role. Theological ways of thinking about or interacting with the world are, on this level, 'social facts' like any other. But theologies may also point to the theoretical or analytic insights that contribute in their own right to the generation of better and more adequate account of human affairs.[20]

The onset of globalization as 'the process of capitalist expansion across national boundaries' upset these men's special connection to God through their care of the land, which I identify as a *contextual theology* rising to the distinction of *contextual theology as a social fact*.[21] Strivings for financial prosperity in the American farming industry collided with cultural norms that were disrupting the local way of life. Subsequently, because residents were sacrificing communal values, suicides among male farmers in rural north-western Oklahoma drastically increased. Hence, a study of a local, state-wide, and regional public health and cultural problem on the micro-level yielded macro-level implications in Ramírez-Ferrerro's text.

Ethnography as epistemology also concerns the positionality of the researcher in the particular culture, church, or community where religious and social phenomena are under study. Dorinne Kondo considers the prevailing power dynamics that are part of the interactions between ethnographers and informants and the ways in which these series of interactions ultimately influence descriptive configurations of culture and community and concludes that the relative positioning of the researcher affects the interpretation of the society that is produced.[22] In this capacity, 'positioning' refers to researchers' familiarity relative to and with their research subjects, with some entering into a community as *emic* (i.e. as an insider) and others as *etic* (i.e. as an outsider) to the social group. Researchers can also be both emic and etic to churches, communities, and cultures. The researcher enters into their work with an epistemological framing of the cultural or social group that affects the formulation of new knowledge.

The religion and science debate is often characterized as contentious because of each discipline's claims to absolute truth. By studying ethnography as epistemology students are given room to wrestle with this topic, which sheds light on issues of social scientific and theological normativity. Religious scholars and theologians who apply qualitative research methods to religious phenomena have stirred the debate with their assertion that applying ethnography to the study of religion turns out a practical ethic.[23] In other words, Scharen proposes, 'the place of knowledge is embedded in forms of life, or to put it simply, in practice.'[24] This is another example of what Pierre Bourdieu named *social habitus*.[25]

More precisely, for religious-studies scholars, the use of qualitative research to explore religious cultures and practices has translated into more nuanced interpretations of the symbols, actions, convictions, and nature of religious adherents and their institutions of worship. For theologians the application of qualitative research methods is a 'turn to culture' that privileges the particularities of congregational practice, beliefs and life to apprehend and make statements about the nature of God and the Church.[26] When researchers transform into observant participants of the embodied practices of church members, they both observe and have access to a God made incarnate, which opens them up to a *carnal theology*.[27]

To initiate conversation about social scientific and theological normativities, students are assigned readings for the first six weeks of the semester that explain why theologians and religious studies scholars now turn to qualitative research to understand religious experience. Alongside that work, students are also assigned readings at the intersection of ecclesiology and ethnography and in the more technical areas of ethnographic research methodology. Each week's required readings are geared to promoting student comparisons of 'social scientific ethnography' and 'theological ethnography'.[28] They are left with the following questions: How are the methodologies similar and how are they different? And, Is theological ethnography a viable means of studying religious conviction and culture? Students are assigned weekly critical thinking and reflection notes to begin to elicit responses to those questions. Byron Wratee contends:

> In the theological world, historical and contemporary perspectives are important in ethnographic research. Theology and theological traditions are mostly inherited. You have to have a firm understanding of historical meaning behind religious practices before you can understand how and why people have perpetuated or revised those practices. Admittedly, current cultural and social norms do dictate '*lived* church.' Nevertheless, 'lived church' is a continuation or tradition-ing of practices.[29]

He also comments:

> Ethnography as a social science explains phenomena through observable efficient causes; theological ethnography may use efficient causes, but it ultimately seeks to explain phenomena through final causes. The difference is *descriptive* versus *normative* claims. Theological ethnography is systematic theology, particularly ecclesiology seen through descriptive and eschatological lens. Scharen and Vigen have convinced me that theological ethnography is a branch of ecclesiology. It is not sociology.

Theologians are merely using ethnographic epistemology and sociological methods to engage in systematic theology. It is not sociology or anthropology, but informed theology. I might be wrong, but that's where I stand.[30]

By the end of the six weeks, students often conclude that both theo-critical ethnography and social scientific ethnography are viable research methods, as different means to produce epistemological data about religious practices, institutions, and cultures that become sources of new knowledge. The students come to this conclusion because of the dialogical character of religion and science, not in spite of it. Nonetheless, there are challenges to using either methodology for interpreting religious and theological belief, practice, and behaviour. When ethnography is epistemology, overcoming theology's association with normative claims becomes improbable.

By virtue of its nature, theology possesses the potential to transcend scientific knowledge, for theology is founded on both what is and what is not observable. Yet social scientific ethnography is based on what is phenomenologically sensed as social experience and, additionally, on reducing the complex into simple terms (i.e. scientific reductionism). Like theology, it can be re-envisioned by what is and what is not observable. As a result, researchers who defend the validity of either or both methodologies face continual valiant struggles.

Yet anthropologist Seeman leaves us with the following thought: 'theology is not just a data field to be mined . . . but a prism that can help me, a [social scientist], to see things I might otherwise have been blind to'.[31] With Seeman's words in mind, Latterell gives his appraisal of how he grows as a sociologist and how his theology students are transformed – stretched and changed – by employing qualitative research like ethnography to theological settings and what theological learnings emerge as a result. He declares:

I incorporate a lot of qualitative studies, and some quantitative research, into my courses. My Sociology of Religion course, for example, draws on the field of (social) anthropology – e.g. Bronislaw Malinowski, Clifford Geertz, W.E.B. DuBois, Susan Kahn, Marla Frederick, and more. I assign a research paper in which I ask students to engage the following prompt: 'Describe the form(s) and social function(s) of religion(s) in relation to a particular group, sphere, or institution.' I introduce corresponding ethnographic research methods, including participant observation and interviews, etc., and many students in the past have completed ethnographic studies of particular communities, groups, or practices in the Atlanta area.

Students are often surprised to learn, on the one hand, how loosely related to individuals' lives and religious praxes the formal beliefs and institutional frameworks of the communities they study are. On the other hand, many students are surprised to learn just how profoundly religious communities, relationships, practices, and ideas can be in the lives of individuals who belong to those communities. These experiences shape students from theoretical or abstract thinkers, to practical and attentive observers of complex and dynamic social phenomena.[32]

The sociology, anthropology, and theology cross-disciplinary encounters that take place during the learning process profoundly stretch the mindsets and disrupt the thoughts and actions of theology students. Latterell's comment suggests the socially transforming nature of theology, outside the realm of the numinous. That transformation can happen especially when theology is incorporated into an investigation of social and cultural processes, processes that are under qualitative study.

## Ethnography as Method

Cultural anthropology is the scientific study of human behaviour, societies, and cultures. The hallmark of cultural anthropology is ethnography. Ethnography is a systematic approach to investigating social relationships, to conducting cross-cultural explorations, and to studying the behavioural characteristics of institutions, communities, persons, and groups. Here, ethnography is an instrument of anthropology and sociology and is a research method used to study culture.

Sociologist Norman Denzin claims: 'The ethnographer who wishes to understand another [subject] has to build up an understanding based on a deep involvement in the subject's world of experience. This means the subject is transformed into a person who is no longer the object of an external voyeuristic gaze.'[33] Denzin's quotation points out the distinguishing feature of ethnographic research method in comparison to other qualitative research methodologies: participant observation. Successful ethnographies are achieved by nurturing trustful relationships with key members of a community and by developing faithful relationships with other members of a cultural group. Subsequently, the primary research instrument for conducting ethnographies is the researcher, whose immersive experience is the method for gaining close proximity to and entrée into daily life activities.

Ethnographers operate as culture bearers and strive to walk in the footsteps of social group members. Being sensitive to the culture (i.e. patterns of behaviour and thinking) of institutions, they are then able to assess and evaluate the power dynamics in social structures. Moreover, as culture bearers, ethnographers employ empathy to see how group members are seeing their own social systems. Ethnographers use of the participant observation method assists community, social groups, and church members to grasp features of their social systems that they see and do not see.

Ethnography as method invariably turns to ethnographic self-reflexivity. Students learn that ethnographic self-reflexivity is a critical component of researchers' positionality: it affords researchers the opportunity to reflect on their experiences of social and cultural immersion. Ethnographic self-reflexivity provides a way for ethnographers to gauge their presumptions and to determine how such preconceptions might shift or contribute to institutional power dynamics. Students are assigned cultural anthropologist and womanist scholar Marla Frederick's *Between Sundays: Black Women and Everyday Struggles of Faith* as one model of scholarship anchored in critical self-reflexivity.[34] Student Wesley Smithart wrote:

> Frederick uses her introduction to explain the importance and sphere of her research along with her own positionality: 'As a practitioner of the faith, I made my inquiry into the spiritual lives of women in a deliberate effort to unpack the dynamics of a lived experience that I have witnessed since childhood' [Frederick, *Between Sundays*, p. 20]. She acknowledges the reality of 'partial truth' in ethnographic work as well as the way positionality informs one's data.[35]

Not only does Smithart point out the significance of engaging in self-reflection as a researcher, but her comments also point to the potential limitations of scientific explorations, particularly when they address ultimate concerns. Regardless of claims to impartiality and neutrality, scientific research might be able to supply only 'partial truths'. Howsoever, I still encourage students to engage in critical self-reflection, asking them to maintain an ethnographic self-reflexivity journal where they capture their feelings, thoughts, and prejudgements as they conduct fieldwork for their basic ethnography. This exercise in self-reflexivity is another prism for collecting and analysing 'data' as well for clarifying information about the lives of religious practitioners in local social contexts such as a community or Church that is captured by the participant observation method and reflected in field notes, interviews, and the life stories of participants.

## Ethnography as Science

Ethnography is social research – the scientific study of humanity and specifically the arts, customs, mindset, behaviour, religion, values (i.e. artefacts) of social groups. In this space, ethnography in a social world achieves the debatable status of a *science* that produces information about the lives of everyday people.[36] Ethnographic research, and qualitative research generally, cannot be conducted outside the norms of science because in this case ethnography is human social research guided by the dictates of positivism.[37] I teach my students the norms of science, explaining that the scientific method uses induction and deduction in the process of approving and disproving theories and approaching but never reaching truth.[38]

And so, I guide Candler's theology students through the scientific method to prepare them to learn how to develop formative theories and contentions as well as primary questions to be investigated via field research. At the same time, I teach them about the recursive processes of deductive and inductive reasoning. Students are taught about using a mixed-methods approach to understand social and congregational life and religious belief and practices. They learn that qualitative and quantitative approaches complement each other and are important to the collection of data. They learn that grounded theory is the outcome of a research process requiring thick description that engages theories to describe social practices and decipher religious and cultural phenomena.

The irony of teaching theology students how to conduct research for a 'theological ethnography' is that they must embrace empiricism to a certain extent in order to realize the process of theo-critical ethnographic research. This might be the only case where science serves religion. Stated another way, this might also be the only case where ethnography as science is in service to the interdisciplinary, humanistic discipline of 'theological ethnography'. However, as theology students sit with new knowledge of and insight into human and lived religion, religious experiences, and the nature of God and the Church as a result of conducting qualitative research as ethnography, they realize there is more than one path to truth – about themselves, people, groups, God, and congregational life. And so, Latterell explains:

By teach[ing] theology students and undergraduate students, I have learned their perspectives and comfort with engaging qualitative research in my class varies less by degree program, and more by their membership in particular religious (or not) communities, families, and so on. Qualitative research case studies tend to disabuse everyone of some of their biases, whether they are biased against religion(s) or biased in favor of a particular religious tradition. Qualitative research adds texture – often untidy, inspiring, perplexing, and intriguing texture – to their preconceived notions and easy assumptions about what religion is.[39]

Sabrina Thomas, an MTS theology student informed by Mary Clark Moschella's *Ethnography as Pastoral Practice: An Introduction* and other assigned readings, concluded the semester surmising that the strength of qualitative research and ethnography for interpretation of social worlds lies in analysis of the power dynamics inherent to social institutions.[40] As well, she highlighted the gift of voice granted to study participants by theological ethnographers who hear the religious narratives and write the stories of people in distinct social and cultural contexts in order to promote social change. Thomas confessed,

There is value in hearing the full range of experiences from those within the group as well as outside of it in order to understand where the seeds of change lie. While we can appreciate the value of disruptive narratives, there is a genuine fear of the interrogation and possible loss of power. For pastoral leaders there seems to be a need to move toward a sense of shared power among congregants and leadership. Pastors and theological ethnographers have to understand that giving marginalized individuals the power to speak is related to the power to change. This power of change is not to be attributed as power loss, but as power gained because these voices aid in understanding where injustices arise within the current power structure and methods in which to eradicate them. Moschella notes that there are links between personal voice and interpersonal change and social transformations. While these transformations are slow, they give way to awareness of one another and also ourselves within our communities.[41]

## Conclusion

As I remember the scene of my dissertation defence six years ago, I can now more definitively answer that query into the nature of ethnography and explain why qualitative research is not solely description or an exercise in journalistic reporting but instead supplies information about our social worlds. I declare ethnography to be (1) an *epistemological method* that uses the intellectual traditions of phenomenology, positivism, social interactionism, and pragmatism to garner interpretations, meaning, and comprehension of human life and cultural groups through the power of social relationships and interactions; (2) a *research method* of anthropology and sociology that uses the researcher as the primary research tool to gain such knowledge; and (3) *social research* (i.e. a science), as a systematic method analysing humanity and cultural phenomena to accumulate reliable knowledge about these social groups, religious practices, and institutions. Ethnography as epistemology, method, and science includes the study of religion and theology and therefore produces generous interpretations and elucidations of our social world.

### Notes

1 Christian Smith, Brandon Vaidyanathan, Nancy Ammerman, José Casanova, Hilary Davidson, Elaine Howard Ecklund, John H. Evans, Mary Ellen Konieczny, Jason A. Springs, Jenny Trinitapoli, and Meredith Whitnah, 'Roundtable on the Sociology of Religion: Twenty-Three Theses on the Status of Religion in American Sociology – A Mellon Working Group Reflection', *Journal of the American Academy of Religion* 81, 4 (2013), 903–38.

2 Smith et al., 'Roundtable', 925–26.

3 Smith et al., 'Roundtable', 909–11, 927.

4 Don Seeman, 'Divinity Inhabits the Social: Ethnography in a Phenomenological Key', in D. Lemons, ed., *Theologically Engaged Anthropology* (New York: Oxford University Press, 2017), 1–31.

5 Pierre Bourdieu, *Pascalian Meditations* (1997), cited in Loïc Wacquant, *Body & Soul: Notebooks of an Apprentice Boxer* (New York: Oxford University Press, 2004), viii; and Pierre Bourdieu, *The Logic of*

*Practice*, trans. Richard Nice (Stanford, CA: Stanford University Press, 1990).

6 Wacquant, *Body & Soul*.

7 Christian Scharen, *Fieldwork in Theology: Exploring the Social Context of God's Work in the World* (Grand Rapids, MI: Baker Academic, 2015), 80–82.

8 Scharen, *Fieldwork*, 80–87.

9 Seeman, 'Divinity', 2.

10 Seeman, 'Divinity', 2.

11 H. Russell Bernard, 'Anthropology and the Social Sciences', *Research Methods in Anthropology: Qualitative and Quantitative Approaches* (5th edn; Lanham, MD: AltaMira Press, 2011), 20.

12 In teaching ethnography, I place 'ethnography' in conversation with 'grounded theory'. Ethnography is a study of the cultural patterns of social groups to offer a 'thick description' – explanation of cultural behaviour, mindset, motivations and shared values, beliefs and actions of groups based on decoding social practices and cultural phenomena. Like ethnography, grounded theory investigates events and social experiences from the perspective of the research subject while comprehending such experiences from the subjects' view. Yet, grounded theory endeavours, more than does ethnography, 'to generate theory that describes basic psychosocial phenomena and to understand how human beings use social interaction to define their reality'. Grounded theory produces middle range theory. 'Middle range theory', a sociological term discussed by Robert K. Merton, is a theory with limited scope that serves to explain a specific set of phenomena. When we speak of middle range theory, we are signalling theory construction, which is distinct from a grand theory that seeks to describe and unpack the meaning of phenomena at a societal level. Middle range theory concentrates on measurable aspects of social reality as opposed to producing theory that can be applied to an entire social world. See Khaldoun Aldiabat and Carole-Lynne Le Navenec, 'Clarification of the Blurred Boundaries between Grounded Theory and Ethnography: Differences and Similarities,' *Turkish Online Journal of Qualitative Inquiry* 2, 3 (2011), 2–3, 6, 8–9, and Margaret D. LeCompte and Jean J. Schensul, *Designing & Conducting Ethnographic Research: An Introduction* (Lanham, MD: AltaMira Press, 2010), 24.

13 Bernard, 'Anthropology and Social Science', 20.

14 Aldiabat and Le Navenec, 'Clarification', 4–5.

15 Barney G. Glaser, *Basics of Grounded Theory Analysis: Emergence vs. Forcing* (1992) in Khaldoun Aldiabat and Carole-Lynne Le Navenec, 'Clarification of the Blurred Boundaries between Grounded Theory and Ethnography: Differences and Similarities', *Turkish Online Journal of Qualitative Inquiry* 2, 3 (July 2011), 5.

16 Justin J. Latterell, interview by Nichole Phillips, at Candler School of Theology, Emory University, Atlanta, GA, 27 February 2017.

17 I use the term 'theo-critical' for researchers who are able to perceive the benefits of using ethnography to offer more comprehensive understandings of theology's turn to culture and away from the conventionality of philosophy and the history of ideas. Further, theo-critical ethnographers are socialized into a classroom culture in which they think critically about social scientific ethnography and ethnographic theology in order to sort through the benefits and drawbacks of both methodologies. Theo-critical ethnographers consider conversations across anthropology, sociology, and theology that propose a more theologically engaged anthropology and socio-theology.

18 Eric Ramírez-Ferrero, *Troubled Fields: Men, Emotions, and the Crisis in American Farming* (New York: Columbia University, 2005).

19 Ramírez-Ferrero, *Troubled Fields*, 161.

20 Seeman, 'Divinity', 3.

21 For the quotation: Ramírez-Ferrero, *Troubled Fields*, 171.

22 Dorinne Kondo, 'Dissolution and Reconstitution of Self: Implications for Anthropological Epistemology,' *Cultural Anthropology* 1, 1 (1986), 75, 84–85.

23 Christian Scharen, 'The Ethnographic Turn in Theology and Ethics,' in *Ethnography as Christian Theology and Ethics*, ed. Christian Scharen and Anna Marie Vigen (New York: Continuum, 2011), 33.

24 Scharen, 'Ethnographic Turn', 33.

25 See Scharen, 'Ethnographic Turn', 28–46.

26 For 'turn to culture' see Scharen, 'Ethnographic Turn', 28.

27 Scharen, 'Ethnographic Turn', 42–44, and Scharen, *Fieldwork*, 104–6. *Carnal theology* derives from the 'practice of dispossession' and is like habitus in that the routine and habitual action of 'emptying oneself' (*kenosis*) should compel individuals to engage social suffering and other social realities and to act more ethically towards other persons.

28 I have developed the term 'theological ethnography' for teaching, learning, and theoretical purposes as distinguishing from what trained anthropologists and sociologists do in conducting 'social scientific ethnography'.

29 Students are asked to engage assigned readings actively and to produce critical reflections on such assigned readings, which I have named 'Interactive Notes'. Byron Wratee, Interactive Notes, 27 January 2016. Used by permission.

30 Wratee, Interactive Notes.

31 Seeman, 'Divinity', 3.

32 Justin J. Latterell, interview by Nichole Phillips, Atlanta, GA, February 27, 2017.

33 Norman K. Denzin, *Interpretive Ethnography: Ethnographic Practices for the 21st Century* (Thousand Oaks, CA: Sage, 1997), 35.

34 Marla F. Frederick, *Between Sundays: Black Women and Everyday Struggles of Faith* (Berkeley, CA: University of California Press, 2003).

35 Wesley Smithart, 'Developing a Roadmap (i.e. Research Design) using Mixed Methods – Qualitative, Quantitative Methods, and Interviewing', Interactive Notes. Used by permission.

36 Identifying ethnography as a science is contestable because of broader conversations happening in social scientific disciplines, particularly anthropology and sociology, with regard to positivism. Positivism is a philosophy of science that counts knowledge as valid when it has been subjected to scientific inquiry and testing of hypotheses – known as the scientific method. The scientific method is the general procedure for generating, testing, and validating scientific knowledge via the 'hypothetico-deductive method.' Thomas Schweizer has laid out a history of, and other information about, the positivist thrust in anthropology; see Thomas Schweizer, 'Epistemology: The Nature and Validation of Anthropological Knowledge', in *Handbook of Methods in Cultural Anthropology*, ed. H. Russell Bernard (Lanham, MD: AltaMira Press, 1998), 39–87. He argues that the positivism of Auguste Comte is not the narrow-minded depiction of data collection and acceptance of the status quo that we experience today. Schweizer has embraced the 'historical' and original interpretation of the term that has not fully survived into the modern century. When he speaks of positivism he is putting forward a 'diverse and analytic philosophy of science rooted in clarity of language, empirical inquiry, the validation of truth claims by means of rational logic, and one that is research-oriented seeking to establish laws or quasi-laws of human nature that can explain historical events and processes' (45–46). This form of positivism is an analytic philosophy of science meant to explain nature, society and culture. It can be applied to the scientific disciplines and/or the humanities. Similar to Schweizer, sociologist Norman K. Denzin reports on the 'positivist resistance' to qualitative research, which would include ethnography; see Norman K. Denzin and Yvonne S. Lincoln, 'Introduction: The Discipline and Practice of Qualitative Research' in *The Sage Handbook of Qualitative Research*, eds Norman K. Denzin and Yvonne S. Lincoln (Thousand Oaks, CA: Sage Publications, 2011), 1–20. Denzin argues that qualitative research embraces two tensions at the same time. The first is more broadly interpretive, postexperimental, and postmodern. The second holds more positivist, postpositivist, and naturalistic conceptions of human experience and its analysis. Yet, both tensions can be combined in the same study (6). Both Schweizer and Denzin elaborate on and reveal the internal struggles in the social sciences, especially anthropology and sociology, with respect to naming 'qualitative research' as 'quasi'-positivistic

(i.e. scientific) or not. Such disciplinary wrangling bears upon decisions social scientists and others make regarding 'ethnography as a science'.

37 Anthropologist H. Russell Bernard describes positivism as a system that transcends theology and metaphysics (i.e. explanation of social phenomenon by immaterial forces like the mind, spirit, or a deity). Positivism contends that sensory experience is the only admissible basis of knowledge and that the scientific method as well as the hierarchy of the sciences, beginning with mathematics and ending with sociology, verifies knowledge. It is a rejection of theism, rationalism, and metaphysics.

38 Bernard, 'Anthropology', 4–9.

39 Justin J. Latterell, interview by Nichole Phillips, Atlanta, GA, 27 February 2017.

40 Mary Clark Moschella, *Ethnography as a Pastoral Practice: An Introduction* (3rd edn; Cleveland, OH: Pilgrim Press, 2008).

41 Sabrina Thomas, 'Who Should Use Ethnography?' Interactive Notes, 2016. Used by permission.

# 12

# Qualitative Research: The Invaluable Tool in Pastoral Ministry

## BERNARDINE KETELAARS

The methods of qualitative research are utilized in my teaching at St Peter's Seminary in London, Ontario, where, in addition to other responsibilities, I serve as Director of Pastoral Formation. In addition to overseeing the field education placements through which the students often interact with individuals or groups and then reflect on experiences theologically, I also teach a course entitled 'Mission and Ministry in the Church of the Twenty-first Century' – formerly 'Missiology and Evangelization' – in which the students are asked to implement the qualitative research method in their main assignment, which will be described below. In the few years that I have utilized this method in the classroom, students have indicated that the experience has proven to be invaluable to them and their ministry.

Prior to coming to St Peter's Seminary, I served for 20 years as executive assistant to the bishop of the diocese of London, and for seven years before that as a parish secretary. In both roles, a constant was the gathering of numbers and statistics for various reports, such as parish censuses and the Quinquennial Report, which was sent to the Vatican ahead of the bishop's visit with the pope. Quantitative surveys and questionnaires were the methods of choice when seeking the number of registered versus active parishioners, when preparing sacramental reports, or when procuring the required information for the reports to be sent to Rome. The numbers were tools utilized by diocesan leadership and administration as they considered the necessary course of action. What I came to realize, however, was that we were not always fully informed as to what was causing the fluctuation in the numbers garnered for the various reports or studies. Quantitative studies were utilized at a higher rate as we began to experience the phenomenon of individuals and families withdrawing from their faith communities. It was obvious that this phenomenon was not unique to the Roman Catholic Church; most mainline Christian Churches were experiencing similar trends. What concerned me, however, was that decisions were being made based primarily on the numbers, with the leadership not always seeking the cause for the results which were presented. The 'lived experience' of those walking away was not being considered.[1] Metaphorically we might say that an epidemic was occurring, but a diagnosis was being made and a treatment prescribed prior to examination and comprehension of all the symptoms.

While serving as the executive assistant to the bishop, I attended numerous meetings at which I would take minutes. Listening intently to the discussions around the current trends, I began to consider more deeply the decline in the number of Catholic Christians partaking in the worship and community life of the Church. I could not help but question how we were going to reverse this trend if we did not know what was feeding this phenomenon, the factors causing this epidemic. It was then that I finalized my topic for my doctoral thesis: implementing qualitative research, I would begin listening to the stories of individuals who no longer practised their faith in the Roman Catholic Church. There was much speculation as to the causes for this phenomenon in the Church, such as priests not being free to marry or the restriction which prohibited women from being ordained, but questions that would seek out the facts were not being asked. On the flip side, if a faith community was doing well, growing in leaps and bounds, it was not always known what the community offered that attracted individuals and families to their house of worship. Even if the question did come up for discussion among those recognizing the trend, no actions were taken to reach out to discover and comprehend the lived experience.

In 2003 the diocese of London began to take the necessary steps to cluster some parishes and suppress others in order to move toward forming more vibrant communities of faith.[2] This reality was being experienced in a number of dioceses throughout North America, including, for example, the archdioceses of Boston and Detroit.[3] Many factors made this restructuring necessary: the financial climate and its effects on the day-to-day life of the parish communities; aging church buildings requiring major renovations; a decrease in the number of Catholics attending Mass and celebrating the sacraments; and a fall in the numbers of those responding to the call of ordained ministry while the average age of priests in active ministry was rising. These are only a few of the factors influencing the culture at the time.

A couple of years after I began my doctoral studies, the diocese of London invited a planning consultant – whose services had been utilized in the past by the diocese – to prepare a statistical projections and analysis report. The report states:

> In terms of average weekly Mass attendance, one sometimes hears a figure of approximately 450,000 to 475,000 Catholics identified as residing within the Diocese of London by 2010. Based on 2010 average weekend mass attendance of 64,656 individuals, this would result in an average participation range by London Diocese Catholics of 13.6% to 14.4% per weekend average.[4]

Though the reality of declining church attendance was not surprising, one could not help but be alarmed when the numbers were presented in black and white. The statistical projections and analysis report made real that which had been suspected all along. Filled out with data, trends could be noted. All of this information was necessary as the diocese of London was considering its next steps. What did not sit well with me, however, was that the study ended here; no one was asking those who were part of the statistics the question *why?* Why did they feel the need to withdraw; what indicators were they receiving that made them search elsewhere or disconnect from 'organized religion' altogether? Two and a half years prior to the publication of the report, I decided that my doctoral work would seek to address this issue, to ask why and determine what was feeding this phenomenon. My study was entitled 'Harkening to the Voices of the Lost Ones: Attending to the Stories of Baptized Roman Catholics No Longer Participating in the Worship and Community Life of the Church'. Who are the 'Lost Ones'?

> The *Lost Ones* are the 'dispersed children of God' (John 11.52). It is important to note that these 'dispersed children' are not lost to God but to the community in which they had previously worshipped. They are those who have slowly withdrawn from the practice of their faith or who at one point intentionally broke any ties with the Church. They are those who no longer feel welcomed by the universal Church or by the local community of faith. They are the *disenchanted, the disheartened, and the disillusioned*. The *Lost Ones* are those baptized into the faith, who no longer participate in the worship and community life of the Roman Catholic Church, and whose stories need to be heard if any form of reconciliation or reunion is deemed possible.[5]

## Finding and Implementing the Method

During my doctoral studies, I was introduced to John Creswell's book *Qualitative Inquiry and Research Design: Choosing Among Five Approaches*, through which I discovered various methods of qualitative research.[6] Upon reviewing the 'contrasting characteristics' of the various approaches proposed by Creswell, I recognized that the method required for a comprehensive study of this trend would be hermeneutic phenomenology. This method would lead me to a deeper understanding of the lived experience of those who had withdrawn from the worship and community life of the Church. The core reasons for this phenomenon might be discovered if the narratives were analysed using Creswell's 'simplified version of the Stevick-Colaizzi-Keen method discussed by Clark E. Moustakas'.[7]

The next step was to conduct a search for participants who met certain criteria pertinent to the study: (1) were 18 years of age or older; (2) had been baptized in the Roman Catholic Church and prior to their withdrawal had attended Mass on a weekly basis; (3) had been away from the Roman Catholic Church for more than three years; and (4) were interested in sharing their faith experience through a one-on-one interview. The search resulted in 18 willing participants – ten women and eight men between the ages of 20 and 75. In order to obtain a non-biased approach, family members and close acquaintances were excluded from the study.

It was imperative that the interviews be held in a safe and welcoming environment. To that end they did not take place in a church building or in any of the diocesan offices; they were conducted in a study lab at the Cardinal Carter Library, King's University College, London, Ontario. In a room with windows looking into the library, the participants never felt secluded – this met the requirements of the diocese of London's *Safe Environment Policy*.[8] If the library was not convenient for the participant, other arrangements were made, for example an interview over Skype or a meeting at a place proposed by the participant that still adhered to the *Safe Environment Policy*.

The participants were made aware of my role at the Diocesan Centre prior to the interviews. I sensed that my not being in a leadership position within the diocese left the participants comfortable, allowing them to freely share their experiences. In an attempt to keep the participants relaxed, our time together was not overly structured. In addition, they were assured that they could review and approve the typed transcript of their interview prior to my moving forward; this provided the participant with the opportunity not only to assess what they had said, but also to add anything they might have missed or delete any segment they did not wish kept in the copy I would be referring to during the research process. Upon meeting the participants, most of them for the first time, I welcomed them, reviewed the consent process, and turned on the tape recorder to begin the time of sharing. The conversation began with a few preliminary questions but then the participant was free to tell their story. During this time, unless immediate clarification was required by either the participant or the researcher, they were neither interrupted nor prompted. If certain issues were not made clear during the sharing of their lived experience, I would address these matters prior to asking the closing questions. The shortest interview lasted 13 minutes, and the longest almost an hour and a half; the average time was around the one-hour mark.

## Holy Conversation

I felt privileged to have listened to these stories and viewed our time together as *holy conversation*. My practising attentive and intentional listening was imperative. As the researcher, I needed not only to listen to what was being said, but also to be attentive to body language and hesitancies, while remaining attuned to what was *not* being said. Henri Nouwen refers to this type of listening as 'spiritual hospitality':

> To listen is very hard, because it asks of us so much interior stability that we no longer need to prove ourselves by speeches, arguments, statements, or declarations. True listeners no longer have an inner need to make their presence known. They are free to receive, to welcome, to accept. Listening is much more than allowing another to talk while waiting for a chance to respond. Listening is paying full attention to others and welcoming them into our very beings. The beauty of listening is that those who are listened to start feeling accepted, start taking their words more seriously and discovering their own true selves. Listening is a form of spiritual hospitality by which you invite strangers to become friends, to get to know their inner selves more fully, and even to dare to be silent with you.[9]

This reflection by Nouwen is paralleled by Max van Manen, a professor of qualitative research methods at the University of Alberta, who views research as a 'caring act'.[10] What transpired from this time of holy conversation was a richer understanding of why individuals and families were withdrawing from the Church, and most of the participants expressed their gratitude for this opportunity to share their story and take the time to reflect on what had led them to their current faith practice or lack thereof. At the beginning of my doctoral research, a couple of colleagues questioned the reasoning behind such a study, noting we already knew the reasons for the withdrawal of baptized Catholics from the Church. Reasons cited included, but were not limited to, the Church's stance on life issues and homosexuality, the need to allow for women to be ordained and/or married priests, and the abuse scandal. Having completed the study, I could recognize that although these issues were mentioned throughout several of the stories shared, for the most part they were not the reasons given for the participants' final break from the Church community. The issues were more intimate and personal, more pastoral than doctrinal.

Four common threads were woven through the research. Topping the list, the lack of hospitality and community within the parishes resounded many times during these periods of conversation; when these conditions were lacking, nothing remained to compel the participants to return to the church building . . . not even the Eucharist. In addition, I heard that spirituality was not dead – whether or not the participant had joined another faith community, spirituality was still being expressed and lived in a variety of ways. One participant stated, 'Just because I don't go to church every week doesn't mean I don't believe in God. I do pray.' The need for ongoing faith formation and the importance of vibrant homilies that would connect sacred Scripture with today's culture were other issues repeatedly identified throughout the interviews. The findings reached by utilizing qualitative methods in research confirmed my initial intuition that delving into the lived experience of this phenomenon was needed in order to uncover the factors causing the epidemic. Those who participated in the project were no longer simply a statistic. Even though this was a relatively small sample, my research provided pastoral insights for diocesan and parish leaders.

## Qualitative Research as a Tool in Pastoral Formation

The themes and concerns heard loud and clear throughout the sharing of lived experiences, and through further reflection, provided me with much to consider as I prepared for a new career that focused on the formation of future priests and lay ecclesial ministers. In my role as Director of Lay Formation and Director of Field Education and as a teacher of mission and ministry, resounding in my mind and heart I felt the need to prepare men and women who would desire to minister in a way that might seem radical and counter-cultural. Rather than seeking authority and power, focusing solely on administrative and temporal issues, and closing doors to those who do not fit the mould, these men and women must hold within their hearts the desire to minister as Jesus did: to go to the peripheries, to seek out those who are wandering, to be a voice of hope, and to welcome with outstretched arms those who approach them when there seems to be nowhere else for them to turn.

Reflecting on the benefits gained throughout my doctoral studies, it became clear that to achieve this goal I would need to make qualitative research methods central in my courses. In the field education placements, students are invited to be truly attentive to the ones to whom they are ministering; one aim is to develop the skills related to the ministry of presence and intentional listening. The ministry of presence is essential – sometimes there is simply nothing more that one can do. The ministries provided by the seminarians and lay students include, but are not limited to, (1) ministry to young people, provided primarily to elementary school pupils, (2) sacramental preparation, which can also be offered at the elementary school level but more often those in formation are invited to accompany candidates and catechumens journeying through the Rite of Christian Initiation for Adults process; and (3) pastoral outreach, which includes ministering to the homebound and to those in long-term-care facilities, hospitals, hospice, soup kitchens, men's missions, and L'Arche.[11] Regardless of the ministry in which the students are involved, all take part in theological reflection workshops. In addition to introducing the first-year theology students to the art of theological reflection, the workshops bring together those in like ministries for a time of shared reflection. Though a number of sources are referenced in these workshops, my main resource is *The Art of Theological Reflection* by John De Beer and Patricia O'Connor Killen.[12] This time of reflection and sharing leads the students to appropriate what they have experienced and heard in order to grow in a deeper understanding of effective outreach ministry. It provides them with the opportunity to ask questions such as: What did I experience? What was I able to offer? What did I receive in return? How did I handle that situation? Where was God in this meeting? And, if necessary, how could I handle a similar situation more effectively in the future? The input received through the discussions and reflections allows those in formation to reflect theologically on lived experiences – both their own and that of those to whom they are ministering – and then to further reflect on the experiences privately through journalling, prayer, sacred Scripture, and the rich traditions offered by the Church.

The Mission and Ministry course offered to the transitional deacons (those preparing for priestly ordination) and lay students provides an opportunity to utilize qualitative research. Applying a mode of adult education, the students are asked to read and reflect on course-related articles. Once in the classroom they are invited to share what new awareness they have gleaned from the article, what questions they were left asking, and how they could apply what they had read to today's pastoral situation in the local church. The seminarians returning from their Pastoral Year (one year in a parish under the supervision and mentorship of a pastor) can reflect on related events which occurred during their time of ministry in the parish. The sharing has been enriching at all levels, particularly as the students wrestle with changing cultural realities and seek to provide a more effective form of outreach to those to whom they will minister. Again they are afforded the opportunity to appropriate their own lived experience.

The main assignment in this course is to go out to a growing and vibrant church community – regardless of faith denomination – and discover what it is that is attracting new worshippers. (I offer this assignment because my dissertation and related studies indicate that many individuals who have withdrawn from the worship and community life of the Catholic Church find themselves attracted to other faith communities.) Asked to connect with a member of the pastoral team (ordained or lay), the student must enter into dialogue to determine what it is that makes the faith community viable and vibrant and to establish what methods of outreach, both within their boundaries and beyond, they provide. The student is encouraged to attend a service if possible and to interact with some of the church members to obtain their reasons for belonging to the community and their perspectives on what may or may not be working in the growing of the faith community.

As they are encouraged to go beyond their comfort level, stretch their boundaries, and connect with a community of faith somewhat foreign to them, some students have challenged this assignment, questioning its rationale. It is encouraging, however, that in the end all have given themselves fully to this assignment. Some have shared that this experience has led them to understand more fully the need for ecumenical dialogue; others noted ongoing relationships that were established. The in-class presentations led to lively discussions, integrating these lived experiences, as the students begin to consider and envision their role as dynamic priests and lay ecclesial ministers. I still recall one of the transitional deacons commenting at the end of his presentation that this exercise had helped him realize what should and should not be done in certain pastoral situations. A lay student who met former Catholics at the church she had connected with re-emphasized the need to be attentive listeners when ministering to those entrusted to one's care. The application of qualitative research has allowed those in ministry formation to realize that they are not alone, that they do not have to reinvent the wheel, and that outreach and dialogue open the door to new possibilities in ministry. I believe Norman K. Denzin and Yvonna S. Lincoln defined *qualitative research* best:

> It is a situated activity that locates the observer in the world. It consists of a set of interpretive, material practices that make the world visible. These practices transform the world . . . qualitative researchers study things in their natural settings, attempting to make sense of, or interpret, phenomena in terms of the meanings people bring to them.[13]

Students who learn to be intentional listeners and observers in the world develop the capacity to interact and interpret meaning in the context of ministry.

## Effective Pastoral Ministry and Outreach

In conclusion, it must be made clear that the use of qualitative research does not come at the cost of eliminating quantitative research. Facts, figures, and statistics are important pieces of the entire picture, but they do not provide the whole. The Church is a living entity, with living and breathing beings. What they have lived and experienced is just as important as, if not more than, the numbers that compose those statistics.

Perhaps what has been most beneficial in utilizing qualitative research in both my doctoral studies and in teaching future ministers of the Church is the realization that, in doing so, we can move from a deductive ecclesiology to an inductive ecclesiology.[14] Effective pastoral ministry and outreach should not be seen as a top-down venture provided by someone who presumes to know what is required for the well-being of those to whom they are ministering. In fact, in the model provided for us by Jesus we are called to serve, not dominate. To serve effectively we must meet the people to whom we are to minister wherever they are in their faith journeys, listen to their stories, and seek to fulfil their spiritual needs while at all times remaining faithful to the teachings of the Church.

*Notes*

1 On 'lived experience' see Max van Manen, *Researching Lived Experience: Human Science for an Action Sensitive Pedagogy* (London, ON: Althouse Press, University of Western Ontario, 1990).

2 'Suppress' is the canonical term for closure; see *The Code of Canon Law,* canon 515 §2, http://www.vatican.va/archive/ENG1104/__P1U. HTM.

3 See http://www.bostoncatholic.org/uploadedFiles/BostonCatholicorg /Parishes_And_People/rcab-parishesclosed-welcomingparishes12012011. pdf and http://www.aod.org/parishes/sacramental-records/closed -parishes/.

4 F. J. Galloway Associates – Management and Planning Consultants, *The Roman Catholic Diocese of London 2011 Pastoral & Personnel Planning Statistical Projections and Analysis Report* (London, ON: 15 September 2011), 3–13, https://dol.ca/documents/2016/10/Full_Report. pdf.

5 Bernardine Ketelaars, 'Harkening to the Voices of the Lost Ones: Attending to the Stories of Baptized Roman Catholics No Longer Participating in the Worship and Community Life of the Church' (PhD Thesis, University of Toronto, 2015), 5.

6 John W. Creswell, *Qualitative Inquiry and Research Design: Choosing among Five Approaches* (2nd edn; Los Angeles: Sage, 2005).

7 Creswell, *Qualitative Inquiry*, 78–79.

8 Diocese of London, *A Safe Environment Policy for the Diocese of London* (London, ON: Diocese of London, 2008; updated October 2016), 14, see http://wp.dol.ca/webportal/uploads/14Policy-Final.pdf.

9 Henri Nouwen, *Bread for the Journey: A Daybook of Wisdom and Faith* (New York: HarperCollins, 1997), 80.

10 Van Manen, *Researching Lived Experience*, 30–31.

11 L'Arche International was founded by Jean Vanier, Phillipe Seux, and Raphaël Simi in Trosly-Breuil, France, in 1964. The mission of L'Arche is 'to make known the gifts of people with intellectual disabilities, working toward a more human society'; see https://www.larche.org/. Our students connect with L'Arche London, in Ontario; see http://larchelondon.ca/. See also Paul Lakeland, *Church – Engaging Theology: Catholic Perspectives.* Collegeville, MN: Liturgical Press.

12 Patricia O'Connell Killen and John de Beer, *The Art of Theological Reflection* (New York: Crossroad, 1994).

13 Norman K. Denzin and Yvonna S. Lincoln, eds, *The Sage Handbook of Qualitative Research* (3rd edn; Thousand Oaks, CA: Sage, 2005), 36.

# PART 3

# Integrating Qualitative Research into Theological Education

# 13

# Qualitative Research in Theological Curricula

## DAVID M. MELLOTT

As a seminary student in the 1980s and early 1990s, I struggled with theological education because I was given very few tools or frameworks to help me grasp and understand the diversity of theological and religious worlds. That lacuna in my education was what guided my discernment process when it came time to look for a doctoral programme. Qualitative research methods changed the ways I theologize, the ways that I teach theology, and the ways that I go about developing programmes in theology.[1]

I have had the opportunity, with the support of faculty colleagues, of integrating qualitative research methods into Master of Divinity and Doctor of Ministry degree programmes. When qualitative research methods are introduced at an early stage of the degree programme, they have the potential to fundamentally shape how our students think about the world, create knowledge, and theologize. In this essay I will share some of the ways that qualitative research has shown up in our programme and the impact it has had on our students.[2]

As my descriptions illustrate, integrating qualitative research into a theological degree programme can have a far-ranging impact. I would argue that it has the power to destabilize hegemonic systems of thought, pedagogical practices, and pastoral practice. While the changes can be challenging for students and teacher alike, inviting students to practise basic methods of qualitative research becomes a powerful opportunity for students to pay attention to their epistemic frameworks and how they create knowledge claims.

## Introducing Master's Degree Students to Qualitative Research Methods

At Lancaster Theological Seminary, in Lancaster, Pennsylvania, we began integrating qualitative research exercises into the Introduction to Seminary course long before it was acceptable in theological circles. For nearly a decade I opened the first day of the first class in the Master of Divinity degree programme by sharing with the students one personal artefact from my faculty office. Over the years I have presented a variety of objects, including a statue of Mother Mary, Seat of Wisdom; a rainbow flag; a painting of the Trinity from New Mexico; and a picture of me shaking hands with Pope John Paul II. I ask the students, 'If you came into my office and saw this object displayed there what would you think?' I am always eager to hear what the students say. In most cases students will share observations or conclusions that they have drawn about me based on the object:

> I would think that you were Catholic.
> I would think that you are a spiritual person. I would think that you were gay.
> I would think that you were part of a play about Noah and the Ark. The picture of the Trinity looks scary.
> I would think that you grew up in New Mexico. I would think that you were bragging about having met a pope.
> You must be wealthy because you met the pope and you have the picture mounted in an expensive-looking frame.
> I would wonder why a faculty member in a Protestant seminary had a picture of him and the pope hanging in his office.

In a few cases students will offer questions about me and the object:

> Where did you get the statue?
> Why do you have a rainbow flag? Where do you use it?
> Who painted the picture of the Trinity? How did you get it?
> When did you meet the pope? How did that happen?
> What was the pope saying to you in the picture?

Over the years I have found that students are much more likely to draw conclusions about me than raise questions. Most students are comfortable with their interpretive skills and confident in their assessment of what things mean. As we proceed with the exercise we discuss the difference between making a statement about something and asking a question. When we dig deeper into one of the statements made about me and the given object, students quickly realize that what they are thinking often says more about them and their assumptions than it says about me. Then we examine some of the questions that occurred to them and we look for any assumptions embedded in those questions. For example, when a student sees the statue of Mary, she may consider the question 'Does he like Mary?' but the student may still struggle to appreciate that that particular question represents her interests, and perhaps not mine. The statue could be important to me for a number of reasons. It might have been a gift from a parent, grandparent, or priest. In fact, I may not have any connection to Mary at all. I intentionally select objects I suspect could be provocative or questionable for some students because the seminary wants to empower them to look at the wide landscape of the practice of religion and to give them tools that will allow them to engage those practices thoughtfully. Most of our new students are not aware of just how diverse the Christian body is. Those that are aware can be resistant to paying attention to some forms of Christianity outside their own.

We open the course and the programme with this object exercise because in the following exercise we take students to a series of churches around the city, giving them an opportunity to practise the art of asking research questions.[3] We divide the students into four teams. Following the categories of material Christianity outlined by Colleen McDannell in her book *Material Christianity: Religion and Popular Culture in America*, each team looks at one of the four areas: artefacts, landscape, architecture, and art.[4] After giving the students about 30 minutes to comb the church interior and grounds, we gather them for a conversation with a member of the pastoral staff. Students are instructed to ask questions about the community based on the materials that they observed. We also instruct them to practise crafting questions that will allow the values and commitments of the community to surface. This is not the moment for the students to share their story, instruct the pastor, or make a theological point that is important to them. Their task is to learn what kind of religious world this community is constructing and how that religious world impacts members and those in the wider community.

Among each new class there is always a continuum of resistance to visiting some of the churches. Some Christian students express discomfort with going into a Unitarian Universalist Church. Some heterosexual students resist visiting the Metropolitan Community Church – the 'gay church' because of its focused ministry with people who are gay, lesbian, bisexual, and transgender. The students who express this resistance allow us to talk about the possible assumption that to take seriously the religious practices of those who are different from us is to indicate that we agree with them. To help the students examine their resistance I invoke the following statement from Robert Orsi in his book *Between Heaven and Earth: The Religious Worlds People Make and the Scholars Who Study Them*, where he writes:

We may not condone or celebrate the religious practices of others – and let me emphasize this here because it is always misunderstood: to work toward some understanding(s) of troubling religious phenomena is not to endorse or sanction them . . . – but we cannot dismiss them as inhuman, so alien to us that they cannot be understood or approached, only contained or obliterated (which is what the language of good/bad religion accomplishes, the obliteration of the other by desire, need, or fear). The point is rather to bring the other into fuller focus within the circumstances of his or her history, relationships, and experiences. It is chastening and liberating to stand in an attitude of disciplined openness and attentiveness before a religious practice or idea or another era or culture on which we do not impose our wishes, dreams, or anxieties.[5]

Over the course of the week we visit four or five churches. After each church visit we debrief with the students about their experience. In the debriefing process we encourage students to pay attention to the words they use, the questions they ask, and the anxieties they bring to the task of theological reflection. At Lancaster Theological Seminary, preparing people for theological studies begins with helping students identify their theological location and understand that others will be different from them. Many of those locations are very far from theirs. In the end this brief and focused introduction to qualitative research methods is part of how we frame theological studies in our curriculum. Throughout the degree programme we return to those elements of the framework for further development and exploration, as illustrated below.

## Introducing Doctor of Ministry Degree Students to Qualitative Research Methods

Master's degree level students in theology are not the only ones to benefit from exploring the contributions of qualitative research methods to theology and the practice of ministry. Doctor of Ministry students can find many resources and opportunities as well.[6] The Doctor of Ministry degree is a professional degree, not an academic degree, that requires ministerial experience and master's level theological studies. The degree is intended to help pastoral practitioners increase the quality of their ministerial practice and make a contribution to the wider Church.

Doctor of Ministry students are typically encouraged to delve deeper into their ministerial context and to take several steps back from their ministry as they engage in theological reflection on ministerial practice. Unless they have a college or master's degree level background in qualitative research, they are similar to their master's level counterparts in their tendency to make assumptions about people, practices, beliefs, and religious artefacts. In many cases, they are even quicker to make their assessments because they arrive with significant pastoral experience in which they are expected to offer the right or best perspective on the theological or spiritual matter at hand. In other words, they have experience of being treated as an expert, whether or not they see themselves that way.

These doctoral students also arrive with many questions about the practice of ministry that have arisen out of either a significant gap between the theology espoused by their denomination and the perspectives of their congregants or a need for an approach that will help them respond to the pastoral and spiritual needs of their communities. The religious worlds of their people and how to engage those worlds are often at the centre of their doctoral studies. In many cases the practitioner wants to find a way to use human experience to challenge or reconstruct theological claims or to create a space in which the particularities of human experience can be noticed and honoured.

The needs of these pastoral leaders and the general purpose of the Doctor of Ministry degree make for a culture ripe for engaging qualitative research methods. I find it most helpful to situate the use of these research methods within the context of how we understand theological reflection. In *The Art of Theological Reflection*, Patricia O'Connell Killen and John de Beer define theological reflection as

> the discipline of exploring individual and corporate experience in conversation with the wisdom of a religious heritage. The conversation is a genuine dialogue that seeks to hear from our own beliefs, actions, and perspectives, as well as those of the tradition. It respects the integrity of both. Theological reflection therefore may confirm, challenge, clarify, and expand how we understand our own experience and how we understand the religious tradition. The outcome is new truth and meaning for living.[7]

I have found that doctoral students find this definition a helpful bridge between their previous academic studies in theology and their need to engage human experience. Killen and de Beer emphasize the importance of both experience and theological traditions when it comes to theological reflections, which gives the students permission to explore methodologies and methods that could help them identify and gather experiences in a way that can prove meaningful. At this point the students are poised to experiment with qualitative research and discern the differences among the various qualitative methods.

In our initial required course in the Doctor of Ministry programme we introduce students to qualitative research methods not only through reading ethnographies, but also through using a common pastoral practice as an opportunity to practise some of the skills needed to do qualitative research. We focus on the pastoral visit.

Initially most of the ministers express some resistance to focusing on the pastoral visit. Some do pastoral visits regularly. Others have replaced visits with office hours. In most cases the ministers do not see anything to be gained by a second look at the pastoral visit.

In this assignment we begin by asking the students to develop questions that they would like to ask their congregants. We limit them to three. We lead the group through a process in which they listen to each other's proposals and then decide on a final list of three. This process alone is a learning moment because some pastoral contexts hinder some questions from being asked. For example, a chaplain working in a prison once expressed discomfort when a question about frequency of church attendance was proposed. One of the most telling questions that the ministers typically ask is 'What are you most proud of?' The ministers are nearly always surprised when they hear the variety of answers. Many respondents say 'my children', 'ownership of my home', 'my degree', or 'my job'. Rarely does the Church or faith or anything church related appear in response to this question.

The pastoral visits take place at the home of the congregant, and the pastor is expected to take note of the inside of the house and how the artefacts (furniture, photos, memorabilia, etc.) of the home are arranged. Again, the pastors are often astounded at what they see when they pay attention closely. Even among those who have been doing pastoral visits to shut-ins on a regular basis, many have never stepped inside the *homes* of their congregants. When the ministers do, they experience an immediate gap between the lives of their congregants and the way in which spirituality and a life of faith are approached in the Church. I remember one pastor reporting that he had done his five pastoral visits and all five homes had 50-inch televisions. He was shocked by the experience because several of those congregants had come to visit him about financial problems. His assessment was that his preaching and ministry needed to be completely reassessed in light of what he had learned. He admitted that his discussion of Christian discipleship was far more theoretical and rarely connected with the struggles and issues of daily living.

This revised version of a pastoral visit is not a qualitative research method, but it was a stepping stone for these students toward collecting the life stories of their congregants, which is a qualitative research method. After the ministers become aware of what qualitative research methods can open up for their consideration and reflection, they are eager to use these methods, not only in their doctoral projects, but also in their ministry. After doing the five assigned visits one pastor decided to do pastoral visits to the homes of all of his parishioners because he wanted to learn more about the people in his church. And his parishioners wanted him to visit their homes too. They were eager to share with him their answers to his interview questions.

## The Formational Impact of Introducing Students to Qualitative Research Methods

There are several places where I see our introducing master's and doctoral students to qualitative research methods having a strong formational impact on seminarians. Students expand their epistemic frameworks. They learn how to read context. And students practise the spiritual discipline of standing non-judgementally before the religious beliefs and practices of others without imposing their own needs. In this second section I will explore each of these.

### Epistemic Frameworks

Most students arrive at seminary unable to articulate clearly their epistemic framework. They are not aware that they are balancing personal experience, inherited customs, scientific theories, biblical testimony, etc. in the creation of their theological and philosophical world-views. Introducing qualitative research methods allows students to explore personal and communal experience in structured ways, producing streams of knowledge that they may have ignored earlier.

For some students, human experience will always dominate their epistemic framework. For them, studying rational arguments and historical precedent seems irrelevant to their ministerial goals. Nonetheless these students do not know how to produce knowledge that is based on qualitative research. The opening course provides students with a few basic skills to get them started and usually energizes these students to do more qualitative research in other courses. For other students, human experience is a distraction to the sturdy work of studying, defending, preaching, and teaching Christian teachings. These students are challenged by the ways in which the practices and beliefs of some do not fit into the categories established by those with privilege. Even when these students understand that there are other ways of being Christian and other ways of talking about God, they can be quick to dismiss them if the epistemic framework favours human experience over what they consider to be the religious heritage of Christianity.

Regardless of the direction from which students arrive at the practice of qualitative research, they all struggle with the integration of voices that come from sacred texts, historians, critics, and contemporary practitioners, including their own. The beauty of introducing students to qualitative research is that it forces them to struggle with these voices. This is not to say that this challenge is absent when all of the voices come from books. The issue of how to include one's own voice can be a struggle in that case too. But the results of qualitative research introduce the experiences of a wider population who rarely fit into the neat categories established by theologians or scholars of religion. Students are forced to deal with the lack of clarity, the messiness, and the risk associated with the practice of religion.

*Reading Context*

Teaching students how to read and interpret contexts is central to theological studies, whether it is directed toward academic research or professional development. My experience at Lancaster Theological Seminary has shown me that introducing students to qualitative research teaches them to interpret the contexts beyond the scope of textual interpretation. I find that students are compelled to pay greater attention to the lives of congregants by hearing the testimonies of others, even though they are unsure how to investigate or to analyse those comments.

One of the major places where students get a chance to practise some of these skill sets is when they take their cross-cultural trip. Students in the Master of Divinity degree are required to participate in a two-week immersion trip authorized by the seminary, usually in an African, Asian, or Middle Eastern country or in the Caribbean. In preparation for those experiences, we charge students to use these trips as opportunities to learn how people very different from them live, make meaning, and engage their faith. We ask them to listen for the metaphors, stories, images, and symbols that the people in these countries use to create their worlds, theologically and philosophically. In 2016 students went to the island of Hispaniola. During a presentation to a congregation in the city, I was delighted to hear a seminarian traveller talk about how the people eat a lot of rice and beans. He quickly noted, 'In the United States many of us would think of rice and beans as the food of the poor. That's not the case in Haiti and the Dominican Republic. It's simply a staple of their diet.' The student's comments about his trip perfectly illustrated how his exposure to a qualitative research approach to education helped shape his ability to read the cultural contexts of Haiti and the Dominican Republic. This student was able to see that the way in which Americans interpret their lives is different from the ways in which Haitians and Dominicans interpret theirs. As a consequence of his paying attention in this way to the lives of the people of Hispaniola, the student was able to represent their world-view respectfully while challenging assumptions held by some in the United States.

## Standing Non-judgementally before the Practices and Beliefs of Others

My current context is extremely ecumenical and diverse. In fact, at Lancaster Theological Seminary we intentionally cultivate a community that is diverse in race, ethnicity, theology, denomination, gender, sexual orientation, class, ability, and financial status. Students at the seminary cannot escape the reality of diversity within Christianity, religion, or humanity. The challenge for students, however, is what to do, how to be, and what to think in light of this diversity. Even students who appreciate diversity struggle with what to do with the significant level of religious and theological diversity that exists within Christianity alone. The compulsion to seek a singular, right answer to every theological quandary is strong. And rightfully, students become clear that some theological teachings and practices are destructive. Not every theological position can be in alignment with the Gospel, no matter our interpretation. When students encounter this reality, they are forced to wrestle with the question 'Who is allowed to decide what is in alignment with the Gospel?'

When we introduce students to qualitative research methods, we provide them with a method by which they can seek out, listen to, and engage a variety of beliefs and practices without compromising their own commitments and values. Invoking the passage from Robert Orsi that I included above helps students to understand that acknowledging – non-judgementally – the realty, space, and contributions of others must become part of our own spiritual discipline. To speak of this as a spiritual practice has allowed students to see the deeper contributions that qualitative research can bring to their studies and to their ministries.

By teaching students this pattern of thinking, question asking, and listening as part of the work of theology, we get to another question that is at the heart of the formation of spiritual leaders:

Who am I in relationship to others? How a minister answers this question is crucial to her or his ministry. Part of how one answers this question will be shaped by one's denominational and theological context. For example, Catholic priests and Protestant ministers may do many of the same things, but the role of each within their community is typically very different. Priests and ministers function differently in the spiritual structures of their denominations. In some forms of ministry, listening to the faithful is important, but the priority is to shape the conscience and identity of the believer to align with the teaching of the Church. This differs greatly from the ministry practised in contexts in which diversity of faith is accepted, and sometimes encouraged. Or to think of this conversation in another way – students who understand their role to be to police the religious world will not be able to listen and study carefully religious worlds that do not conform to their rubric for orthodoxy. By contrast, for students who understand their role to be as religious consultants for those who seek to deepen and express their faith, developing the skills of non-judgemental listening will be core to their formation.

## Including Qualitative Research Methods Changes Theology

We shouldn't romanticize or take lightly how much the task of theology and teaching theology could be changed by the integration of qualitative research methods.[8] Many students will be challenged, from different angles, about what to do with experience-based information. Even doctoral students who come with an appreciation for the lived experiences of religious practitioners will likely struggle with these methods. If they can understand the importance of this challenge, their theological reflections will be enriched and their pastoral practice will be enhanced. As noted above, for some students personal experience is the rubric by which they evaluate theological claims. Those students will be challenged when they are expected to bring experience into conversation with classic texts and voices, including the Bible. These students can feel that their experience gets lost or discounted quickly when historical or scholarly texts deal exclusively with rational, linear arguments. There may be little room for the student to find themselves in the conversation.

For other students, experience-based information is of little value. These students will be challenged to appreciate why experience brings value to the process of theological reflection. These students can become irritated when they think that historic theological arguments are being interrupted or set aside because of the contradictory experience of some religious practitioners. Some believe the inclusion of human experience in our theologizing will undermine fidelity to church teaching. Many of these students will find qualitative research and its results to be a waste of time and a distraction.

Even if students lean in one of these directions, integrating qualitative research methods into a theological curriculum means that they will be confronted with the ongoing theological task of bringing multiple voices into conversation with one another. Emerging theologians who want to integrate the voices of religious practitioners into their work will need to decide how much weight they will give to biblical texts, how much weight they will give to human experience, how much weight they will give to theological claims made over the centuries, and how much weight they will give to psychological, anthropological, and sociological theories. In addition to which voice or voices get prioritized in our theological reflections, theologians will be pushed to consider the extent to which they will privilege one voice or set of voices. For example, when the experiences of religious practitioners contradict or critique scholarly opinion, how will the theologian negotiate these differences? Integrating the experiences and voices of people who build and navigate religious worlds is not the same as bringing a variety of scholarly voices together in a scholarly argument. Qualitative research can push theologians to reconsider what we think is worthy of our attention when we are eager to make all-encompassing claims about God and things religious.

Adding qualitative research to a theology programme will change the entire epistemic framework of the students' education. It will also do something else. It will invite them to explore the quality of their pastoral relationships and the variety of ways that they can engage pastoral ministry. Students who learn to appreciate qualitative research should think carefully about the extent to which they integrate the experience of congregants and others into their preaching, teaching, and pastoral care. Perhaps they will spend time listening not only to the Bible and historical theological claims, but also to the voices of those all around them.

## Notes

1 My book *I Was and I Am Dust: Penitente Practices as a Way of Knowing* (Collegeville, MN: Liturgical Press, 2009) is an extended argument of how qualitative research is important for the academic study of theology.

2 Even though we are currently working through a redesign of the curriculum, we remain committed to integrating qualitative research methods into the programme.

3 We have limited our visits to Christian and Unitarian Universalist Churches because a key value of our master's level degree programmes is to help students appreciate the importance and gift of diversity within Christianity. The same exercise could be done when visiting mosques, temples, synagogues, etc.

4 Colleen McDannell, *Material Christianity: Religion and Popular Culture in America* (New Haven, CT: Yale University Press, 1995), 2.

5 Robert Orsi, *Between Heaven and Earth: The Religious Worlds People Make and the Scholars Who Study Them* (Princeton, NJ: Princeton University Press, 2005), 7–8.

6 Students in academic doctoral programmes would benefit from exploring what qualitative research would contribute to their work. See Mellott, *I Was and I Am Dust* for a wider discussion.

7 Patricia O'Connell Killen and John De Beer, *The Art of Theological Reflection* (New York: Crossroad, 1994), viii.

8 Many practical matters need attention and they are dealt with in other chapters of this book. I have focused here on the epistemological changes and theological opportunities that arise.

# 14

# Wonder and the Divine Dance:
# The Lived Reality of Qualitative
# Research within a Master
# of Divinity Curriculum

JOSEPH (JODY) H. CLARKE

Atlantic School of Theology (AST) is a fully accredited theological school within the community of schools affiliated with the Association of Theological Schools. It is an ecumenical university located in Halifax, Nova Scotia. AST was formed by the amalgamation of Holy Heart Seminary, the theological faculty of the University of King's College, and the faculty of Pine Hill Divinity Hall. The university became its own degree-granting institution by an act of the provincial legislature in 1974. Since that time, AST has carved out an identity as a progressive graduate theological university. In recent years, it has intentionally woven qualitative research methodology into the fabric of its Master of Divinity (MDiv) curriculum. The purpose of this chapter is to outline how qualitative inquiry has made its way into the MDiv curriculum and the impact that this integration has had on the academic life of the university.

The migration of qualitative research extends beyond the theoretical study of various research methodologies and into the life blood of AST's MDiv programme. As a result of this movement, the curriculum now more fully unites life experience and theological reflection. This chapter will discuss this development and highlight numerous discoveries made as AST gave expression to the central tenets of qualitative research. These findings include the use of qualitative research in the development of evocative questions; the ways that qualitative research can foster a sense of wonder; the propensity of qualitative inquiry to decrease the distance between ourselves and the other; and, finally, the opportunities that qualitative research offers for participation in a divine dance, one that is deeply relational, transformative, and revelatory.

The inclusion of qualitative research in the curriculum was not at the head of the university's agenda as the faculty and students set out on a journey to revise the MDiv programme. The expedition began just prior to the turn of the millennium as AST decided to initiate a process of intentional institutional discernment. Initially the focus of this discernment period was on themes and trends in theological education. The process consisted of three components: a bi-weekly faculty seminar, a bi-weekly student seminar, and a series of shared encounters with artists, musicians, and community leaders. The encounters spanned the fall and winter semesters. This rhythm of seminar/ encounter/seminar enabled the seminar members to analyse their experiences and then develop new lines of inquiry as they prepared for the next visit. In order to respect the integrity of the people whom AST visited, a number of ethical protocols were put in place. Each setting was contacted several weeks prior to the visit. The people being interviewed were informed about the nature of the conversation. It was suggested that should they consent, then the meeting would take place at time and location determined by those being visited. They were informed that the meeting could be terminated at any time. All of those who were interviewed were asked if their statements could be recorded and used by the university at a later date. It is worth noting that everyone who was contacted agreed to a visit and that every visit exceeded the allotted time.

The classroom seminars engaged in a survey of numerous educational and transformational theories. The curriculum that had guided AST through the 1980s and 1990s was built around action-reflection liberationist theory. The university had been influenced by the work of James Cone, Paulo Freire, Gustavo Gutiérrez, Dorothee Sölle, and Rosemary Radford Ruether. The 'hermeneutic circle', the process of interpretation in which an individual's understanding makes reference to its historical, literal, and cultural context, was at the forefront of AST's field education programme, a programme that was integrated into the other theological disciplines.[1] Within the faculty seminar there was a notion that this model was still effective and could continue to serve AST well into the future. Yet despite our best intentions in implementing a curriculum that possessed a commitment to consciousness-raising, a feeling arose that even critical thought could become its own calcified orthodoxy.[2]

To enrich critical thought, seminar participants came to understand that it was important for theological reflection to be done within the context of a wider series of conversations. With that idea in mind, AST set out on a mission to listen to the rhythms and pulses of the lives of people who share the geography of Canada's east coast. It was hoped that these conversations might reveal perspectives that AST could draw upon in reshaping the MDiv curriculum. Sections of these conversations were recorded by the project's research assistant and two faculty members who led the discernment process. This engagement with the wider cultural context gave the discernment venture buoyancy and vitality. Instantly the data made an impact on the imaginations of the seminar participants.

AST shares many realities with other constituencies within Atlantic Canada. We have to be frugal and resourceful in the management of our resources; we have to be resilient; and we have to rely on each other. Given these common realities, AST faculty and students initiated several multifocal conversations with our neighbours here in the Atlantic region. These conversations came from time in the coal mines of Cape Breton and subsequently with former miners and their families; from time huddled on the deck of a scallop dragger, imaging the world occupied by those who go down to the sea in ships; and from time spent sitting in silence and then in deep conversation with people of Canada's First Nations. In the unnerving presence of the transcendent, we stood in the thin places that are held sacred by African-Nova Scotians. We talked with the former mayor of a fishing community that was devastated by Canada's 1992 moratorium on Atlantic cod fishing (which remains in place today); we also spent time walking in the company of poets, painters, artisans, and musicians.

At the same time as these encounters were taking place, participants turned their attention to the work of Canadian philosopher Charles Taylor. In *The Malaise of Modernity* (1991), Taylor explored how Western notions of individuality, religion, and political philosophy were formed and how they might fail. One such failing is born of instrumental reason, which Taylor defines as 'the kind of rationality we draw on when we calculate the most economical application of means to a given end'.[3] It creates a disenchantment with the world, as any sense of the sacred is sacrificed on the altar of 'cost-benefit' analysis.

Taylor's text quickly became a valuable resource in the discernment process. In addition to the moral blunder born of instrumental reason, Taylor raises two other concerns. The second is the drift to individualism, in which the self becomes the sole point of reference. Taylor argues that this drift leads to a loss of meaning. The third concern builds on the previous two. With the strict adherence to instrumentalism and the loss of a moral horizon beyond the self, there is a subsequent loss of political will. In building on the work of Alexis de Tocqueville, Taylor noted that

> a society in which people end up as the kind of individuals who are 'enclosed in their own hearts' is one where few will want to participate actively in self-government. They will prefer to stay at home and enjoy the satisfactions of private life, as long as the government of the day produces the means to these satisfactions and distributes them widely.[4]

The seminars were disciplined and reflective. The encounters were wild, uncomfortable, and unpredictable. They were experiences akin to being in the wilderness. The wildness came in standing on the shoreline of a blustery lake, just off a nondescript secondary highway, where generations of African-Nova Scotians have been baptized. The discomfort – and there was a great deal of discomfort throughout the entire discernment process – came when the First Nations community of Chapel Island narratively surveyed the Lake Bras d'Or region of Cape Breton and shared with us the collective grief at the loss of access to the land once wandered over by their ancestors. Access to the streams, rivers, and mountains has been denied to generations of Indigenous people, who can now only observe a land that they once inhabited. Unpredictability came as faculty and students found some dimension of their assumed worlds altered with each new encounter.

In conjunction with the encounters, the seminars continued to work with Taylor's analysis in an effort to move past instrumental reason. They returned to liberation-oriented theories with fresh ears. In this return, seminar participants found Freire's dialectical model of learning dynamically significant.[5] This model invites a climate of co-inquiry within which students, teachers, and the learning context enter into conversation. Through dialogue, seminar participants sought out meaning, tested assumptions, and remained open to having their theological assumptions altered and their world-views sharpened. Working in conjunction with the encounters, the seminars were creating an environment charged with transformative energy.

## The Birth of the Question and the Genesis of Wonder

Inadvertently the encounter experiences were raising awareness and proving to be an antidote to the concerns raised by Taylor's writings in seminar discussions. Seminar participants noticed that churches and communities, when they confine themselves to their own world or ecclesial view, could evince character that had given Taylor cause for concern. Regardless of how progressive they assumed their position to be, they remained focused on proof-texting their assumptions. We were learning that creating an evocative learning environment was key to freeing people from the tyranny of a closed imagination. The encounters were not intended to solve problems. They were developed to cultivate new relationships and seek fresh perspectives. The fresh perspectives that were found led participants into a place of 'wonder'. Heidegger noted, 'even astonishment does not fulfill what we intend with the word "wonder": and what we are trying to understand as a basic disposition, the one that transports us into the beginning of genuine thinking'.[6]

Wonder-filled thinking demands that the encounter be deep and rich. Such encounters – the truly dangerous ones – are predicated upon respect and a desire for connection. Participants understood implicitly that the connecting questions needed to target more than cognitive insight. They recognized that questions that invited the other to respond with gravity contained an emotive element. A feeling-based question has the capacity to carry the conversation into the realm of the unconscious, where the self is less guarded. The proto-questions were built around two words, *feel* and *like*. What does it feel like to work in a coal mine? What does it feel like to live in this community? What does it feel like to be on board your ship during a winter storm? The combining of 'feel' with 'like' was intended to invite the respondent to offer an analogy or a metaphor. However, the faculty and students were concerned whether even the 'feel-like' questions would have sufficient 'grit' to enter into places of deeper meaning.

At this point those involved in the process realized the importance of well-constructed qualitative questions. Questions were written and rewritten. Ideally questions will open up the conversation. The need for painstaking attention to the development of open-ended questions became the first major insight that AST would amalgamate into its new curriculum. As faculty and students forged the questions that would guide their research, one evocative underlying question came into view, intended to reach to the heart of the encounter – What moves (or stirs) you? This became the first question posed. Subsequent questions were raised by faculty and students, with all questions required to reflect the spirit of the visit.

Emboldened by this question, seminar participants dived into the encounters with a sense of excitement. This phase of the process was the university's first foray into conducting qualitative research. The immersions were built around a desire to understand what moves the people who have shaped the emotional and cultural landscape of Atlantic Canada. The question of what moves a people has the potential to take us just beneath the surface, where deep connections are possible and where meaning can be created and shared. The question instantly bore fruit. A former coal miner answered 'music'. A Roman Catholic priest with a long history of social activism from the same region of Cape Breton offered the same response, fiddle in hand. Like the coal miner and social activist, the former mayor replied with a single term, 'the ocean'. The word passed over trembling lips as his eyes filled with tears. The Chief of a First Nations community responded with a long period of silence. Then he rose from his seat in the community hall and took the AST delegation on a walk. We walked by the lake, the rolling hills, and the land where his people had once freely hunted and fished. These were the first cautious steps into a new kind of conversation.

Epistemologically AST was shifting its focus from answering questions to practising the art of asking questions. Of equal importance was the recognition that the best questions were those that led us to the birthplace of meaning. This was the first movement toward what Max van Manen describes as phenomenological methodology. Van Manen writes that the discipline of phenomenology 'directs its gaze toward the regions where meaning and understandings originate, well up, and percolate through the porous membranes of past sedimentation – then infuse, permeate, infect, touch, stir us, and exercise a formative and affective effect on our being'.[7]

The 'formative and affective effect' that van Manen refers to is dynamic in nature. A dynamic structure is created when two (or more) forces engage each other. The structure can be thought of as a tension arch, much like that which passes between two electrical poles. For example, the responses to the meaning-based question offered respectively by the miner, the priest, and the First Nations Chief each form a tension arch. One pole consists of the integrity found in the unique responses to the question.

But the images they offer, such as music, the ocean, and silence point to something beyond, something just over the horizon. As such, these terms give rise to a wonder-based sensibility. This is where the second pole exists. For example, what is it about music that moves a man who toils in coal mines, or a priest who spends his life in the service of social justice? What is the relationship between music and social transformation? What is it about the ocean that stirs the heart of a man who lives next to the sea? Why does silence contain so much power for the First Nations Chief? For those involved in encounter-based experiences, their emerging curiosity was being transformed into a wonder-based sensibility.

Building on the work of Heidegger, van Manen writes, 'wonder is a disposition that has a dispositional effect: it dislocates and displaces us. Wonder is not to be confused with amazement, marveling, admiration, curiosity, or fascination.'[8] In fact, wonder picks researchers up and deposits them in a new land, one that affirms the past but senses the presence of something else. It serves as a passageway. Rowan Williams, reflecting on the nature of words, illuminates this point with a graphic illustration:

> Many years ago, I heard a distinguished sculptor saying that he had discovered his vocation when visiting a gallery in his teens. 'I knew,' he said 'that there was something missing from that gallery, and it was *my work*.' The gallery had been showing a set of exhibition pieces designed to lead up to the work of Rodin; the teenage visitor has sensed that he knew *how to go on* from Rodin, so that his work would be the obvious next step in a story. You could say that he did not 'agree' that Rodin should be where the story ended; but that does not add up to a rejection of Rodin, and that indeed was as far as possible from the young man's intention.[9]

If the discipline of sculpting concluded with Rodin, then despite his brilliance he could be considered a failure. In the imagination of one sculptor, Rodin's work created a tension arch with an unforeseen future. The dynamic energy of the tension arch was alive and well within the encounters. As with Rodin, music, silence, and the ocean are not where the stories ended. Participants now equipped with a meaning-based question, were beginning to access a world full of wonder. Wonder naturally produces new questions. The tension arch affected the being of those who allowed themselves to be touched by the lived reality of others. The practical application of this emerging orientation, born of qualitative inquiry, properly belongs to any theological school that wishes to inspire its students to touch the hem of the human condition. For example, a pastor asks a bereaved mother how she is feeling in relation to the death of her child. The mother response, 'There are no words.' Her answer is complete and accurate. And yet a further question unearths other truths. 'If there were words, what words would you use?' the pastor gently asks. The mother, either consciously or unconsciously sensing the pastor's genuine concern for her, replies, 'devastated, shattered, empty'.[10]

Layers of meaning reside in expressions such as 'devastated, shattered, empty'. By moving toward a world that contains such descriptors, the pastor, like AST's research participants during their encounters, sojourns in a land fraught with danger and uncertainty. Yet this is precisely the pathway to discovery. Returning to the coal miner, a follow-up question is posed by the students: 'What is it about music that is moving?' In response one miner said:

> In the winter time it is common not to see daylight for months on end. We'd go into the mine before dawn and you wouldn't get out 'til after dark. So, music is the only thing that gives you any sense of light. You gotta have it. Otherwise, I think you'd die.

The response offers numerous insights. Music is more than a tune or a song. For this miner it is a matter of 'life and death'. The words uncover a reality about the nature of mining. They also convey the deeper meaning for the miner, that without music his mortality is at stake. This depth of connection is equally true for the mayor, who said, once he had collected himself, 'The ocean is alive and we know it well. And it is never the same. It is always speaking to you. It is our job to listen.'[11]

An appreciation of the value of wonder leads the researcher in the direction of meaning. As such, wonder serves as a way of shedding light. It presses into human experience, and in so doing contributes to the illumination of a larger world-view. Essentially, what began as a wandering process for AST was now bringing those involved with the discernment process to a place of wonder. As the school embraced the seminars and encounter experiences, the seminar participants came to recognize the animating energy found in deep inquiry. They also began to appreciate that this form of engagement had consequences for the larger theoretical mission of the school.

## Wonder and Qualitative Research

Thus far the focus of this chapter has been on AST's gradual and serendipitous foray into the world of qualitative research. The embryonic research methodology, built on the search for meaning, resulted in an encounter with wonder. John Creswell notes that qualitative research 'consists of interpretive, material practices that make the world visible. These practices transform the world.'[12] This transformed world in which AST now found itself was characterized by a pervasive sense of the sacred. The encounters brought assumptions and expectations into question as they expanded the world-view of participants. As researchers, we were being pushed by wonder to a place where we were becoming overwhelmed 'by awe and perplexity – such as when something familiar has turned profoundly unfamiliar, when our gaze had been drawn by the gaze of something that stares back at us'.[13] The cohabitants of our region were sharing their experiences and supplying us with stories of transformation, heartache, and resilience. The encounters were humbling and invigorating. This emerging perspective constitutes a significant movement in the formation of a rigorous pastoral identity as the student and faculty participants recognized they needed to relinquish portions of their assumed world. It was invigorating because with this surrender came the freedom to be comfortable with uncertainty.

To develop a capacity to live with uncertainty, indeed to relish such opportunities, is starkly counter-cultural. This is particularly true in light of the epidemic of anxiety that has a firm grip on contemporary culture. The first victim of anxiety is curiosity. Anxiety drives people on a desperate search for certainty and thus supports the rise of individual and cultural relativism. This reaction to anxiety can be heard in the way a society justifies itself for the purpose of maintaining a status quo. Those who maintain the status quo, in turn, applaud themselves for their openness and irrevocable certainty. Jonathan Schofer notes that the impulses of relativism are layered and can 'claim knowledge of others, the desire to affirm our own values as right, the desire to have a firm underpinning for our values, and the desire for clarity in times of ambiguity'.[14] This form of relativism leads to a non-critical posture within which individuals tend to believe that they know enough and that their values and assumptions about the world are free of projection and distortion. According to Schofer, the antidote to this form of relativism is found in the virtues that counter such tendencies, such as 'various forms of humility, diligence in learning, receptiveness, and tolerance for ambiguity'.[15] Humility, a commitment to learning, a receptivity to the radical reality of otherness, and an ability to tolerate uncertainty characterize the birth of a fertile imagination. These 'virtues' also describe the qualities of the consummate theological student.

As AST's discernment processed matured, it became clear that the new MDiv curriculum should contain a disciplined practice whereby students are encouraged to adopt an attitude of curious and open inquiry and a capacity to sit in the resulting ambiguity. As Mary Clark Moschella has pointed out, theological education has 'long stressed listening skills as a critical dimension of care and counseling'.[16] Moschella believes that deep down listening 'is a liberating practice, a practice that validates and honors another person's experience, insight, and soul'.[17] Music liberates the soul of the miner. The ocean gives shape to the life blood of one who chooses to live and die on its shores. Landscapes free the imagination of a First Nations' Chief. The caring inquiry of a pastor unearths some tiny portion of a mother's grief.

The emphasis on the power of listening forms a cornerstone of Moschella's text *Ethnography as Pastoral Practice: An Introduction*. Ethnography, a form of social research in which the practitioner gets 'to know the people in a particular place, interact with them and form relationships', is one of the five classical disciplines within the broader field of qualitative inquiry.[18] The others are phenomenology, grounded theory, case study, and narrative research. According to Creswell, ethnographic research 'involves extended observations of the group, most often through participant observation, in which the researcher is immersed in the day-to-day lives of the people and observes and interviews the group participants. Ethnographers study the meaning of the behaviour, the language, and the interaction among members of the culture-sharing group.'[19] The central thesis of Moschella's book is that ethnography can be a vehicle for congregational transformation. Moschella maintains that the 'humble journey of listening to the religious and spiritual lives of people through pastoral ethnography can lead to a place of life-giving change with a faith community and beyond'.[20]

At the time of this discernment process, those involved with selecting and arranging the encounters did not consider the degree to which these brief visits might affect the lives of those we visited. For example, we had not thought about the degree to which the questions might open old wounds or unearth repressed memories. Seminar participants were becoming aware that the responses to 'what moves you?' were providing us with new notions about our being neighbours and about the impact of forces that move our neighbours on how AST goes about the business of providing graduate theological education within Atlantic Canada.

AST's encounters were short and sharp, lasting between two and five hours. In the world of ethnographic research the encounters were too brief to be considered a full blown piece of ethnographic research. However, the encounters were proving to be thematically consistent with the ethnographic methodology espoused by Moschella, in that they brought about transformation in all those who entered into them. For the members of the seminar there was a growing sense of excitement. Interestingly, the people who shared with us their stories, uniformly expressed an appreciation for being heard. As the First Nations Chief noted, 'most people who come here from the universities want to study us. You want to talk with us, that is a different thing.'

In the search for meaning, qualitative inquiry has the potential to create deeper understanding and, in doing so, transform those who engage it. The sculptor in Williams's account so understood Rodin that he took up the mantle of the master, an act that transformed his life. Understanding 'involves seeing that there is now something further to be said/done; that there is a future for *this* particular line of engagement. It is very different from a penetration into the inner workings of an object so as to lay bare its "essential" mechanism.'[21] As with this sculptor's encounter, the seminar participants understood that there were implications for what they were discovering that pushed them into the future. A future that holds prophetic possibilities.

## Bridging the Gap and Perichoresis in Action

Qualitative researcher and educational theorist Thomas Schwandt notes that communication philosopher Marshall McLuhan has argued that the Western world is becoming 'intensely individualist and fragmented'.[22] Taylor has maintained that the act of seeking out the other contravenes instrumentalism, individualism, and the origins of hopelessness.[23] Taylor and McLuhan agree that the drift to self-centredness makes relationships 'revocable' and creates a culture of isolation. This slide to isolationism contains a self-fulfilling prophecy in the belief that isolation is good. Pierce Hibbs suggests that our society has become maimed by sin born of the Western belief that 'we are better off if we have our own space'.[24] From that suggestion follows the argument that gaps between people are good because they provide people with their own space. The experience of the AST community as it stood in close proximity to the other is that our appreciation of the world, and our place in it, was increasing. Qualitative inquiry is intensely relational and serves as a remedy for fragmentation. The intense nature of such engagement answers the call of Taylor, who concluded *The Malaise of Modernity* by calling for a 'complex, many-leveled struggle, intellectual, spiritual, and political, in which the debates in the public arena interlink with those in a host of institutional settings'.[25]

In the quest for meaning, qualitative research methods can create a bridge that decreases the distances between people and creates understanding. This is not to suggest that qualitative research is the remedy for the many ills plaguing the Western world. It is to say that the approaches and methods employed by qualitative research promote an interdependent and relational way of being that stands counter to the independence and self-sufficiency found in much of the Western world today. As such, qualitative research can be considered an invaluable tool for understanding and constructing a more relationally oriented world. Referencing the work of Kierkegaard, Sartre, Buber, and Nussbaum, Schwandt argues 'for an ethic of closeness, of care, of proximity, or of relatedness, and hold(s) that morality must be theorized from an *experiential* basis, specifically in the experience of the I–thou relationship'.[26] This radical relatedness or vulnerable attentiveness opens us to a profound reality where, in living out an ethic of closeness, we find ourselves creating a world characterized by a desire for connection.

AST's quest to participate in the construction of a relationally oriented world is an act both loving and prophetic. During the debriefing sessions that followed each visit, researchers regularly noted that something about the visit was 'holy' or 'sacred'. The term that comes closest to capturing the spiritual dimension of the project is *perichoresis*, which describes the fluidity of the relationship between the three persons of the Trinity. Hibbs states that 'because the Trinity is the archetype of distinct persons in perfect unity, it should come as no surprise that the doctrine of perichoresis illuminates the nature of language and provides the antidote to autonomy and isolationism'.[27]

The antidote Hibbs is referring to is found in caring and respectful interactions. Pamela Cooper-White suggests that perichoresis can be described as a divine dance that captures 'a compelling image for the dynamic, energy, and multiplicity-in-unity inherent in the symbol of the Trinity'.[28] The dance communicates its essence in movement. The dance is self-communicating and responsive. It respects the integrity of the multiple realities while underscoring the longing for connection. In the example of the bereaved mother, her words 'devastated, shattered, empty' are self-revelatory. The pastor responds, and in the exchange greater unity is achieved. Their realities remain distinct and yet in the interaction something has changed. In theological education, as Hibbs notes, we are 'bound to a God who dwells in self-communion, a God who speaks to himself and to his creatures. God's perfect self-communion is the archetype for our creaturely communion. And this is especially important to remember in a world where communion is the goal, but rarely the norm.'[29] The mother initially said, 'There are no words.' The pastor, as researcher, invited her to form images. This was an intimate act. The mother accepted the invitation and in the subsequent revelation created a new depth of understanding.

## Conclusion and Outcomes

Individualism, isolationism, and hopelessness fuel anxiety and feed the cultural malignancies of personal and social relativism. As AST began the process of reimagining its MDiv programme, it seemed apparent that a new curriculum needed to honour the theological disciplines of theology, scriptural studies, history, and practical theology while providing an opportunity for students to construct questions that could lead them to meaningful encounters with others. Such encounters can lead participants on a journey predicated on a spirit of discovery.

In the end AST's discernment process gave rise to a curriculum that embedded qualitative approaches within various parts of its academic offerings, particularly in field education. However, AST's major commitment to qualitative research was found in the development of two new courses. The first is an introductory course in which students examine various research methodologies and are encouraged to think of themselves as 'researchers'. The hope is that graduates will gain the skills to conduct rudimentary and ethically appropriate research within the larger church context. The second significant investment in qualitative research comes in the final year of the MDiv programme, when students undertake a two-credit, two-semester course entitled 'The Graduate Research Project'. This course requires that each student explores a question or issue in ministry that has captured their attention and is of consequence to them as a researcher and to their faith tradition. With supervision and guidance, students are expected to develop and execute a piece of original qualitative research. The student-researchers are expected to present their findings to a larger public audience. It is worth noting that the presentations have taken on a festive feel and are now one of AST's banner events. The annual presentations attract hundreds of people onto the university's campus.

Over the years presentations have included an exploration of the pastoral identity of those called to bi-vocational ministry; the experiences of young single women in ministry; the spiritual themes found in body art; how new technology affects the experience of worship; the transformative dimension of music in worship; the experience of prayer in the three Abrahamic faith traditions; the experience of physicians and medically assisted death; the lived reality of black women in roles of ecclesial leadership in Canada; faith and public life; the spiritual life of people who come to the Church later in life; the very real world of competition among clergy; the experience of church closures; the experience of church amalgamations; the spirituality found in daily rituals; the role of small group work in the transformation of a congregation; congregational life without a paid accountable pastor; the spirituality of older women; eco-theology and the practice of prayer.

As stated at the outset, qualitative research methodology is now built into AST's MDiv curriculum. Its migration was the result of a happy accident in which the university worked feverishly to find a question that would enable us to make deep connections with cohabitants of Atlantic Canada. These encounters proved to be AST's first rudimentary foray into the worlds of phenomenological and ethnographic research. AST came out of the period of curricular discernment with a commitment to achieving three goals above and beyond the normal expectations of a divinity degree: (1) to cultivate in students the discipline and artistry necessary to finding a key question of meaning, (2) to help students-researchers realize that in creating and asking evocative questions, they are challenging a social order that affirms instrumentalism and isolationism while closing a gap between themselves and others, and (3) through the experiences of interacting with others to highlight for students that reaching out in a spirit of genuine curiosity opens doors and builds bridges. Through their experiences with qualitative research approaches and tools, AST students are learning that meaningful encounters created by insightful questions humbly shared have the potential to change the fabric of our society.

## Notes

1 The idea of the hermeneutic circle, with the individual part only comprehensible within the whole, comes from the work of Friedrich Schleiermacher, Wilhem Dilthey, Martin Heidegger, and Hans-Georg Gadamer.

2 Paulo Freire, *Pedagogy of the Oppressed* (1970) (New York: Continuum, 1982), 20.

3 Charles Taylor, *The Malaise of Modernity* (Concord: Canadian Broadcasting Corporation, 1991), 5.

4 Taylor, *Malaise*, 9.

5 Freire, *Pedagogy of the Oppressed*.

6 Martin Heidegger, *Basic Questions of Philosophy: Selected 'Problems' of 'Logic'* (Bloomington, IN: Indiana University Press, 1994), 143.

7 Max van Manen, *Phenomenology of Practice: Meaning-Giving Methods in Phenomenological Research and Writing* (Walnut Creek, CA: Left Coast Press, 2014), 26–27.

8 Van Manen, *Phenomenology of Practice*, 37.

9 Rowan Williams, *The Edge of Words: God and the Habits of Language* (London: Bloomsbury, 2014), 71.

10 The conversation took place on 4 October 1993, in Lower Sackville, Nova Scotia. The name has been omitted for privacy. It is used by permission.

11 The quotations contained in this paper were gathered in fall 1998 and winter 1999. They are used by permission.

12 John W. Creswell, *Qualitative Inquiry and Research Design* (3rd edn; Thousand Oaks, CA: Sage, 2013), 43.

13 Van Manen, *Phenomenology of Practice*, 360.

14 Jonathan Wyn Schofer, 'Virtues and Vices of Relativism', *Journal of Religious Ethics* 36, 4 (2008), 712.

15 Schofer, 'Virtues and Vices', 712.

16 Mary Clark Moschella, *Ethnography as a Pastoral Practice: An Introduction* (3rd edn; Cleveland, OH: Pilgrim Press, 2008), p. 12.

17 Moschella, *Ethnography*, 13.

18 For the quotation see Moschella, *Ethnography*, 26.

19 Creswell, *Qualitative Inquiry*, 90.

20 Moschella, *Ethnography*, 235.

21 Williams, *Edge of Words*, 79.

22 Thomas A. Schwandt, 'Three Epistemological Stances for Qualitative Inquiry: Interpretivism, Hermeneutics and Social Constructionism', in *The Landscapes of Qualitative Research*, ed. Norman K. Denzin and Yvonne S. Lincoln (Thousand Oaks, CA: Sage, 2003), 315.

23 Taylor, *Malaise*, 10.

24 Pierce Taylor Hibbs, 'Closing the Gaps: Perichoresis and the Nature of Language', *Westminster Theological Journal* 78, 2 (2016).

25 Taylor, *Malaise*, 120.

26 Schwandt, 'Three Epistemological Stances', 317. Italics in original.

27 Hibbs, 'Closing the Gaps', 303.

28 Pamela Cooper-White, *Braided Selves: Collected Essays on Multiplicity, God, and Persons* (Eugene, OR: Cascade Books, 2011), 120–21.

29 Hibbs, 'Closing the Gaps', 322.

# PART 4

# Valediction

# 15

# The Gift and Challenge of Qualitative Methods for Pastoral Formation

## SUSAN WILLHAUCK

A professor mentor of mine in theological school introduced me to congregational study and ethnographic research, and I have used those tools in parishes. In particular, some years ago I conducted interviews and surveys and focus groups in a struggling congregation. These groups had an impact on discernment and on reshaping the congregation's vision for youth ministry; they also solidified for me my identity and role as their minister, as I engaged in pastoral practices of listening, subverting my own assumptions, elevating under-heard voices, and framing challenging questions. Congregants described the process as providing a freeing sense of becoming 'unstuck'. I have found learning and practising qualitative research to be a precious gift for pastoral formation in the development of pastoral identity and leadership. It has been so in my own work, and other authors in this volume attest to this gift as well. A treasured gift must be given and received well, and a sense of responsibility passed along with it. The gift of qualitative research goes beyond the formal use of research tools in a congregational setting, however. It is also a gift of profound encounter with others, a gift that leads to one's own self-giving in response to the Gospel call. In this chapter I explore giving and receiving in the teaching and learning of qualitative methods and the challenges that accompany that gifting. Here I lay out a framework for qualitative method in theology and discuss pedagogical challenges that have arisen both in my own teaching and through research that I have done on qualitative research in theological education.

## One School's Experience

I teach in the pastoral theology department at Atlantic School of Theology (AST). One of the courses I teach each year is the Graduate Research Seminar for final year Master of Divinity and Master of Arts students (see Jody Clarke's chapter in this volume for background on the development of the course within the curriculum at AST). It is a two-term course that provides final-year students (both on campus and with distance learners) with an opportunity for in-depth exploration of a question or issue in ministry that has captured their imagination and will make a difference for the Church.

As the students are active in ministry in their field placements, each of them selects a dilemma in ministry that is ripe with consequences for both the student and the particular ministry and can be explored in a field setting. The Graduate Seminar invites students to engage with a variety of theological disciplines as they come to a deeper understanding of the dynamic forces that move within communities of faith and agencies of social responsibility. The overall goal is to equip students to function effectively as leaders within such contexts. Students are challenged to see themselves as researchers and agents of change while becoming competent in theological engagement, social analysis, and spiritual assessment. In the conviction that pastoral ministry is a site of ongoing research into human systems and congregational practice and that research is itself an act of ministry, faculty hope to achieve what Mary Clark Moschella has described in a course syllabus as giving leaders 'ears to hear' the voices of ordinary persons as they practise their faith.

Our belief at AST is that through engaging in pastoral ethnography, a religious leader can help a community articulate its corporate faith stories in their cultural complexity. Part of our mandate at AST came from our founding denominations (Roman Catholic Church,

Anglican Church of Canada, and United Church of Canada), which wanted our graduates to go into ministry in their various parishes with certain competencies, particularly in leadership. The judicatories wanted to quell the tide of decline in churches. They were saying, 'Send us good leaders who can transform the Church.' Our rationale for requiring the course was that the experience of taking the bull by the horns and directing a research project would indeed contribute to the students' formation as leaders.

In surveys that our school asks alumni to complete five years after they have graduated, most of those who are serving in ministry agree that their graduate project helped prepare them to assess their context of ministry and equipped them for leadership. But I sought further analysis and my curiosity led me to wonder what other faculty and institutions were doing with regard to teaching qualitative research, and why. Therefore, in 2016 I applied for and received a grant from the Wabash Center for Teaching and Learning in Theology and Religion to research how teaching qualitative research methods in schools of theology helps develop leadership capacities. Through surveys and interviews (which I shall describe later) and an on-site symposium with faculty I also sought to delineate how students learn and use qualitative methods and what pedagogical practices are effective in achieving learning goals.

In my own case I found a pedagogical challenge in that for some of my students the Graduate Seminar produced enormous anxiety. The thought of designing and implementing a seven-month project was very daunting for some. And some students were not convinced of its value. I wanted to be able to help students better understand the purpose and benefits of the use of qualitative methods in theological education and to guide them through their projects to experience the joys of research. Though some students complain that the course requires too much work in the time that they have and some may resist for other reasons, for the most part the faculty sees great value in the course and many fine projects have resulted. In particular, the faculty values students' developing the ability to listen carefully, with patience, in the spirit of curiosity, and having the experience of staying with a sustained question over the course of two terms. The course also challenges students to move outside their comfort zones by not allowing them to depend on prior experience or what they are already good at doing. Before I delve into pedagogical concerns, at this point I will orient us in a rationale for the important role of qualitative research in theology. Those with substantial background in qualitative research may not need this excursion and may want to skip ahead, but anyone considering engaging qualitative research in their teaching or theological study may be after some basic assumptions behind this method.

## Qualitative Methods in Theology

Qualitative research is one within a cluster of social science methodologies employed in diverse theological fields, including systematic theology, ethics, liturgical studies and pastoral and/or practical theology. As a result of a turn to experience and context, theologians of all stripes are employing qualitative research to understand how people interpret their lives, how they make meaning. Research is a form of deep listening and caring and interpreting in order that we act faithfully to live out the conviction of the Gospel. It is about being attentive to what is going on – about listening and observing in order to be transformational. I like to think of it as a kind of Zen practice. In *Ethnography as a Pastoral Practice: An Introduction*, Mary Clark Moschella writes that religious leaders can 'harness the power of social research to transform a group's common life and its purposeful work in the world'. By sharing their research results with their congregation, leaders can 'stimulate more honest theological reflection and trusting relationships . . . this process sows the seeds for spiritual and social transformation within the faith community and beyond'.[1] When these things occur, we recognize that Christianity is a communal practice and understand that God is present in and works through human experience.

A major methodological shift in the twentieth century was toward theological inquiry that grounds itself in the human experience of individuals and communities who are doing theology. This shift places an emphasis on or uses the language of practical theology or praxis or context. Simply put, the contextual shift stood in contrast to the explication of doctrine, or to exegetical studies/the historical critical method, where the primary task of theology was to exegete the texts and tradition. An often-quoted description of qualitative research is 'an umbrella term covering an array of interpretive techniques which seek to describe, decode, translate, and otherwise come to terms with the meaning, not the frequency, of certain more or less naturally occurring phenomena in the social world'.[2] Qualitative researchers are interested in understanding the meanings people have constructed, that is, how people make sense of their world and the experiences they have in the world. Again, this sees Christianity not as a set of propositions with the theological task primarily to unpack these propositions, but as communal practice. This is not to value human experience above the Gospel, but to understand that the Gospel is an embodied act and to see God as present in and working through human experience.

There is, however, the question of authority or normativity in qualitative research. How do peoples' experiences stack up against doctrinal suppositions and authority? A 'people's theology' has to be correlated with other sources of authority for our theological claims, guarding against the unquestioned authority of the 'I'. We take Scripture, tradition, and liturgy as primary resources but also use social science methods, historical and textual hermeneutics and critical theories. Yet, according to Siroj Sorajjakool, qualitative research can counter the devaluation of local knowledge – it can de-colonialize knowledge, where knowledge is seen as stemming from only one authority.[3] It sees experience as an important alternate text and can cause students and teachers to question understandings and uses of power that produce certain circumstances. Elaine Graham, Heather Walton, and Frances Ward discuss the move from applied theology to theological reflection, looking to the self and the interior life as 'the primary space in which theological awareness is generated and nurtured'. They write of exploring a 'theology by heart' of the living human document, to use the famous phrase coined by Anton Boisen, considered to be the founder of clinical pastoral education.[4]

Theology uses qualitative method to explore and critically evaluate the performance of faith to interpret the practices that social scientists call 'habitus', those things that are second nature, unspoken, but firmly entrenched patterns of behaviour. There is often a gap between theology and practice. Just because people profess to believe certain things, or to follow a particular theology, does not mean that they act on that theology – that they actually do what they say or practise what they preach. Right belief does not always lead to right action. We often think that if we can just get our thinking straight, then right action will follow, but that does not always happen. For example, a Church might talk about the love of God for all people but turn away homeless visitors on Sunday morning. Qualitative research methods help us understand not only the gaps between theology and lived practices, but also the practices that do reflect embedded theologies. Instead of a pastoral leader using theological reasoning to persuade a congregation to affirm their own agenda for faithful action, qualitative methods such as ethnography engage the congregation in its own interpretive practice through theological reflection. It is research that is undertaken to improve the quality of practice. For, as James Hopewell observed, 'Despite our aspirations, congregations are not timeless havens of congenial views or values. By congregating, human beings are implicated in a plot, in a corporate historicity that links us to a specific past, that thickens and unfolds a particular present, and that holds out a future open to transformation.'[5]

Qualitative research methods are built on a post-positivistic phenomenological world-view that assumes that reality is socially constructed through individual or collective definitions of the situation. The purpose of qualitative research is to understand the current social situation from the point of view of the participants, which leads the researcher to become 'immersed' in the phenomenon of interest. Now, qualitative method has its critics too – some say it is not scientific but mere storytelling. Yes, it is written in narrative form, but that does not mean it cannot be rigorous. Stories are important sources of data. Faith and religious experience are narrative in nature, communicated in stories whose use is therefore integral to the method.

## Qualitative Research as *Kenōsis*

In *Fieldwork in Theology: Exploring the Social Context of God's Work in the World*, Christian Scharen offers qualitative method or 'fieldwork in theology' as a tool for 'getting involved in' or waking up to what God is doing in the world.[6] He argues that Christians seeking to understand the 'complexity of this beautiful and broken world' must engage in the disciplined craft of fieldwork in theology. To explicate this point, he identifies two main positions on how Christians should regard the world. One is that the Church withdraws from the world in order to form a clear Christian identity over against the world. He situates within this approach Stanley Hauerwas and William Willimon, who proposed in their 1989 book *Resident Aliens* that we are called not to help people, but to follow Jesus. Another school of thought is represented by Donald MacKinnon and Rowan Williams, for example, who see following Jesus (discipleship) as a radical self-emptying (*kenōsis*), an act of self-giving that Rowan Williams called the 'practice of dispossession'. He writes of a 'sending God' who sends Jesus and who in the Spirit sends us.[7] The practice of dispossession is an act of giving ourselves away, of holding nothing back. The Christian colony is not complete; rather we acknowledge its incompleteness, which 'drives the Church's openness to the other and in fact to the whole world'.[8] I have found that the notion of a practice of dispossession resonates with the students and helps them come to a deeper understanding of their call and of their role in relationship to those whom they will serve.

## Research Summary

My research into teaching qualitative research has convinced me that in theological education we are good at teaching about the Christian tradition. We are good at teaching students how to think critically and clearly. We are good at many things. But how well do we help students understand how people will react to what they are doing and saying? How will the people respond? How will they accept or reject the faith? How well do we help students appreciate people's narratives and see and hear the measure of depth of their lives, to understand how they interpret their significance? We are good at teaching the methods, the how-to, the mechanics of qualitative research. We have tried to convey the wisdom of this approach, but we have not accounted for whether the students believe that it has an impact on them; we have not understood well how the students learn or do not learn, are formed or not. This difficulty was echoed in my grant research.

To learn more about how and where qualitative research is taught in theological education I surveyed 52 faculty and interviewed 14 of them (the project was confined to the United States and Canada). That the presence of qualitative methods in theological schools is more extensive is evident from the Ecclesiology and Ethnography Network.[9] I learned that there is a huge interest in qualitative research in theological education. Several faculty spoke of the growing trend toward embracing context and experience and toward the use of qualitative research as a result. The problem is knowing how to use qualitative research, how to implement it in the curriculum. Most teaching of qualitative research is currently done in Doctor of Ministry programmes, but increasingly it takes place in Master of Divinity programmes as well. Faculty have students use research skills like interviewing, direct and participant observation, and collecting and organizing data in courses across the disciplines. Some of those interviewed responded that they did not teach qualitative methods per se, but they did do qualitative research themselves and brought their research into their teaching.

## Goals for Teaching Qualitative Research

When I asked faculty about their specific goals in teaching qualitative research, their responses followed four major themes: contextualization, communication, reflection/reflexivity, and vocation. In terms of contextualization, faculty believe that it is important to be able to contextualize theology, to correlate theology and experience. They consistently identified the ability to employ analytical skills to assess a context, to acknowledge the habitus, issues, and systems at work, and to recognize patterns in a congregation and their theological significance. Teaching qualitative research can also encourage connections between schools of theology and other social institutions, such as prisons and social agencies.

The theme of communication included the goals of listening and asking the right questions and getting below the surface to explore the multiple right answers within a congregation. Those interviewed emphasized the significance of interpretive skills across cultures for understanding the narratives of a congregation, to see how members make meaning and for students to be able to appreciate what they find. The communication may go beyond congregations, as students may engage in research in other social contexts.

Other goals could be described as reflexive in nature – how qualitative research affects the person doing it. Faculty see value in students' increased self-awareness in knowing where they are and how their experiences affect them. This self-awareness involves the students' recognizing their own assumptions and learning not to jump to immediate evaluation and to resist the urge to fix things. Some respondents expressed the importance of learning about and leading theological reflection on how God is present in the community's practice. Qualitative research is also a point of departure for personal transformation, by encouraging vulnerability and challenging expectations. Qualitative research disrupts students' complacency, which in turn teaches them how to disrupt prophetically and pastorally. It teaches about difference, trains in the arts of listening and asking questions, in moving beyond what is immediately seen. It can challenge a 'whitewashed' view of social action and help students understand theologies other than their own. Another rationale is that qualitative research incarnates learning comparable to a spiritual discipline as a counter practice to disincarnate or distancing social practices such as hiding behind rules or policy. In terms of the formation of pastoral identity, I learned that qualitative research aids the formation of ministers as good pastoral leaders in that it teaches the suspension of preconceptions and challenges canon or accepted norms. Given the discussion of theological normativity, that tension remains. It helps students understand themselves and others at a visceral level, exposing their own biases. As Scharen commented, 'Seeing people as they are and not as we imagine they ought to be is harder than it looks.'[10] In place of pronouncements that are about what ought to be or what we want to receive, qualitative research enhances our ability to interrupt and unsettle. Students connect qualitative research to their ministry contexts most directly through learning, listening, and interviewing skills that transfer to pastoral care and to preaching and teaching through better knowledge of their community.

Lastly, some goals were vocation related. The faculty I interviewed wanted students to see that research is a theological and spiritual practice that forms the researcher into a pastoral leader and contributes to vocational clarity. One goal was the development of habits and ways of being and doing that would facilitate the student's calling, to promote an incarnational theology and leadership modelled on Jesus. Some faculty gave specific examples of qualitative research their students had done that the students claimed had had an impact on their formation for ministry – a phenomenological study of how women with severe illnesses felt they were treated by the Church; an ethnography of a Catholic parish and how it responded to large numbers of immigrants from Mexico; a grounded-theory study of parents of youth and the sexuality and sex education of their teens: a phenomenological study of how Pentecostals experience the sacraments and how participation in them impacts their spirituality.

## Pedagogical Gifts and Challenges

While the faculty I interviewed sensed that learning qualitative research was valuable for ministerial leadership, none of them felt confident that recognition was more than anecdotal. More than one person suggested that to be concerned about whether students are 'applying' what they learn in seminary is what Paulo Freire called the 'banking method' of education.[11] But there is pressure on schools from denominational leadership and accrediting bodies to teach skills and assess outcomes and the students 'buy' into that approach. On the one hand faculty are challenged to engage students in ways that move beyond straight lines of direct application. On the other hand, many students are interested only in contemporary experience, and not in tradition, and while empirical research can get at such experience, there is also a need to correlate with tradition (returning us to the issue of authority and normativity).

There was consensus among theological faculty whom I interviewed and who participated in the grant symposium that they resisted applying or transferring learning to job skills or performance because of the difficulty in defining good performance and leadership in ministry. They questioned the notion that there ought to be capacities or skills that can be learned and 'applied' to ministry as well as the assumption or expectation that 'one learns this in order to do that'. Correct practice does not always follow from the application of theory. In *Adult Learning: Linking Theory and Practice*, Sharan Merriam and Laura Bierema provide a helpful analysis of adult learning theories and perspectives that facilitate the relational dynamic of theory and practice aiming for learning that changes how we know and aims to move toward social change. There are various kinds of emancipatory social change, and sometimes congregations or organizations need such transformation in their cultural context.[12] Natalie Wigg-Stevenson has suggested that the desire for application is a hangover from the banking model of education. She writes:

Despite the fact that most educators now know at least the basic gist of Freire's theory, if only by osmosis, the dominant practices of teaching and learning in most theological institutions . . . nevertheless tend to prioritize a model oriented toward expert teachers filling up 'receptacle' students with vital information about the theological traditions. Despite the fact that we might want to raise students' critical consciousness in

order to facilitate their capacity to transform those same traditions, our pedagogies can often struggle to reflect that desire.
Teaching liberation is really difficult, as is learning liberation.
And in a culture that increasingly instrumentalizes education
toward capitalist ends, not to mention the rapidly dwindling
resources for supporting theological education, it often feels
like we don't have the time or space to 'get beyond the basics'.[13]

Rather than skills, theological faculty prefer to talk about practices of leadership that come more through transformative
learning, theological reflection, and self-reflexivity, favouring a
language that speaks of developing an ethnographic disposition.[14]
I learned that faculty think that qualitative research is important
for congregational settings, for doing social and cultural analysis.
It is a form of ecclesiology in that it helps students understand the
nature of the Church from the perspective of the local context.
Qualitative research can help students analyse that social context, see how it can be different, and perhaps be instrumental in
knowledge production in that context. Understanding research
as a disposition rather than a mechanistic how-to or set of tools
helps us construct more appropriate strategies for teaching it.

There was consensus among the faculty that students enter into
qualitative research sceptically and fearfully, as many theology
students have no background in research. Theological students
often lack the language for qualitative research because it is not
what they do in the rest of the curriculum. Theological students
usually do not have an innate sense of coding and analysis, and
we need to convey their usefulness in terms of ministry – in identifying themes and issues and reflecting theologically on them.
Qualitative research sends students into unfamiliar territory from
which they learn not information but how things work (or do not
work), awareness that they bring to their own contexts. But there
are few, if any, direct correlations (I learn this so I can do that).
Qualitative research can raise the leadership bar by growing
students' capacity to help people work together. But sometimes
one needs to stand alone in the cause of something that is right,
which takes an inner strength. Qualitative method can stress the

participatory aspect of ministry without losing its prophetic component. For Wigg-Stevenson,

> Ethnography entails a form of reflexive, critical consciousness in relation to context, whereby its practitioner learns both how to produce knowledge in that context, and even to transform that knowledge thereby transforming the context around it.[15]

Some participants spoke about the need to integrate qualitative research more throughout their curriculum and ministry formation. Faculty voiced that the explicit nature of what they were doing and why they were doing it needs to be conveyed more clearly if the students are to benefit from their learning. The challenge lies in how to communicate these issues effectively. Faculty named as challenges writing good and valid questions that lead to the data and also teaching students how to analyse their data and not simply report it – how to move beyond description to theological reflection. Some advocated the use of software in data analysis.

There are practical challenges as well, such as the timeframe within which qualitative methods must be taught and a project carried out. The curriculum's other requirements allow usually just one or two semesters. Creative ways to make space were given, along with ideas of how to use qualitative research other than in full courses on this topic. One participant suggested it would help if qualitative research were part of the ethos of the school and not just something that one or two people do, which would require the backing of school administration in terms of both workload for faculty and budget considerations. Fuller integration of qualitative research would make it less alien to students. Sample size and field research are also issues related to available time: the timeframe will often require that student research be based on a small, select sample and a nearby context. Students have other courses too and can rarely immerse themselves in one place; as a result they may appear to fly in, collect data, and leave again.

Research ethics boards/internal review boards are a necessary challenge for student research. Not all theological schools who teach qualitative research have such boards, and when the faculty serves this function, the board will be internal rather than external. Ethical concerns and concerns about liability are very serious. Procedures for gaining informed consent must be in place. Some respondents wondered if students are even qualified to carry out qualitative research and, indeed, what makes someone qualified.

Faculty also raised the difficulties of evaluating student research. Some indicated that they used rubrics in their internship/contextual education programmes, with benchmarks for assessment in field research. But how to evaluate research is not self-evident. A public project presentation? An oral defence? An e-portfolio (as several faculty used)? Little is done to assess the outcome of teaching/learning qualitative methods. Some schools use exit interviews and alumni surveys to assess their curriculum in general terms. Such evaluation and assessment pertain to both student learning and faculty teaching and record the social privilege and power that faculty may bring. Our asking students what they have learned lets us know if we are teaching what we think we are. Allowing feedback as a means of dialogue is crucial, while using multiple modes of assessment yields more complete understanding. We can use evaluation as creating space focused less on judgement and more on learning from each other and model that for students. Standard course evaluations might supply only superficial information, but teachers can be encouraged to add more specific questions. One specific suggestion proposed that students be asked throughout the term to assess themselves and the teaching. Participants agreed that current evaluation/assessment measures for long-term learning are unsatisfactory, with little beyond the occasional alumni survey.

We need to gain greater clarity about what qualitative research does and its role in theological education, in order that we might better communicate its value to naysayers. We need to create institutional space for doing this scholarly work, recognizing that qualitative research may take longer than other courses or forms of research. We need to communicate more clearly that research is a theological act and spiritual practice. We need to resolve for students the tension between hustling for credits and checking boxes for ordination, on the one hand, to experiences of personal transformation at the level of the soul, on the other. And we need greater cross-institutional conversations about teaching qualitative research, so that we might exchange ideas, refine our teaching practices, and learn from each other.

I close with what one student recently told me about doing qualitative research. They said that the experience had showed them what it means to look back deep into our history and then forward into our future. They said that because we live in challenging times for the Church, we have to re-examine our role in society. The Church is doing many good things, but there are many more ways in which the Church falls short or fails. As the times change, the Church has to change too. In qualitative research, this student said, we look at tradition and theology and their value and power for good, and we evaluate ourselves to see how we might move forward in kingdom-building ways.

From the critical pedagogy of Henry Giroux, we learn that it is only when we engage in conversation that we can imagine change.[16] We do not have to be this way; we can be something else. Theological schools are agents of transformation when we who are educators teach and learn about what is possible through the exquisite gift of qualitative research.

## Notes

1 Mary Clark Moschella, *Ethnography as a Pastoral Practice: An Introduction* (Cleveland, OH: Pilgrim Press, 2008), xi.

2 John Van Maanen, 'Reclaiming Qualitative Methods for Organizational Research: A Preface', *Administrative Science Quarterly* 24, 4 (1979), 520.

3 Siroj Sorajjakool, 'Qualitative Research and Pedagogy', Wabash AST Symposium paper, Halifax, NS, 24–26 May 2016.

4 Elaine Graham, Heather Walton, and Frances Ward, *Theological Reflection: Methods* (London: SCM Press, 2005), 2, 18.

5 James F. Hopewell, *Congregation: Stories and Structures* (Philadelphia, PA: Fortress Press, 1987), 160.

6 Christian Scharen, *Fieldwork in Theology: Exploring the Social Context of God's Work in the World* (Grand Rapids, MI: Baker Academic, 2015), xv.

7 Rowan Williams, *A Ray of Darkness: Sermons and Reflections* (Cambridge, MA: Cowley, 1995), 231; Scharen, *Fieldwork*, 12.

8 Scharen, *Fieldwork*, 13.

9 See www.ecclesiologyandethnography.com.

10 American Academy of Religion Ethnography Workshop, AAR Annual Meeting, San Antonio, TX, 19–22 Nov. 2016.

11 Paulo Freire, *Pedagogy of the Oppressed* (New York: Continuum, 1970), 71–72.

12 Sharan B. Merriam and Laura L. Bierema, *Adult Learning: Linking Theory and Practice* (San Francisco, CA: Jossey-Bass, 2014), 83–84, 88.

13 Natalie Wigg-Stevenson, 'From Theological Application to Theological Transformation: Ethnography as Critical Reflexive Practice', Wabash AST Symposium paper, Halifax, NS, 24–26 May 2016.

14 Thomas Edward Frank, *The Soul of the Congregation: An Invitation to Congregational Reflection* (Nashville, TN: Abingdon Press, 2000), 57.

15 Wigg-Stevenson, 'From Theological Application'.

16 Clare Doyle and Amarjit Singh, *Reading and Teaching Henry Giroux* (New York: Peter Lang, 2006), 142.

# Select Bibliography

Adams, Tony E., Stacy Holman Jones, and Carolyn Ellis. *Autoethnography: Understanding Qualitative Research*. New York: Oxford University Press, 2015.

Adkins, A. W. H. '*Theoria* versus *Praxis* in the *Nicomachean Ethics* and the *Republic*', *Classical Philology* 73, 4 (1978), 297–313.

Adler, Gary, Tricia Bruce, and Brian Starks, eds. *American Parishes: Remaking Local Catholicism*. New York: Fordham University, forthcoming.

Afdal, Geir S. *Researching Religious Education as Social Practice*. Munster: Waxmann, 2010.

Agar, Michael H. *The Professional Stranger*. 2nd edn. San Diego, CA: Academic Press, 1980.

Aldiabat, Khaldoun, and Carole-Lynne Le Navenec. 'Clarification of the Blurred Boundaries between Grounded Theory and Ethnography: Differences and Similarities', *Turkish Online Journal of Qualitative Inquiry* 2, 3 (2011), 1–13.

Allen, Christina. 'What's Wrong with the Golden Rule? Conundrums of Conducting Ethical Research in Cyberspace', *Information Society* 12, 2 (1996), 175–88.

Andrews, Dale P. 'African American Practical Theology'. In *Opening the Field of Practical Theology: An Introduction*, edited by Kathleen A. Cahalan and Gordon S. Mikoski, 11–29. New York: Rowman & Littlefield, 2014.

Apple, Michael. *Ideology and Curriculum*. New York: Routledge, 1990.

Asquith, Glenn H., Jr. 'Anton T. Boisen and the Study of "Living Human Documents"', *Journal of Presbyterian History* 60, 3 (1982), 244–65.

Auerbach, Erich. *Mimesis: The Representation of Reality in Western Literature*. Princeton, NJ and Oxford: Princeton University Press, 2003.

Baker, Christopher R. *The Hybrid Church in the City: Third Space Thinking*. 2nd edn. London: SCM Press, 2009.

Ballard, Paul, and John Pritchard. *Practical Theology in Action*. London: SPCK, 1996.

Banner, Michael. *Ethics of Everyday Life: Moral Theology, Social Anthropology, and the Imagination of the Human.* Oxford: Oxford University Press, 2014.

Bass, Dorothy C., Kathleen A. Cahalan, Bonnie J. Miller-McLemore, James R. Nieman, and Christian B. Scharen. *Christian Practical Wisdom: What It Is and Why It Matters.* Grand Rapids, MI: Eerdmans, 2016.

Battle, Michael. 'Liberation'. In *The Blackwell Companion to Christian Spirituality*, edited by Arthur Holder, 515–31. Malden, MA: Wiley-Blackwell, 2011.

Beaudoin, Tom. 'Why Does Practice Matter Theologically?' In *Conundrums in Practical Theology*, edited by Joyce Ann Mercer and Bonnie J. Miller-McLemore, 8–31. Leiden: Brill, 2016.

Bennett, Zoë. *Using the Bible in Practical Theology: Historical and Contemporary Perspectives.* Abingdon: Ashgate, 2013.

Bennett, Zoë, and Lyall, David. 'The Professional Doctorate in Practical Theology: A New Model of Doctoral Research in the UK', *Reflective Practice: Formation and Supervision in Ministry* 34 (2014), 190–203.

Bennett, Zoë, Elaine Graham, Stephen Pattison, and Heather Walton. *Invitation to Research in Practical Theology.* London: Routledge, 2018.

Bernard, H. Russell. 'Anthropology and the Social Sciences'. *Research Methods in Anthropology: Qualitative and Quantitative Approaches*, 1–22. 5th edn. Lanham, MD: AltaMira Press, 2011.

Berry, David M. 'Internet Research: Privacy, Ethics and Alienation: An Open Source Approach', *Internet Research* 14, 4 (2004), 323–32.

Bird, Frederick, and Laurie Lamoureux Scholes. 'Research Ethics'. In *The Routledge Handbook of Research Methods in the Study of Religion*, edited by Michael Stausberg and Steven Engler, 81–105. London: Routledge, 2013.

Boal, Augusto. *Theatre of the Oppressed.* London: Pluto Press, 2000.

Bold, Christine. *Using Narrative in Research.* London: Sage, 2011.

Bondi, Liz, David Carr, Chris Clark, and Cecelia Clegg, eds. *Towards Professional Wisdom: Practical Deliberation in the People Professions.* Farnham: Ashgate, 2011.

Bourdieu, Pierre. *The Logic of Practice.* Translated by Richard Nice. Stanford, CA: Stanford University Press, 1990.

Bourdieu, Pierre. *Outline of a Theory of Practice.* Translated by Richard Nice. Cambridge: Cambridge University Press, 1972.

Bourdieu, Pierre. *The Weight of the World: Social Suffering in Contemporary Society.* Translated by Priscilla Pankhurst Ferguson. Stanford, CA: Stanford University Press, 1999.

Brayboy, Bryan M., and Donna Deyhle. 'Insider–Outsider: Researchers in American Indian Communities', *Theory into Practice* 39, 3 (2000), 163–68.

Bretherton, Luke. *Christianity and Contemporary Politics: The Conditions and Possibilities of Faithful Witness*. Malden, MA, and Oxford: Wiley-Blackwell, 2010.

Bretherton, Luke. *Resurrecting Democracy: Faith, Citizenship, and the Politics of a Common Life*. New York: Cambridge University Press, 2015.

Bristol, Laurette S. M. *Plantation Pedagogy: A Postcolonial and Global Perspective*. New York: Peter Lang, 2012.

Browning, Don, S. *A Fundamental Practical Theology: Descriptive and Strategic Proposals*. Minneapolis, MN: Fortress Press, 1991.

Cahalan, Kathleen A. 'Roman Catholic Pastoral Theology'. In *Opening the Field of Practical Theology*, edited by Kathleen A. Cahalan and Gordon S. Mikoski, 217–32. Lanham, MD: Rowman & Littlefield, 2014.

Cahalan, Kathleen, Edward Foley, and Gordon S. Mikoski, eds. *Integrating Work in Theological Education*. Eugene, OR: Pickwick, 2017.

Cameron, Helen. *Talking about God in Practice: Theological Action Research and Practical Theology*. London: SCM Press, 2010.

Cannon, Katie G. *Black Womanist Ethics*. Atlanta, GA: Scholars Press, 1988.

Carroll, Jackson. *God's Potters: Pastoral Leadership and the Shaping of Congregations*. Grand Rapids, MI: Eerdmans, 2006.

Castellano, Marlene Brant. 'Updating Aboriginal Traditions of Knowledge'. In *Indigenous Knowledges in Global Contexts: Multiple Readings of Our World*, edited by George J. Sefa Dei, Budd L. Hall, and Dorothy Goldin Rosenberg, 21–36. Toronto: University of Toronto Press.

Charles Marsh, Peter Slade, and Sarah Azaransky, eds. *Lived Theology: New Perspectives on Method, Style, and Pedagogy*. New York: Oxford University Press, 2017.

Charmaz, Kathy. *Constructing Grounded Theory: A Practical Guide through Qualitative Analysis*. New York: Sage, 2006.

Christiano, Kevin, William H. Swatos, Jr., and Peter Kivisto. *Sociology of Religion: Contemporary Developments*. 3rd edn. Lanham, MD: Rowman & Littlefield, 2016.

Cimperman, Maria. *Social Analysis for the 21st Century*. Maryknoll, NY: Orbis, 2015.

Clifford, James, and George E. Marcus, eds. *Writing Culture: The Poetics and Politics of Ethnography*. Berkeley, Los Angeles, and London: University of California Press, 1986.

Conde-Frazier, Elizabeth. 'Participatory Action Research: Practical Theology for Social Justice', *Religious Education* 101, 3 (2006), 321–29.

Conrell, Stephen, and Douglass Hartmann. *Ethnicity and Race: Making Identities in a Changing World*. 2nd edn. Thousand Oaks, CA: Pine Forge Press, 2007.

Cooper, John M. 'The Relevance of Moral Theory to Moral Improvement in Epictetus'. In *The Philosophy of Epictetus*, edited by Theodore Scaltsas and Andrew S. Mason, 9–19. Oxford and New York: Oxford University Press, 2007.

Cooper-White, Pamela. *Braided Selves: Collected Essays on Multiplicity, God, and Persons*. Eugene, OR: Cascade Books, 2011.

Costley, Carol, Geoffrey Elliott, and Paul Gibbs. *Doing Work-based Research: Approaches to Enquiry for Insider-Researchers*. London: Sage, 2010.

Creswell, John W. *Qualitative Inquiry and Research Design*. 3rd edn. Thousand Oaks, CA: Sage, 2013.

Csinos, David M. *Children's Ministry that Fits: Beyond One-Size-Fits-All Approaches to Ministry with Children*. Eugene, OR: Wipf & Stock, 2011.

Denzin, Norman K. *Interpretive Ethnography: Ethnographic Practices for the 21st Century*. Thousand Oaks, CA: Sage, 1997.

Denzin, Norman K. *Performance Ethnography: Critical Pedagogy and the Politics of Culture*. Thousand Islands, CA: Sage, 2003.

Denzin, Norman K., and Yvonna S. Lincoln, eds. *The Sage Handbook of Qualitative Research*. 3rd edn. Thousand Oaks, CA: Sage, 2005.

Derrida, Jacques. *Given Time: 1: Counterfeit Money*. Translated by Peggy Kamuf. Chicago, IL: Chicago University Press, 1992.

Derrida, Jacques. 'Hospitality'. In *Acts of Religion*, edited by Gil Anidjar, 356–420. New York and London: Routledge, 2002.

Douglas, Kelly Brown. *The Black Christ*. New York: Orbis Books, 1994.

Douglas, Kelly Brown. *What's Faith Got to Do With It? Black Bodies/ Christian Souls*. Maryknoll, NY: Orbis Books, 2005.

Driskill, Joseph D. 'Spirituality and the Formation of Pastoral Counselors', *American Journal of Pastoral Counseling* 8, 3/4 (2006), 69–85.

Dussel, Enrique D. 'Theology of Liberation and Marxism'. In *Mysterium Liberationis: Fundamental Concepts of Liberation Theology*, edited by Ignacio Ellacuría and Jon Sobrino, 85–102. Maryknoll, NY: Orbis, 1993.

Fanon, Frantz. *Black Skin, White Masks*. Translated by Charles Lam Markmann. New York: Grove Press, 1967.

Farley, Edward. *Practicing Gospel: Unconventional Thoughts on the Church's Ministry*. Louisville, KY: Westminster John Knox, 2003.

Fell, Tony, Kevin Flint, and Ian Haines. *Professional doctorates in the UK, 2011*. Lichfield: UK Council for Graduate Education, 2011.

Fichter, Joseph. *One-Man Research: Reminiscences of a Catholic Sociologist*. New York: Wiley, 1973.

Finlay, Linda. 'Negotiating the Swamp: The Opportunity and Challenge of Reflexivity in Research Practice', *Qualitative Research* 2, 2 (2002), 209–30.

Fisk, Anna. *Sex, Sin, and Ourselves: Encounters in Feminist Theology and Contemporary Women's Literature*. Eugene, OR: Pickwick Publications, 2014.

Forrester, Duncan B. *Truthful Action: Explorations in Practical Theology*. Edinburgh: T&T Clark, 2000.

Foucault, Michel. *The Hermeneutics of the Subject: Lectures at the Collège De France, 1981–1982*. Translated by Graham Burchell. New York: Picador, 2005.

Foucault, Michel. 'Subjectivity and Truth'. In *The Politics of Truth*. New York: Semiotext, 1997.

Frederick, Marla. *Between Sundays: Black Women and Everyday Struggles of Faith*. Berkeley, CA: University of California Press, 2003.

Freire, Ana Maria Araujo, and Donaldo Macedo. *The Paulo Freire Reader*. New York: Continuum, 2000.

Freire, Paulo. *Education for Critical Consciousness*. New York: Continuum, 1990.

Freire, Paulo. *Pedagogy of the Oppressed*. Translated by Myra Bergman Ramos. 4th edn. New York: Bloomsbury Academic, 2018.

Freire, Paulo. *The Politics of Education: Culture, Power and Liberation*. South Hadley, MA: Bergin & Garvey, 1985.

Ganzevoort, R. Ruard, and Johan Roeland, 'Lived Religion: The Praxis of Practical Theology', *International Journal of Practical Theology* 18, 1 (2014), 91–101.

Garrigan, Siobhán. *The Real Peace Process: Worship, Politics, and the End of Sectarianism*. London: Equinox, 2010.

Geertz, Clifford. *The Interpretation of Cultures*. New York: Basic Books, 1973.

Gerkin, Charles. *Widening the Horizons: Pastoral Responses to a Fragmented Society*. Louisville, KY: Westminster John Knox, 1986.

Gibson, Rich. 'Paulo Freire and Pedagogy for Social Justice', *Theory and Research in Social Education* 27, 2 (1991), 129–59.

Giroux, Henry A. *On Critical Pedagogy*. New York: Continuum, 2011.

Giroux, Henry A. 'Paulo Freire and the Politics of Postcolonialism', *Journal of Advanced Composition* 12, 1 (1992), 15–26.

Glaser, Barney G. *Basis of Grounded Theory Analysis: Emergence vs. Forcing*. Mill Valley, CA: Sociology Press, 1992.

Graham, Elaine. 'Feminist Theory'. In *The Wiley-Blackwell Companion to Practical Theology*, edited by Bonnie J. Miller-McLemore, 193–203. Malden, MA: Wiley-Blackwell, 2011.

Graham, Elaine. 'Research Report: Is Practical Theology a Form of "Action Research"?' *International Journal of Practical Theology* 17 (2013), 148–78.

Graham, Elaine. *Transforming Practice: Pastoral Theology in Age of Uncertainty*. Eugene, OR: Wipf & Stock, 2002.

Graham, Elaine, Heather Walton, and Frances Ward. *Theological Reflection: Methods*. London: SCM Press, 2005.

Grinyer, Anne. 'The Anonymity of Research Participants: Assumptions, Ethics, and Practicalities', *Pan-Pacific Management Review* 12, 1 (2009), 49–58.

Groome, Thomas. *Christian Religious Education*. San Francisco, CA: Jossey-Bass, 1999.

Groome, Thomas. *Sharing Faith: A Comprehensive Approach to Religious Education and Pastoral Ministry. The Way of Shared Praxis*. San Francisco, CA: Harper, 1991.

Gubi, Peter Madison. 'Assessing the Perceived Value of Reflexive Groups for Supporting Clergy in the Church of England', *Journal of Mental Health, Religion and Culture* 19, 4 (2016), 769–80.

Gupta, Akhil, and James Ferguson, eds. *Anthropological Locations: Boundaries and Grounds of a Field Science*. Berkeley, CA: University of California Press, 1997.

Gutiérrez, Gustavo. *A Theology of Liberation*. New York: Orbis, 1973.

Hadot, Pierre. *Philosophy as a Way of Life*. Edited by Arnold I. Davidson. Malden, MA, and Oxford: Blackwell, 1995.

Harré, Rom, and Grant Gillett. *The Discursive Mind*. London: Sage, 1994.

Healy, Nicholas H. *Church, World, and the Christian Life: Practical-Prophetic Ecclesiology*. New York: Cambridge University Press, 2000.

Helopoulos, Jason. *The New Pastor's Handbook: Help and Encouragement for the First Years of Ministry*. Ada, MI: Baker Books, 2015.

Henderson, Hayley. 'Toward an Ethnographic Sensibility in Urban Research', *Australian Planner* 53, 1 (2016), 28–36.

'Henry Giroux: The Necessity of Critical Pedagogy in Dark Times'. Interview by Jose Maria Barroso Tristan. *truthout*, 6 Feb. 2013. http://www.truth-out.org/news/item/14331-a-critical-interview-with-henry-giroux.

Henriksen Jan-Olav, ed. *Difficult Normativity: Normative Dimensions in Research on Religion and Theology*. Frankfurt am Main: Peter Lang, 2011.

Holmes, Barbara A. *Joy Unspeakable: Contemplative Practices of the Black Church*. Minneapolis, MN: Fortress Press, 2004.

Hoover, Brett C. 'Power in the Parish'. In *American Parishes*, edited by Gary Adler, Tricia Bruce, and Brian Starks. New York: Fordham University Press, forthcoming.

Hoover, Brett C. *The Shared Parish: Latinos, Anglos, and the Future of US Catholicism*. New York: NYU Press, 2014.

Hopkins, Dwight N. *Being Human: Race, Culture and Religion*. Minneapolis, MN: Fortress Press, 2005.

Horkheimer Max. *Critical Theory: Selected Essays*. New York: Continuum, 2002.

Howell, Paul. 'From *Rain Man* to *Sherlock*: Theological Reflections on Metaphor and ASD', *Practical Theology* 8, 2 (2015), 143–53.

Iderström, Jonas, and Tone S. Kaufman, eds. *What Really Matters? Scandinavian Perspectives on Ecclesiology and Ethnography*. Eugene, OR: Pickwick, 2018.

Ignatius. *The Spiritual Exercises of St Ignatius*. Translated by George E. Ganns. Chicago, IL: Loyola Press, 2009.

Irzarry, Jose. 'The Religious Educator as Cultural Spec-Actor: Researching Self in Intercultural Pedagogy', *Religious Education* 98, 3 (2003), 365–81.

Kaufman, Tone S. 'From the Outside, Within, or Inbetween? Normativity at Work in Empirical Practical Theological Research'. In *Conundrums in Practical Theology*, edited by Joyce Ann Mercer and Bonnie J. Miller-McLemore, 134–62. Leiden: Brill, 2016.

Kaufman, Tone S. *A New Old Spirituality? A Qualitative Study of Clergy Spirituality in the Nordic Context*. Eugene, OR: Pickwick, 2017.

Kaufman, Tone S. 'Normativity as Pitfall or Ally? Reflexivity as an Interpretive Resource in Ecclesiological and Ethnographic Research', *Ecclesial Practices: Journal of Ecclesiology and Ethnography* 2 (2015), 91–107.

Ketelaars, Bernardine. 'Harkening to the Voices of the Lost Ones: Attending to the Stories of Baptized Roman Catholics No Longer Participating in the Worship and Community Life of the Church'. Doctoral thesis, University of Toronto, 2015, https://tspace.library.utoronto.ca/handle/1807/70994.

Killen, Patricia O'Connell, and John De Beer. *The Art of Theological Reflection*. New York: Crossroad, 1994.

Kincheloe, Joe L., Peter McLaren, Shirley R. Steinburg. 'Critical Pedagogy and Qualitative Research: Moving to the Bricolage'. In *The Sage Handbook of Qualitative Research*, edited by Norman K. Denzin and Yvonna S. Lincoln, 163–77. 3rd edn. Thousand Oaks, CA: Sage, 2005.

Kleinman, Sherryl, and Martha A. Copp. *Emotions and Fieldwork*. Newbury Park, CA, London, and New Delhi: Sage, 1993.

Kovach, Margaret. 'Emerging from the Margins: Indigenous Methodologies'. In *Research as Resistance: Critical, Indigenous, and Anti-Oppressive Approaches*, edited by Leslie Brown and Susan Strega, 19–36. Toronto: Canadian Scholars' Press, 2005.

Lambek, Michael. *The Ethical Condition: Essays on Action, Person, & Value*. Chicago, IL and London: University of Chicago Press, 2015.

Lao Tzu. *Tao Te Ching*. Translated by Victor H. Mair. New York: Bantam Books, 1990.

Lao Tzu. *The Way of Lao Tzu (Tao-te ching)*. Translated by Wing-Tsit Chan. Upper Saddle River, NJ: Prentice Hall, 1963.

LaSalle-Klein, Robert. *Blood and Ink: Ignatio Ellacuria, Jon Sobrino, and the Jesuit Martyrs of the University of Central America*. Maryknoll, NY: Orbis, 2014.

LeCompte, Margaret D., and Jean J. Schensul. *Designing and Conducting Ethnographic Research: An Introduction*. Lanham, MD: AltaMira Press, 2010.

Lee-Treweek, Geraldine, and Stephanie Linkogle, eds. *Dangers in the Field: Ethics and Risk in Social Research*. London and New York: Routledge, 2000.

Leonardo, Zeus. *Race, Whiteness, and Education*. New York: Routledge, 2009.

Liebert, Elizabeth. 'Supervision as Widening the Horizons'. In *Supervision of Spiritual Directors: Engaging the Holy Mystery*, edited by Mary Rose Bumpus and Rebecca Bradburn Langer, 125–46. Harrisburg, PA: Morehouse Publishing, 2005.

Llewellyn, Dawn. *Reading, Feminism, and Spirituality: Troubling the Waves*. London: Palgrave, 2015.

Lowman, Emma Battell, and Adam J. Barker, A. *Settler: Identity and Colonialism in 21st Century Canada*. Halifax, NS: Fernwood Publishing, 2015.

Luckmann, Thomas, and Peter Berger. *The Social Construction of Reality: A Treatise in the Sociology of Knowledge*. New York: Anchor, 1966.

McClintock Fulkerson, Mary. *Places of Redemption: Theology for a Worldly Church*. Oxford: Oxford University Press, 2007.

McDannell, Colleen. *Material Christianity: Religion and Popular Culture in America*. New Haven, CT: Yale University Press, 1995.

McGranahan, Carole. 'What is Ethnography? Teaching Ethnographic Sensibilities without Fieldwork', *Teaching Anthropology* 4 (2014), 23–36.

MacIntyre, Alasdair. *After Virtue: A Study in Moral Theory*. London and New York: Bloomsbury Academic, 1981.

McRobbie, Angela. 'The Politics of Feminist Research: Between Talk, Text and Action', *Feminist Review* 12, 1 (1982), 46–57.

Malinowski, Bronislaw. *Argonauts of the Western Pacific* (1922). London: Routledge & Kegan Paul, 1966.

Marcus, George E., and Michael M. J. Fischer, *Anthropology as Cultural Critique: An Experimental Moment in the Human Sciences*. Chicago, IL: University of Chicago Press, 1986.

Mason, Jennifer. *Qualitative Researching*. London: Sage, 2002.

Meneses, Eloise, Lindy Backues, David Bronkema, Eric Flett, and Benjamin L. Hartley. 'Engaging the Religiously Committed Other: Anthropologists and Theologians in Dialogue', *Current Anthropology* 55, 1 (2014), 82–104.

Mercer, Joyce Ann, and Bonnie J. Miller-McLemore, eds. *Conundrums in Practical Theology*. Leiden: Brill, 2016.

Merriam, Sharan B., and Laura L. Bierema. *Adult Learning: Linking Theory and Practice*. San Francisco, CA: Jossey-Bass, 2014.

Milbank, John. 'Can a Gift Be Given? Prolegomena to a Future Trinitarian Metaphysic', *Modern Theology* 11, 1 (1995), 119–61.

Milbank, John. 'The Transcendality of Gift: A Summary in Answer to 12 Questions', *Revista Portuguesa de Filosofia* 65 (2009), 887–97.

Miller-McLemore, Bonnie J. *In the Midst of Chaos: Caring for Children as a Spiritual Practice*. San Francisco, CA: Wiley Bass, 2007.

Miller-McLemore, Bonnie J. 'The Living Human Web: Pastoral Theology at the Turn of the Century'. In *Through the Eyes of Women: Insights for Pastoral Care*, edited by Jeanne Stevenson-Moessner, 9–26. Minneapolis, MN: Fortress Press, 1996.

Monette, Maurice L. 'Paulo Freire and Other Unheard Voices', *Religious Education*, 74, 2 (1979), 543–54.

Moore, Allen J., ed. *Religious Education as Social Transformation*. Birmingham, AL: Religious Education Press, 1989.

Morris, Wayne, ed. *Acedia and the Transformation of Spiritual Malaise: Essays in Honour of Fr Martin McAlinden*. Chester: Chester University Press, forthcoming.

Moschella, Mary Clark. 'Enlivening Local Stories through Pastoral Ethnography'. In *Teaching Our Story: Narrative Leadership and Pastoral Formation*, edited by Larry A. Goleman, 67–86. Herndon, VA: Alban, 2010.

Moschella, Mary Clark. *Ethnography as a Pastoral Practice: An Introduction*. 3rd edn. Cleveland, OH: Pilgrim Press, 2008.

Moschella, Mary Clark. 'Practice Matters'. In *Pastoral Theology and Care: Critical Trajectories in Theory and Practice*, edited by Nancy J. Ramsay, 5–29. Chichester: John Wiley & Sons, 2018.

Nakrathat, A. *Udom suksa Thai nai rob satawat* (A century of Thai higher education). Bangkok: Sathabun Ram Jit, 2014.

Nangle, Joseph. *Engaged Spirituality: Faith Life in the Heart of the Empire*. Maryknoll, NY: Orbis Books, 2008.

Nash, Dennison, and Ronald Wintraub. 'The Emergence of Self-Consciousness in Ethnography', *Current Anthropology* 13, 5 (1972), 527–42.

Neyland, Daniel. *Organizational Ethnography*. London: Sage, 2008.

Nouwen, Henri, *Bread for the Journey: A Daybook of Wisdom and Faith*. New York: HarperCollins, 1997.

Omi, Michael, and Howard Winant. *Racial Formation in the United States*. 2nd edn. New York: Routledge, 1994.

Orsi, Robert. *Between Heaven and Earth: The Religious Worlds People Make and the Scholars Who Study Them*. Princeton, NJ: Princeton University Press, 2005.

Ospino, Hosffman. *Hispanic Ministry in Catholic Parishes*. Boston, MA: Boston College, 2014.

Outlaw, Lucius. *Critical Social Theory in the Interests of Black Folks.* Lanham, MD: Rowman & Littlefield, 2005.

Parachin, Janet W. *Engaged Spirituality: Ten Lives of Contemplation and Action.* St Louis, MO: Chalice Press, 1999.

Pattison, Stephen. *The Faith of the Managers.* London: Cassell, 1997.

Piper, Helen, and Heather Simons. 'Ethical Responsibility in Social Research'. In *Research Methods in the Social Sciences*, edited by Bridget Somekh and Cathy Lewin, 56–64. London: Sage, 2005.

Powdermaker, Hortense. *Stranger and Friend: The Way of an Anthropologist.* New York and London: W. W. Norton, 1966.

Prainsack, Barbara, and Ayo Wahlberg. 'Ethnographic Sensibility at the Interface of STS, Policy Studies, and the Social Study of Medicine', *BioSocieties* 8, 3 (2013), 336–59.

Ramírez-Ferrero, E. *Troubled Fields: Men, Emotions, and the Crisis in American Farming.* New York: Columbia University, 2005.

Ramsay, Nancy J., ed. *Pastoral Theology and Care: Critical Trajectories in Theory and Practice.* Chichester: John Wiley and Sons, 2018.

Randolph, R. Sean. *The United States and Thailand: Alliance Dynamics, 1950–1985.* Berkeley, CA: Institute of East Asian Studies, University of California, 1986.

Reddie, Anthony G. *Acting in Solidarity: Reflections in Critical Christianity.* London: DLT, 2005.

Reddie, Anthony G. *Black Theology in Transatlantic Dialogue.* Basingstoke and New York: Palgrave Macmillan, 2006.

Ribbens, Jane. 'Interviewing: An "Unnatural Situation"'? *Women's Studies International Forum* 12, 6 (1989), 579–92.

Rizvi, Fazal, and Bob Lingard. *Globalizing Education Policy.* London: Routledge, 2010.

Scharen, Christian. '"Judicious Narratives", or Ethnography as Ecclesiology'. *Scottish Journal of Theology* 58, 2 (2005), 125–42.

Scharen, Christian. *Fieldwork in Theology: Exploring the Social Context of God's Work in the World.* Grand Rapids, MI: Baker Academic, 2015.

Scharen, Christian, and Anna Marie Vigen, eds. *Ethnography as Christian Theology and Ethics.* London and New York: Continuum, 2011.

Schneiders, Sandra. 'The Study of Christian Spirituality: Contours and Dynamics of a Discipline', *Christian Spirituality Bulletin* 6, 1 (1998), 3–21.

Schofer, Jonathan Wyn. 'Virtues and Vices of Relativism', *Journal of Religious Ethics* 36, 4 (2008), 709–15.

Seeman, Don. 'Divinity Inhabits the Social: Ethnography in a Phenomenological Key'. In *Theologically Engaged Anthropology*, edited by Derrick Lemons, 1–31. New York: Oxford University Press, 2017.

Seneca, *On Benefits.* Translated by Miriam Griffin and Brad Inwood. Chicago, IL: University of Chicago Press, 2014.

Slee, Nicola. *Women's Faith Development: Patterns and Processes.* Aldershot: Ashgate, 2004.

Slee, Nicola, Fran Porter, and Anne Philips, eds. *The Faith Lives of Women and Girls.* Abingdon: Ashgate, 2013.

Slee, Nicola, Fran Porter, and Anne Philips, eds. *Researching Female Faith: Qualitative Research Methods.* London: Routledge, 2018.

Slingerland, Edward. *Effortless Action: Wu-Wei as Conceptual Metaphor and Spiritual Ideal in Early China.* Oxford and New York: Oxford University Press, 2007.

Smith, Christian, Brandon Vaidyanathan, Nancy Ammerman, José Casanova, Hilary Davidson, Elaine Howard Ecklund, John H. Evans, Mary Ellen Konieczny, Jason A. Springs, Jenny Trinitapoli, and Meredith Whitnah. 'Roundtable on the Sociology of Religion: Twenty-Three Theses on the Status of Religion in American Sociology – A Mellon Working Group Reflection', *Journal of the American Academy of Religion* 81, 4 (2013), 903–38.

Sölle, Dorothee. *The Silent Cry: Mysticism and Resistance.* Minneapolis, MN: Augsburg Fortress Press, 2001.

Spicker, Paul. 'Research without Consent'. *Social Research Update,* 51 (2007), http://sru.soc.surrey.ac.uk/SRU51.pdf.

Sprague, Joey, *Feminist Methodologies for Critical Researchers: Bridging differences.* 2nd edn. Lanham, MD: Rowman & Littlefield, 2016.

Stanley, Liz. *Knowing Feminisms: On Academic Borders, Territories and Tribes.* Thousand Oaks, CA: Sage, 1997.

Stewart, Charles. 'Secularism as an Impediment to Anthropological Research', *Social Anthropology* 9, 3 (2001), 323–28.

Stipe, Claude E. 'Anthropologists versus Missionaries: The Influence of Presuppositions', *Current Anthropology* 21, 2 (1980), 165–79.

Stoller, Paul. *The Cinematic Griot.* Chicago, IL and London: University of Chicago Press, 1992.

Stoller, Paul. *Sensuous Scholarship.* Philadelphia, PA: University of Pennsylvania Press, 1997.

Stoller, Paul. *The Taste of Ethnographic Things.* Philadelphia, PA: University of Pennsylvania Press, 1989.

Stuerzenhofecker, Katja. 'Transforming Practical Theological Education in the Changing Context of Non-confessional Higher Education'. Doctor of Professional Studies dissertation, University of Chester, 2016. http://chesterrep.openrepository.com/cdr/handle/10034/620544#

Swinton, John, and Harriet Mowat. *Practical Theology and Qualitative Research.* London: SCM Press, 2016.

Tanner, Kathryn. *Theories of Culture: A New Agenda for Theology*. Minneapolis, MN: Fortress Press, 1997.

Taussig, Michael. *Mimesis and Alterity: A Particular History of the Senses*. New York and London: Routledge, 1993.

Taylor, Charles. *The Malaise of Modernity*. Concord: Canadian Broadcasting Corporation, 1991.

Taylor, John. *Classics and the Bible: Hospitality and Recognition*. London: Duckworth, 2007.

Thomas, Jim. 'When Cyberresearch Goes Awry: The Ethics of the Rimm "Cyberporn": Study', *Information Society* 12, 2 (1996), 189–97.

Tikly, Leon P. 'Education and the New Imperialism'. In *Postcolonial Challenges in Higher Education*, edited by Roland Sintos Coloma, 23–45. New York: Peter Lang, 2009.

Townes, Emile M. *Womanist Ethics and the Cultural Production of Evil*. New York: Palgrave Macmillan, 2006.

Townes, Emile M. *Womanist Justice, Womanist Hope*. Atlanta, GA: Scholars Press, 1993.

Tracy, David. *The Analogical Imagination: Christian Theology and the Culture of Pluralism*. New York: Crossroad, 1981.

van Manen, Max. *Phenomenology of Practice: Meaning-Giving Methods in Phenomenological Research and Writing*. Walnut Creek, CA: Left Coast Press, 2014.

van Manen, Max. *Researching Lived Experience: Human Science for an Action Sensitive Pedagogy*. London, ON: Althouse Press, University of Western Ontario, 1990.

Visweswaran, Kamala. *Fictions of Feminist Ethnography*. Minneapolis, MN: University of Minnesota Press, 1994.

Wacquant, Loïc. *Body & Soul: Notebooks of an Apprentice Boxer*. New York: Oxford University Press, 2004.

Walton, Heather, ed. *Literature and Theology: New Interdisciplinary Spaces*. Ashgate: Farnham, 2011.

Wigg-Stevenson, Natalie. *Ethnographic Theology: An Inquiry into the Production of Theological Knowledge*. New York: Palgrave Macmillan, 2014.

Wigg-Stevenson, Natalie. 'From Proclamation to Conversation: Ethnographic Disruptions to Theological Normativity', *Palgrave Communications: Radical Theologies* (2015), 1–9. http://www.palgrave-journals.com/articles/palcomms201524.

Wigg-Stevenson, Natalie. 'You Don't Look Like a Baptist Minister: An Autoethnographic Retrieval of "Women's Experience" as an Analytic Category for Feminist Theology', *Feminist Theology* 25, 2 (2017), 182–97.

Wijsen, Frans, Peter Henriot, and Rodrigo Mejía, eds. *The Pastoral Circle Revisited: A Critical Quest for Truth and Transformation*. Maryknoll, NY: Orbis, 2005.

Wiles, Rose, Graham Crow, Sue Heath, and Vikki Charles. 'The Management of Confidentiality and Anonymity in Social Research', *International Journal of Social Research Methodology* 11, 5 (2008), 417–28.

Williams, Rowan. *The Edge of Words: God and the Habits of Language*. London: Bloomsbury, 2014.

Williams, Rowan. *A Ray of Darkness: Sermons and Reflections*, Cambridge, MA: Cowley, 1995.

Willows, David. *Divine Knowledge: A Kierkegaardian Perspective on Christian Education*. Aldershot: Ashgate, 2001.

Woodward, James, and Stephen Pattison, eds. *The Blackwell Reader in Pastoral and Practical Theology*. Oxford: Blackwell, 2000.

# Index of Names and Subjects

Simons, Helen 47
*skholé* 5–6
Slade, Peter xvii
Smithart, Wesley 200
Snyder, Timothy 68
social justice xxvii, 151, 152, 154
  leaders 163
social media 64–5
social mobility 19–20, 25, 27–8
sociology
  of the body 186
  and Catholic social teaching 135
  of religion xxvi, 133, 138, 145–6,
  185–7
Sorajjakool, Siroj xx–xxi, 261
spiritual hospitality xxix, 213–14
spirituality
  African American 152
  desert 153
  engaged xxvii, 150–67
  teaching with qualitative research
  149–67
Stoller, Paul 84, 89, 92
Swatos, William 145–6
Swinton, John xxiv, 181

Taussig, Michael 17 n22
Taylor, Charles xxxii, 240, 249–50
Thailand xx–xxi, 19–33
theatre of the oppressed 122–3
*them* and *us* thinking 120–28
theological reflection 19, 33, 39–
  40, 66, 124–5, 135–6, 145–6
  defined 228–9
  workshops 216
theology
  applied 4
  by children 63, 65–6, 71–2
  communal 65–7
  and ethics xviii
  evaluation 234–5
  four voices 177–9
  as Gospel mimesis 15

lived xvii
  pastoral 134, 147
  as playbook and gamefilm 13
  practical xix, 134
  three publics 42
  *see also* liberation theology
*theoria*, in Aristotle 6
theory vs. practice 7–12
thick description 13, 113–14, 130,
  161, 191, 201, 204 n12
Thomas, Sabrina 202
Tipton, Steven xxix
Tracy, David 42
transformative pedagogy xxxiii,
  100–116
Trinity 250–51

Uganda xix–xx, xxiii, 83–4, 87–90
University of Chester 40
University of Notre Dame 3–4

van Manen, Max xxix, 214, 243–4
Vatican Council (II) 137
Vigen, Aana Marie xvii, xviii
Visweswaran, Kamala 55
vocation
  pastoral 266
  of a sculptor 244–5
vocations, religious xxvii

Whitmore, Todd xix–xx, xxiii–xxiv
Wigg-Stevenson, Natalie xxiv–xxv,
  63, 68, 173, 180–81, 267–9
Willhauck, Susan xxxii–xxxiii
Williams, Rowan xxxiii, 244, 263
Willimon, William 263
wonder 242, 244–8
Wratee, Byron 196–7
writing 6–7

xenophobia 124–8

Younge, Gary 125